THE SONG
OF SONGS

Other Continental Commentaries from Fortress Press

Genesis 1–11
Claus Westermann

Genesis 12–36
Claus Westermann

Genesis 37–50
Claus Westermann

Psalms 1–59
Hans-Joachim Kraus

Psalms 60–150
Hans-Joachim Kraus

Isaiah 1–12
Hans Walter Wolff

Obadiah and Jonah
Hans Wolter Wolff

Haggai
Hans Walter Wolff

Micah
Hans Walter Wolff

Matthew 1–7
Ulrich Luz

Galatians
Dieter Lührmann

Revelation
Jürgen Roloff

Othmar Keel

THE SONG
OF SONGS

A Continental Commentary

Translated by
Frederick J. Gaiser

FORTRESS PRESS
MINNEAPOLIS

For Esther Leu and Hans Heinrich Schmid

THE SONG OF SONGS
A Continental Commentary

First Fortress Press edition 1994.

Translated from *Das Hohelied*, published by Theologischer Verlag Zürich in the Züricher Bibelkommentare series.

Scripture quotations, unless otherwise noted, are from the New Revised Standard Version of the Bible, copyright © 1989 by the Division of Christian Education of the National Council of the Churches of Christ in the United States of America.

Library of Congress Cataloging-in-Publication Data

Keel, Othmar, 1937–
 [Hohelied. English]
 The Song of Songs : a Continental commentary / Othmar Keel ; translated
 by Frederick J. Gaiser.—1st Fortress Press ed.
  p. cm.—
 Includes bibliographical references and indexes.
 ISBN 0—8006—9507—0 :
 1. Bible. O.T. Song of Solomon–Commentaries. I. Title.
 BS1485.3.K4413 1994
 223′.9077—dc20   93–11518
                                                          CIP

The paper used in this publication meets the minimum requirements of American National Standard for Information Sciences—Permanence of Paper for Printed Library Materials, ANSI Z329.48–1984.   ∞™

Manufactured in the U.S.A.   AF 1–9507

98 97 96 95 94 1 2 3 4 5 6 7 8 9 10

Contents

Contents

Preface

[It is impossible for me] to despise that which is mistakenly called physical love; it is the substance of a sacrament, and I pay it the same respect I give to the unconsecrated bread, also the substance of a sacrament; the separation of love into so-called physical love and the other kind is open to criticism, perhaps inadmissible; no love is either purely physical or purely of the other kind; both always contain a portion of the other, even if only a tiny one. We are neither pure spirits nor pure bodies, and it may be that the angels envy us our ever-changing mixture of both.

Heinrich Böll, *Brief an einen jungen Katholiken*

The Song of Songs has so much drama, so many experiences of longing and love, of good fortune and sorrow, that one can certainly enjoy the poems without lengthy commentary. They are effective in themselves, and long-winded explanations can only disturb the reader's personal appropriation of them. But one who comes to treasure these poems, and reads them again and again will eventually be directed by something in the text—perhaps a change in speaker or a particular simile or metaphor—to ask questions about what the songs really mean, about whether a particular interpretation is correct. These are, after all, poems from a distant and foreign world. So an expert who has studied that world and its languages will be summoned to begin an intellectual endeavor that will always be limited to particular issues. It can only provide interpretive helps and can never replace the poems themselves.

The present commentary has innumerable predecessors, and, even though the debate with them is limited, I did not want to omit it altogether. The interpreter stands in the midst of a serious conversation with other interpreters. Above all, I have engaged four recent major commentators: Rudolph, Gerleman, Pope, and Krinetzki (for the complete references, see the bibliography). These scholars represent four important streams of recent exegesis of the Song. Rudolph's commentary remains strongly in the tradition of Herder, Wetzstein (see note 24), and Budde, who used the analogy of modern recent Arab songs from Palestine and Syria to interpret the Song as a collection of folk songs, more or less directly connected with (peasant) wedding feasts. Gerleman understands the Song as literature, with a clear dependence on the love poetry of ancient Egypt. Pope seeks the roots of many of the Song's expressions and metaphors in Northwest Semitic philology and mythology (Ugarit) and in the sacred marriages of Sumer. Krinetzki strongly accents the form of the material and uses depth psychology to attempt to explain its motifs. Because my conversation with these authors is often lively, especially where disagreements are evident, I want to emphasize at the outset that the consensus is broader than the impression that may be given here.

I attempt to pay equal attention to the form and the content of the songs, with indirect reference to the Hebrew text. In order to shed light on the development and analysis of the various motifs I have sought to include both written and iconographic parallels; yet here too the format required that the results of many years of research be made as accessible as possible to the reader. Much of what is presented here is more fully developed in my preliminary study to this work: *Deine Blicke sind Tauben. Zur Metaphorik des Hohen Liedes*, SBS 114/115 (Stuttgart: Katholisches Bibelwerk 1984). But some things are not treated there and are new here—for example, all the observations about the delineation and structure of the individual poems and also much of the material about the background of the motifs. Only 50 of the present 158 illustrations are found in the preliminary study.

In this commentary I cite Hebrew or other foreign languages only when necessary. The traditional terms "perfect" and "imperfect" are used for the two most important forms of the Hebrew verb. In narrative texts, the Hebrew perfect can be rendered with the English imperfect, perfect, or past perfect; in the case of verbs signifying the mental or physical state of the subject (verbal adjectives) and verbs of perception, it often has a present sense. Finally, the perfect can also vividly portray future events as though in the present. The Hebrew imperfect is employed chiefly for repeated and continuous actions in the past and present, for future transactions and events, and to give modal meanings (should, may, can, etc.).

I am grateful to my friend and colleague, Dominique Barthélemy; conversations with him about introductory questions, especially regarding the process of canonization, were invariably profitable. As always, and with more love than ever, my wife contributed a large number of the drawings. The book is dedicated to our sister-in-law, Esther Leu, and our friend, Hans Heinrich Schmid.

Othmar Keel

Translator's Preface

Whereas Professor Keel provides his own German translation of the Hebrew text of the Song, this English version makes use of the NRSV as the standard translation. Where Keel's translation differs markedly from the NRSV, the latter is replaced with an English rendering of the former. Such material is enclosed in brackets. Words in parentheses are additions to the Hebrew text made by Keel in his German translation. Angle brackets signal material that Keel deems to be a gloss.

Professor Keel provided his own translation of the Egyptian texts cited. Here standard English translations have been used whenever possible, seeking the version that best renders Keel's meaning. Where no English version was adequate, Keel's German has been translated into English. This material is enclosed in brackets. Other parentheses and brackets in nonbiblical texts are those of the several translations cited and do not, therefore, have uniform meaning in the present commentary.

Standard English translations of the Egyptian love songs do not use completely uniform reference systems. For consistency, the system employed throughout this book is that of M. V. Fox (*The Song of Songs and the Ancient Egyptian Love Songs* [Madison: University of Wisconsin Press, 1985]), even when the translation itself comes from another source.

Where English and Hebrew versification in biblical texts differs, the Hebrew references are included in parentheses, e.g., Cant. 7:1 (2).

In the narrative, Song of Songs is regularly abbreviated Song. In textual references, the standard abbreviation, Cant., is used.

Frederick J. Gaiser

ix

Introduction

Origins and Allegorizing of the Song of Songs

If one encountered the Song anywhere but in the Bible, one would hardly hesitate to call it a collection of love songs—which of course would be basically correct. The singular form of the title ("the Song of Songs") seems to suggest a unified composition, but the term "Song" is frequently used collectively in Hebrew (see the commentary on 1:1a). The title at the beginning of Hosea ("The word of the Lord that came to Hosea") or Isaiah ("The vision of Isaiah") leads no one to read the book of Hosea as a single poem or the book of Isaiah as a single vision, even though the separate sections of these books are not clearly distinguished from one another (in contrast, say, to the book of Psalms).

Neither should the ascription to Solomon disturb the impression that one is dealing here with love songs. Tradition remembers Solomon as the most glorious of all Israelite kings. A large harem and interesting relationships with women come with this territory. Solomon was notorious for both; moreover, he was known as a great songwriter (see the commentary on 1:1b). The rabbis of the first century A.D. thought that Solomon's songs, as contained in the Song, had been collected and written down by the same officials of the Judean king Hezekiah (721–693 B.C.) who had also put together a collection of Solomon's proverbs (Prov. 25:1).[1]

The Cultural Background

Even though the rabbis' supposed date of the collection is questionable, their references to Solomon and the officials of Hezekiah correctly iden-

---

1. Babylonian Talmud, *B.Bat.* 15a; tr. I. Epstein, *The Babylonian Talmud: Seder Nezikin III*, 2 vols. (London: Soncino, 1935) 1:71: "Hezekiah and his colleagues wrote [down] Isaiah, Proverbs, the Song of Songs and Ecclesiastes."

1

tify the milieu that gives rise to these love songs. Thanks to the understanding granted him by God (1 Kgs 3), Solomon was thought to be the wisest of all human beings (1 Kgs 4:29-34 [5:9-14]) and was therefore regarded as the patron of wisdom. Just as the cultic poetry (Psalms) stood under the patronage of David, the wisdom poetry was related to Solomon. Such patronage, however, does not refer to authorship in the modern sense. Reflecting on the course of the world in the third/second century B.C., the Preacher (Ecclesiastes) still speaks in the role of Solomon; even a first-century B.C. Alexandrian book of wisdom written (in Greek!) one thousand years after Solomon carries the title, "The Wisdom of Solomon."

The world under Solomon's patronage was the world of the upper class, of high officials and wisdom teachers who provided their sons and perhaps their daughters an education. The Lamentations of Jeremiah, arising out of the destruction of Jerusalem in 587 B.C., bewail the collapse of this world. There one hears of leaders who have become like deer who find no pasture (Lam. 1:6; cf. Cant. 2:2, 9). Their sons, used to spending their time singing and making (secular) music, are compelled to carry millstones (Lam. 5:13-14). These precious young men are described in Lamentations as "worth their weight in fine gold"; they were "purer than snow, whiter than milk; their bodies were more ruddy than coral, their hair like sapphire" (4:2, 7). These words are strikingly reminiscent of the similar description of the lover in Cant. 5:10-16 (for more on these descriptions, see pp. 18–22).

 The wisdom teacher was the third bearer of religious knowledge in the ancient world, along with the priest, who administered the household of God in the temple and knew its rules precisely, and the prophet, who saw God in dreams and visions and who spoke God's word (Jer. 18:18; Ezek. 7:26). The wise ones did not gain their knowledge like the priests, through patriarchal instruction and contact with the holy, or like the prophets, through God's personal address, but rather through their own alert minds, through observation of the course of everyday affairs, and through attention to the experiences of earlier generations. They regarded humanity and its work, the world and its affairs, as creations of God. Thus both their observations and the rules they formulated about them had theological significance, even when not explicitly stated. Many of their sayings sound quite profane; take, for example, the way they characterize some types of people—like the lazy:

> The lazy person buries a hand in the dish,
>   and will not even bring it back to the mouth. (Prov. 19:24)
> As a door turns on its hinges,
>   so does a lazy person in bed. (Prov. 26:14)

Here are the beginnings of what will develop into modern psychology, into a very broad and differentiated branch of learning.

Love was an area of human life that particularly puzzled the wise:

> Three things are too wonderful for me;
>> four I do not understand:
> the way of an eagle in the sky,
>> the way of a snake on a rock,
>> the way of a ship on the high seas,
>> and the way of a man with a girl. (Prov. 30:18-19)

The focus is clearly on the fourth. What is it that causes the young man to leap upon the mountains and bound over the hills (Cant. 2:8)? Yet for the most part the wise men and the teachers were less interested in the motivation behind such actions than in the dangers thereof. Most of these teachers were apparently elderly. Ezekiel (7:26) replaces "wise" (Jer. 18:18) with "elders." Nevertheless, their instructions in matters of love are remarkably sensuous. Although they naturally paint a dark and terrible picture of the "loose woman" who seduces unsuspecting young men (Proverbs 7), at the same time they urge the student to enjoy his young wife. In language closely related to that of the Song, the wife is described as a lovely deer, a graceful doe. "May her breasts satisfy you at all times; may you be intoxicated always by her love." He is urged to satisfy her so that she does not become disappointed and turn to strangers, who will then drink from his "springs" (Prov. 5:15-20).[2]

Although many wisdom teachers had a positive attitude toward sensual pleasures, as long as these remained within the bonds of marriage, others tended toward a less sensual, more serious portrayal of women and love—for example, the austere Jesus Sirach (ca. 180 B.C.):

> A modest wife adds charm to charm,
>> and no scales can weigh the value of her chastity.
> Like the sun rising in the heights of the Lord,
>> so is the beauty of a good wife in her well-ordered home.
> Like the shining lamp on the holy lampstand,
>> so is a beautiful face on a stately figure.
> Like golden pillars on silver bases,
>> so are shapely legs and steadfast feet.
> My child, keep sound the bloom of your youth,
>> and do not give your strength to strangers.
> [When you have found] a fertile field within the whole plain,
>> [sow it confidently with your own seed to reproduce your family!
> Then your offspring will be near you
>> and your clan will not be scattered about]. (Sir. 26:15-21; cf. also
> Prov. 31:30)

In addition to the danger addressed here, the wise reject adultery primarily because it infringes on the rights of other men.

Yet while the students were scratching these admonitions and similar weighty matters onto one side of their papyri and ostraca (pottery

---

2. In a fine essay, A. M. Dubarle makes many additional observations about the relation between wisdom literature and the Song: "L'amour humain dans le Cantique des cantiques," *RB* 61 (1954) 66–86.

shards used as writing material), they, and those of their teachers who retained something of their youth, were adding a series of love songs to the other side. At least that practice is what one finds in Egypt, and the Egyptian love songs are closer in language and mentality to the Bible's than any others in the ancient Near East. The collection of love songs on Papyrus Chester Beatty I stands alongside a document praising Pharaoh Ramses V (an example of bureaucratic literature) and a record of a cattle sale (another thing the students had to learn about). On the Turin Papyrus one finds love songs on one side and legal protocols on the other; on the Harris Papyrus 500 two entertaining stories are opposite the love songs. All indications are that in Israel too it was the "wise" (i.e., government officials) and their students who composed and perhaps in some cases gathered, wrote down, and circulated the love songs. Their education explains the learned, rich, and differentiated language of the Song; their privileged status explains the familiarity with every kind of luxury so apparent among the Song's authors; their self-assurance explains the freedom to write about individual experiences and feelings.

The Date of Composition

As already explained, the ascription of the songs to Solomon does not indicate authorship in the modern sense; thus, one must depend solely on internal criteria to determine the time of writing, not only of the individual songs but also of the final collection.

Gerleman (76–77) assumes that most of the material did come from the tenth century B.C.—the time of Solomon—because the Solomonic era has been characterized as a period of humanistic enlightenment during which Israel had active contact with Egypt and its love songs (note Solomon's marriage to an Egyptian princess; 1 Kgs 3:1; 7:8; 9:16, 24; 11:1).

But contact between Israel and Egypt was also intensive in the time of King Hezekiah at the end of the eighth century B.C. (Isa. 30:2; 31:1). The praise of Mutirdis, high priestess of Hathor (see note 41), demonstrates that ancient love poetry was not yet a thing of the past in the Egypt of 700 B.C. As mentioned, this was a time of significant literary activity in Judah (Prov. 25:1). The influx of refugees from the Northern Kingdom after the fall of Samaria (722/721 B.C.) would explain the inclusion of material that seems to come from the north (e.g., Cant. 4:8). The end of the eighth century B.C. is also the earliest time to make sense of the many Aramaisms found in the Song. A strong Aramaic influence would probably have shown up first in the Northern Kingdom by way of Damascus. It was assumed in Isaiah's day that every educated Judean knew Aramaic (2 Kgs 18:26); and Isaiah presupposes a widespread acquaintance with love songs when he takes one out of context and uses it to pronounce judgment on Judah (like the Song, it employs the metaphor of the beloved as vineyard; cf. Isa. 5:1 and Cant. 1:6). Notice also how Isaiah rhetorically describes the flirtatiousness of the daughters of Zion, who are so often mentioned in the Song, and who, like the female partner in the Song, "walk with outstretched necks, glancing wantonly with their eyes" (Isa. 3:16–17; see the commentary on Cant. 4:4).

Other motifs in the book are impossible prior to the end of the seventh century B.C. The oasis at En-gedi was not settled and cultivated until then (see the commentary on 1:14b); similarly, many of the terms used for exotic spices and perfumes point to a late preexilic or early exilic date.³ During the same period, Ezekiel, like Isaiah before him, used love songs to gain a hearing for his message (Ezek. 33:32).

But the Song has one Persian loanword (4:13) and perhaps even one from Greek (3:9). Persian loanwords are possible at the earliest in the sixth century B.C. This fact, along with the state of the development of several other ideas, causes many scholars to date the book in the late Persian or even in the Greek period.⁴ Yet no one who knows the ancient Egyptian love songs can fail to see that these are much closer to the Song than the *Idylls* of Theocritus (third century B.C.) and similar Hellenistic poetry.

In my opinion, the collection most nearly fits between the eighth and sixth centuries B.C. At that time ancient Egyptian love literature was still flourishing (a fact that has not been demonstrated for the Hellenistic era; but see n. 42), and ancient Near Eastern motifs were enjoying a final heyday in Israel (see figs. 9, 28–29, 34, 54–55, 57, 85, and 86, among others). This dating does not exclude the possibility that individual words and verses or even whole songs (e.g., 3:9-10d) entered the collection at a later time. As with other OT books, one must assume a rather complicated history behind the formation of the Song; it will be very difficult to ever achieve a high level of certainty about this matter.

The map on page 36, designating the towns and regions mentioned in the Song, helps clarify its geographic origin. Given the several occurrences of Jerusalem in refrains (probably added by the redactor), this city must have been the setting for the final redaction. But because, other than Jerusalem and En-gedi, all Israelite locations mentioned in the Song lie in the Northern Kingdom, and because, other than Kedar, all non-Israelite locations are found even farther north, many of the individual songs must originally have been sung in the northern areas.

Typological and Allegorical Recasting

The oldest example of work on the collection that moves beyond the traditional Hebrew text appears to be the translation into Greek, the Septuagint, which likely took place in the first century B.C. The translator attempted to produce as literal a version as possible, leaving untranslated individual words he did not understand. The Septuagint has no trace of

3. A. Brenner, "Aromatics and Perfumes in the Song of Songs," *JSOT* 25 (1983) 75–81.
4. See H.-P. Müller, "Neige der althebräischen Weisheit: Zum Denken Qohäläts," *ZAW* 90 (1978) 232–33, 259–60; idem, *Vergleich und Metapher im Hohen Lied*, OBO 56 (Fribourg: Universitätsverlag; Göttingen: Vandenhoeck & Ruprecht, 1984) 29; cf. the authors mentioned by Müller and another essay that first appeared in 1985: G. Garbini, "La datazione del 'Cantico dei Cantici,'" *RSO* 56 (1982) 39–46.

allegorizing or spiritualizing the message. Indeed, many times the erotic sense is more blunt than in the original Hebrew. For example, instead of the abstract plural דֹּדִים ("love, joys of love"—1:2, 4; 4:10; 5:1; 7:12 [13]), the Septuagint prefers דַּדַּיִם ("[the two] breasts") and translates accordingly (Gerleman, 77–82).

Three passages in rabbinic texts of the first or second centuries A.D. show that the natural, literal meaning of the Song was still widespread in Judaism at that time. For example, the first saying probably comes from about 90 A.D.: "Our rabbis have taught on Tannaite authority: He who recites a verse of the Song of Songs and turns it into a kind of love-song, and he who recites a verse in the banquet hall not at the proper time [but in a time of carousal] bring evil into the world."[5] When God asks what *should* keep people busy while eating and drinking, the rabbis answer: the appropriate teachings of the law!

Rabbi Aqiba (died 135 A.D.) turns even bigger guns against those who use the Song "profanely": "He who warbles the Song of Songs in a banquet-hall and makes it into a kind of love-song has no portion in the world to come."[6] Most interesting, however, is a tradition placed in the mouth of Rabbi Simeon ben Gamaliel (ca. 140 A.D.):

There were no days better for Israelites than the fifteenth of Ab [in August] and the Day of Atonement [in October]. For on those days Jerusalemite girls go out in borrowed white dresses—so as not to shame those who owned none. All the dresses had to be immersed. And the Jerusalemite girls go out and dance in the vineyards. What did they say? "Fellow, look around and see—choose what you want! Don't look for beauty, look for family." . . . And so it says, *"Go forth you daughters of Zion, and behold King Solomon with the crown with which his mother crowned him in the day of his espousals and in the day of the gladness of his heart"* (Cant. 3:11).[7]

This passage apparently means that at harvest time festivals in the vineyards and orchards gave young men and women a chance to meet; during these festivals portions of the Song were sung (see the commentary on 2:10-13).

How then did allegorical interpretations arise that see, for example, Yahweh in the radiant male lover and Israel in his female counterpart? Certainly not because the Song was originally meant as allegory. It is true that the OT uses relations between men and women as models (metaphors) for the relation between Yahweh and Israel (Hosea 2; Jeremiah 2), occasionally giving these models allegorical development (Ezekiel 16 and 23). But these passages limit the comparison *(tertium comparationis)* to the legal aspects of the relationship, especially to the

5. Babylonian Talmud, *Sanh.* 101a; tr. J. Neusner, *The Talmud of Babylon: An American Translation,* vol. 23c, *Tractate Sanhedrin, Chapters 9–11* (Chico, Calif.: Scholars Press, 1985) 152.
6. Tosefta *Sanh.* 12:10; tr. J. Neusner, *The Tosefta: Fourth Division: Nezikin: The Order of Damages* (New York: Ktav, 1981) 237.
7. Mishnah *Ta'an.* 4:8; tr. J. Neusner, *The Mishnah: A New Translation* (New Haven and London: Yale Univ. Press, 1988) 315–16.

question of faithfulness; they avoid sexual or erotic symbolism. What the author intends to say always either shines clearly through the imagery or is made explicit. This whole tradition is typical of the prophetic literature and limited strictly to it.

But the Song has always been considered a part of the wisdom tradition. In this tradition the relation between man and woman sometimes serves as a model for the relation between student and wisdom. For example, Proverbs 1–9 contrasts Lady Wisdom to the foreign woman, who is depicted as a seductress. The "Solomon" of Wis. 8:2ff. wants to take wisdom for a bride. But here too, as in the case of the prophetic literature, the true meaning of the text remains clear; the limits are maintained.

The Song began to be interpreted allegorically by early Jewish groups like the Pharisaic scribes (and probably the Essenes), at the latest in the second half of the first century B.C. (not first by Rabbi Aqiba at the beginning of the second century A.D.).[8] Allegorizing presupposes that the song had achieved canonical status in its "profane" sense; without this status, allegorizing makes no sense (Rudolph, 83). Allegorizing begins when new circumstances and new ways of thinking can no longer come to grips with an old and honored text. Because of its status the text cannot simply be discarded (just as Greek-speaking Alexandria, e.g., could not discard Homer's *Iliad*), but its contents can no longer be accepted as they are. Thus one claims to have discovered a deeper meaning in the text—a meaning that is only there because one has first inserted it. The canonical status of the Song was based on its Solomonic authorship and its established place in the wisdom literature. Allegorizing became necessary because of the final loss of Israelite independence with the end of the Hasmonean dynasty and the beginning of Roman rule (63 B.C.). The resulting separation of national or "profane" life from religious life was stronger than ever. Once understood as national-religious literature, the canon was seen more and more as cultic-religious literature, and its natural interpretation became more and more offensive to groups rigorously and monomaniacally fixed only on the question of the relationship between Yahweh and Israel. The rabbinic texts cited previously (notes 5–7) show how difficult it was to suppress the natural interpretation. The results of the allegorizers' search for a deeper meaning were arbitrary, unsatisfactory, and often revoltingly grotesque, as any history of interpretation of the Song will show.

I can illustrate this point with two random examples involving Cant. 1:13 ("My beloved is to me a bag of myrrh that lies between my breasts"). Allegorizers take this verse to mean "one thing between two others" which signifies, among other things, either the presence of Yahweh (Shekinah) between the two cherubim above the ark (Rashi, Ibn Ezra) or Christ between the OT and the NT (Philo Carpasius, Cyril of

8. D. Barthélemy, "Comment le Cantique des cantiques est-il devenu canonique?" in *Mélanges bibliques et orientaux en l'honneur de M. Mathias Delcor,* AOAT 215, ed. A. Caquot, S. Légasse, and M. Tardieu (Kevelaer: Butzon & Bercker; Neukirchen-Vluyn: Neukirchener, 1985) 13–22.

7

Alexandria).[9] If two allegorizers ever agree on the interpretation of a verse it is only because one has copied from the other. I will forgo even a brief account of the dramatic shifts in typological and allegorical exegesis. These shifts bear interesting witness to the history of piety and theology, but, as pure inventions, they contribute nothing to a better understanding of the Song.

Yet, despite feverish attempts at suppression by a clerical mentality, the natural interpretation has frequently broken through. The NT has no trace of an allegorical interpretation of the Song. Did the allegorizers understand God better than Jesus did? When the Christian church received the Song from the Pharisaic scribes, who were dominant after the destruction of Jerusalem, the book came with a thoroughly established allegorical sense. Yet Origen (185–253/54 A.D.), who, along with Hyppolytus of Rome, was the first teacher of the church to take up the Song, still saw it clearly as a work of profane poetry. He called it a wedding song (epithalamium)—nothing less than the prototype of all pagan, Greek, and Roman wedding songs. But understood in this literal way the Song, according to Origen, was mere superficial babble, unworthy of God.[10] Like most so-called allegorizers, he basically advocated a typological meaning: what was described as a profane wedding song was actually a model for a higher reality. Yet he did not seem to believe that the Song was originally written in code, as an allegorical portrayal of another reality. Someone inclined toward Platonism can easily regard the whole creation—including the love described in the Song—as an encoded book of divine secrets. One can then read the Song under the slogan, "All earth comprises / Is symbol alone" (Goethe, *Faust, Great Books of the Western World* [Chicago: Encyclopaedia Britannica, Inc., 1952] 294). But that view has nothing to do with exegesis in any precise sense.

How intensely Origen himself still felt the natural, literal meaning of the Song is demonstrated by his urgent warning that it be read only by those who are deaf to the enticements of physical love; otherwise it could seem that the Holy Scriptures were awakening such feelings—a shocking idea! He notes with approval a Jewish regulation that allowed only mature people (over age 30) to read the Song.[11]

Amid all the devaluing, even demonizing, of the body and physical needs, Cyril of Jerusalem (313–387 A.D.) also felt compelled to polemicize against a natural understanding: "For you must not, accepting the vulgar, superficial interpretation of the words, suppose that the Canticle is an expression of carnal, sexual love."[12] Despite the heavy indoctri-

9. For these and other examples, see H. H. Rowley, "The Interpretation of the Song of Songs," *JTS* 38 (1937) 338–39, 343. On the history of interpretation, see Pope, 89–229, and the literature cited there.
10. R. Lawson, *Origen: The Song of Songs: Commentary and Homilies,* ACW 26 (Westminster, Md.: Newman, 1957) 268, 270.
11. J.-P. Migne, *Origenis opera omnia,* vol. 3, PG 13 (Paris: Vrayet, 1862) 63–64; Lawson, *Origen,* 23.
12. J.-P. Migne, *S. P. N. Cyrilli Hierosolymitani opera quae exstant,* PG 33 (Paris:

nation to interpret the Song allegorically or typologically, many in fourth-century Jerusalem were apparently unbiased enough not to find symbols of Jesus' passion in the litter described in 3:9-10d (an interpretation Cyril demanded of his hearers).

But not only plain common sense rejected these unreasonable demands. Exegesis of the Antioch school, less prone to allegory than its counterpart in Alexandria, also had difficulty with such antics. The Antiochians were as little inclined as the Alexandrians or Cyril of Jerusalem to accept the natural and literal meaning of the Song, but they sought another way out. According to a letter of the best-known Antioch exegete, Theodore of Mopsuestia (350–428 A.D.), discussed in 553 A.D. at the fifth Ecumenical Council (the second in Constantinople), the Song was Solomon's homage to pharaoh's daughter, meant to defend his marriage with her; thus, as a purely secular poem, it had no place in the canon. In practice that point was true—it was not then, nor had it ever been, read aloud in synagogue or church.[13] The practice of reading from the Song at Passover, often regarded as ancient, cannot be clearly demonstrated prior to the eighth century A.D. (Rudolph, 77, 93). Theodore of Mopsuestia was naturally not alone in his low estimate of the Song as profane literature; he represented an entire movement. In the ninth century A.D., the Syrian Isho'dad of Hedatta (died ca. 872 A.D.) could still write: "The blessed interpreter [Theodore of Mopsuestia] and all those who followed in his footsteps relate it [the Song of Songs] to the daughter of pharaoh."[14]

In the twelfth century A.D., an anonymous rabbi in northern France posited that the Song was a song of praise written by Solomon about his favorite wife, and even the well-known Ibn Ezra (died 1167) interpreted the Song in a natural sense (though offering also a secondary typological meaning as a defense against attacks by the orthodox).[15] At the turn of the fourteenth century A.D., an anonymous Alemannic poet used verses of the Song as the basis for forty-three "Minnelieder Salomos zu Ehren seiner Geliebten" (love songs of Solomon in honor of his beloved).[16] Similarly, composers of historical novels about medieval times, from J. V. von Scheffel to Umberto Eco, are no doubt correct when they have their young monastic heroes (from Ekkehard to Adson) speak in the words of the Song when touched by unexpected passion. The language of this book seems made to order to express the feelings for which these characters had no words.

Vrayet, 1857) 1141ff.; L. McCauley and A. Stephenson, *The Works of Saint Cyril of Jerusalem*, vol. 2, FC 64 (Washington, D.C.: Catholic Univ. of America Press, 1970) 215.
13. J. D. Mansi, *Sacrorum conciliorum nova et amplissima collectio*, vol. 9 (Florence, 1763; reprint, Paris and Leipzig: H. Welter, 1902) 225ff.
14. G. Diettrich, *Išô'dadh's Stellung in der Auslegungsgeschichte des Alten Testaments*, BZAW 6 (Giessen: Ricker'sche, 1902) xx.
15. Rowley, "Interpretation," 352, n. 4; see other references there and in Rudolph, 93.
16. D. G. Schöber, *Das Hohelied Salomonis aus zwoen deutschen Handschriften, deren Eine in zerschiedene Stücke deutscher Reime über dasselbe, die Andere in einer alt-deutschen Übersetzung davon, besteht* (Augsburg, 1752) 21–49; printed as an appendix in J. G. Herder, *Lieder der Liebe: Die ältesten und schönsten aus dem Morgenlande: Nebst vier und vierzig alten Minneliedern* (Leipzig: Weygandsche, 1778) 156ff.

Nevertheless, in academic circles, even the rise of humanism and the Reformation were unable to breach the solid front of typology and allegory. The humanist Sébastien Chateillon, whose intellectual honesty prohibited him from seeing anything but erotic songs in the Song, concluded therefore (like Theodore of Mopsuestia earlier) that the book did not belong in the canon. Because of this view, Calvin forced him to leave Geneva in 1545, saying, "Our chief disagreement concerns the Song of Songs. He [Chateillon] saw it as a lascivious and obscene poem, in which Solomon describes his shameless love affairs."[17]

A new point of view did not appear until the seventeenth and eighteenth centuries. Hugo Grotius formulated his position on the Song briefly and directly in his "Annotationes ad Vetus Testamentum" (1644): "The Hebrews call this the most noble song because of its many elegant formulations, which are lost by translation into other languages. It is a dialogue of love between Solomon and the daughter of the Egyptian king, enhanced by two choirs—one of young men, another of maidens—who keep watch near the bridal chamber. The marital secrets are concealed here by an honorable cloak of words. This is the reason that the ancient Hebrews wanted this book read only by those about to marry." Everything up to this point was already to be found in Origen. But then Grotius discretely distances himself from the allegorical interest of Origen and his successors (including the reformers). He admits: "In order to make it endure longer, it is believed that Solomon composed this writing with such artistry that without great distortion one could find in it allegories expressing the love of God for his people Israel—as the Targum perceives and demonstrates. . . . But that love was the prototype *[typos]* of the love of Christ for the church." In his own comments, however, Grotius primarily cites parallels from classical authors like Theocritus, Catullus, Horace, Virgil, and many others, mentioning only twice an allegorical or typological interpretation.[18]

Then, in the eighteenth century, many representatives of a literal, natural interpretation of the Song appeared. The most forceful and convincing representative was J. G. Herder; because of his wide knowledge of different peoples it was self-evident to him that the Song was a collection of love songs.[19] Herder also influenced Goethe's evaluation in the "West-Eastern Divan": "We lament the fact that we are permitted no full enjoyment of the fragmentary poems, interwoven into and overladen upon one another as they are. . . . Sometimes we thought to draw something out of the delightful confusion and piece it together, but the enigmatic and inscrutable character of these few pages is precisely what provides their charm and personality."[20] (I have yet to deal with the problem of the composition of the material; see pp. 16–17.)

17. G. Baum, E. Cunitz and E. Reuss, *Ioannis Calvini Opera quae supersunt omnia,* vol. 11, Corpus Reformatorum 39 (Braunschweig: C. A. Schwetschke, 1873) 675.
18. H. Grotius, *Opera omnia theologica,* vol. 1 (Amsterdam, 1679; reprint, Stuttgart and Bad Cannstatt: Frommann, 1972) 267a.
19. Herder, *Lieder der Liebe.*
20. J. W. von Goethe, *Noten und Abhandlungen zum west-östlichen Divan,* vol. 5 of

The nineteenth century saw the last of the allegorical or typological commentaries by significant OT scholars. The typological commentary of Franz Delitzsch appeared in 1851;[21] the allegorical commentary of E. W. Hengstenberg in 1853. Such interpretations continued for approximately another hundred years within the Catholic Church. Then in 1943 Pius XII's encyclical *Divino afflante spiritu* not only allowed but even required attention to literary forms. As a result, after the war a series of works appeared justifying a literal and natural interpretation of the Song.[22] Thus ended the Song's captivity under the capricious rule of a spiritualistic Babylon; all major churches now accept its return to the modest surroundings of home. Just as Israel's deportation to foreign lands produced conscious reflection on its uniqueness and role among the nations, so the Babylonian captivity of the Song has led to a deepened understanding of its specific function within the biblical testimonies about humankind and humanity's relationship to God and the world (see also pp. 30ff.).

Sitz im Leben, Composition, Literary Forms, and Language

Once the Song had been rescued from an existence beyond space and time and brought back down to earth, more detailed questions arose about its cultural milieu.

The *Sitz im Leben*

The traditional notion that the life setting of the Song was Solomon's marriage to the daughter of pharaoh was no longer tenable for the simple reason that nowhere in the book is Solomon directly addressed. He is mentioned only in the third person.

On the basis of the accounts of a Near Eastern specialist, E. Renan noted in 1860 (even before his well-known *Mission en Phénicie,* 1860/61) that the seven-day marriage festivals reported in the OT (Gen. 29:27; Judg. 14:12, 17) were very similar to those celebrated in Arab countries right up to the present. These festivals are accompanied by much singing, which was also already the case in the OT (cf. Jer. 7:34; 16:9; 25:10; 33:11). He saw the Song as the best-known collection of songs for such an occasion.[23] A bit later, the longtime German consul in Damascus, J. G. Wetzstein, advocated the same view, supporting it with ethnological material. Wetzstein had observed how in Hauran, an area south of Damascus, during the seven-day wedding ceremonies the bride and

---

Sämtliche Werke: Jubiläumsausgabe (Stuttgart and Berlin: Cotta, 1905) 150.
21. For more on Delitzsch's view, see the careful and detailed commentary by S. Wagner, *Franz Delitzsch: Leben und Werk,* BEvT 80 (Munich: C. Kaiser, 1978) 285–94.
22. M. A. van den Oudenrijn, *Vom Sinne des Hohenliedes,* BibB (Fribourg: Schweizerischen katholischen Bibelbewegung, 1953); Dubarle, "L'amour humain"; J. P. Audet, "Le sens du Cantique des cantiques," *RB* 62 (1955) 197–221; cf. H. Haag, "Das heutige Verständnis des Hohenliedes in der katholischen Exegese," in *Mélanges Delcor,* 209–19.
23. E. Renan, *Le Cantique des cantiques: Traduit de l'hébreu avec une étude sur le plan, l'ge et le caractâre du poème* (Paris: Michel Lévy Frères, 1860) 86.

groom were enthroned (on a threshing table) and celebrated as king and queen. The songs sung at these ceremonies had many similarities to those in the Song.[24] This interpretation met with considerable approval, both because of its plausibility and because it saw the Song as a hymn to modest and monogamous marriage (see Budde and Würthwein). Nevertheless, its inadequacies did not remain hidden for long: the Song never uses the word "queen" for the bride; the man is never referred to as "groom"; and the only section in which the term "wedding" appears (3:11) was, according to the Mishnah, sung at a festival in the vineyards that had nothing to do with marriage (see note 7 above).

Gustav Dalman, who lived in Palestine for a long time and who possessed a remarkably detailed knowledge of its people and customs, writes in the introduction to his large collection of Palestinian songs (published in 1901 as *Palästinischer Diwan*):

Not all these songs (which descriptively portray the pulchritude of a woman, or, rarely, a man) can be applied directly to a bride and groom; their beauty is generally given less attention. This point does not preclude the existence of regions where things might be done differently—which, according to Wetzstein's accounts, is just the case in the broad environs of Damascus and part of Hauran. But the use of descriptive songs in the marriage rites, as reported there, is by no means a common Palestinian custom, and there is no justification for insisting that even there such usage would be absolutely invariable. Descriptive songs are sung on all kinds of occasions, not only at weddings. Thus they can only be referred to a bridal party when that is directly stipulated. One needs to take this into account when exegeting the Song of Songs, which, based on its content, does not consist of actual wedding songs but rather love songs (which, of course, might have their place also at weddings). (XII)

But the Arab culture of Palestine was not the only new factor to be considered by nineteenth-century Western scholars seeking an appropriate understanding of the Song; there was also the new material from the ancient Near East. Spurred by Napoleon's Egyptian expedition in 1798, ancient Near Eastern research, including the discovery of the world portrayed in its images and the deciphering of hieroglyphics and cuneiform, made an enormous impression on the scholarly world of the nineteenth and early twentieth centuries. The question of how to view the Bible in this newly discovered universe led to protracted and sometimes vehement disagreements. One side regarded the Bible merely as a late and undistinguished witness to the advanced civilization of the ancient Near East; the other tried to maintain as fully as possible the claim that every sentence of the Bible bore witness to a unique revelation. Many scholars, for whom a number of passages in the Song were too artistic, too lofty, or too exotic to be attributed to Palestinian or OT peasant marriage rites, looked for an appropriate *Sitz im Leben* in the newly discovered

24. J. G. Wetzstein, "Die syrische Dreschtafel 4: Die Tafel in der Königswoche," *Bastians Zeitschrift für Ethnologie* 5 (1873) 287–94. The material is also found in F. Delitzsch, *Commentary on the Song of Songs and Ecclesiastes,* tr. M. G. Easton (1877; reprint, Grand Rapids: Eerdmans, 1982) 162–76.

world of the ancient Near East. They thought they found it in the fertility cults depicting affirmations of love between a god and goddess (e.g., the sun-god and the moon-goddess[25] or Isis and Osiris[26]). Most widely accepted were the attempts to explain the Song as a collection of texts from the cult of the Sumerian pair Dumuzi and Inanna—honored among the Akkadians as Tammuz and Ishtar—whose counterparts in Syria were Baal and Anat (or Astarte). To demonstrate the existence of such cults in biblical Israel, one could point not only to the prophetic condemnation of Baal worship but also (for the Mesopotamian form) to a specific reference to women weeping for Tammuz at the north gate of the temple of Jerusalem (Ezek. 8:14). Wittekindt, Haller, and Schmökel wrote their commentaries under the assumption that the texts of the Song came from this cult. The commentaries by Ringgren and Pope still have considerable sympathy for this position, even though they do not represent it directly. One of its chief difficulties is that the Song's presumed main characters are never named; thus, at best, one can see the present text only as a well-expurgated version of such cultic songs. Even apart from the names of the main characters, literary connections are minimal (see pp. 25-30). Above all, one misses any references in the Song to the priests, altars, cleansing rituals, and other cultic matters that appear in the Sumerian sacred marriage songs.[27] In addition, the cultic interpretation presupposes an overall dramatic structure (cultic drama), which for the Song can be achieved only by transposing texts quite arbitrarily (as in Schmökel; see pp. 15-17). Schmökel's commentary (1956) is a recent, though failed, attempt to comprehend the Song as a book of sacred marriage texts.

Either the threshing table (as the rostrum for a simple peasant wedding) or the ancient Near Eastern temple (as the site of a magnificent divine wedding) would provide the Song, each in its own way, with an unequivocal *Sitz im Leben* (every form critic's dream). Either the peasant wedding, with its simple and austere customs, or the *hieros gamos* (sacred marriage), so interesting to students of comparative religion, would be able to satisfy the need for an ethical or religious orientation. Delitzsch even wanted to see in the Song nothing less than a prototype of the inner-Trinitarian "marriage": the bride relates to the bridegroom as the church relates to Christ, and the church relates to Christ as the Son relates to the Father (see note 21). But the actual state of affairs appears to be at once more complex (in regard to literary forms) and more prosaic (in regard to religious or theological intensity).

Ancient Egyptian love songs were first made available to a broad audience in 1874. Parallels to the Song were sought immediately.[28] But in

---

25. W. Erbt, *Die Hebräer: Kanaan im Zeitalter der hebräischen Wanderung und hebräischer Staatengründungen* (Leipzig: Hinrichs'sche, 1906) 196–202.
26. O. Neuschotz de Jassy, *Le Cantique des Cantiques et le mythe d'Osiris-Hetep* (Paris: C. Reinwald, 1914).
27. S. N. Kramer, *The Sacred Marriage Rite: Aspects of Faith, Myth, and Ritual in Ancient Sumer* (Bloomington: Indiana Univ. Press, 1969) 65, 80, 82.
28. C. W. Goodwin, "On Four Songs Contained in an Egyptian Papyrus in the British Museum," *Transactions of the Society of Biblical Archaeology* 3 (1874) 380–88; G.

his 1899 edition of the love songs on the London Papyrus Harris 500, W. M. Müller declared that all the parallels between the Song and Egyptian love songs were insignificant: "Hebrew and Egyptian poetry are just as different as Hebrew and Egyptian thought."[29] Whether OT scholars accepted this position or simply overlooked the Egyptian love poetry, they made only sporadic mention of these important parallels over the next fifty years. Not until Schott published all the then-known Egyptian love songs and related texts in a handy translation (1950) and A. Hermann added his important and impressive study (*Altägyptische Liebesdichtung* [Wiesbaden: Harrassowitz, 1959]) were scholars made aware of this aid to the understanding of OT love songs. In his 1965 commentary, Gerleman interpreted the Song—alas, quite one-sidedly—from the perspective of the Egyptian parallels, rejecting any connection to marriage or to the Near Eastern cults. The valuable book by M. V. Fox, *The Song of Songs and the Ancient Egyptian Love Songs* (Madison: University of Wisconsin Press, 1985), stands in the same tradition (with the same one-sidedness). This work, which arrived too late to be considered here, is not only a comparative literary study but also a full commentary on the Song. For Gerleman and Fox, the poems of the Song—like the ancient Egyptian love songs for Hermann—are love lyrics, formulations of the moods and experiences of lovers, standing in a particular literary tradition and expressed in the language of poetic fiction (note the comments under the rubric *"Ort"* in Gerleman's commentary). Similarly, Dalman had already designated the majority of Palestinian songs in his collection as "the experiences and moods of lovers."[30] The Song's use of elements taken from the repertoire of Near Eastern divinities and sacred marriages, fully ignored by Gerleman, was then convincingly described by H.-P. Müller as a "lyrical reproduction of the mythical" and thus integrated into a lyrical understanding of the Song.[31]

But unless one is willing to read these literary-metaphorical expressions of the lovers' experiences and feelings of longing, pain, and happiness as reports of actual concrete events, the assignment of a *Sitz im Leben,* in the form-critical sense, becomes exceedingly problematic, even impossible. Love poems arise under all kinds of conditions; they are read, recited, and sung under all kinds of conditions—whether for personal pleasure in one's private chamber or for public recognition at a royal festival. Most often, an individual poem does not tell its setting. The search for the *Sitz im Leben* needs to be modified; it makes sense only as a search for the milieu that gave rise to such poetry (see pp. 1–4) and for the origins of the literary forms and metaphors (see pp. 18–30).

These matters are important to understand if one is to interpret

---

Maspero, "Les Chants d'amour du Papyrus de Turin et du Papyrus Harris," *JA* 8/1 (1883) 47; G. C. Pola, *L'imitazione egiziana nel Cantico dei Cantici* (Turin, 1896).

29. W. M. Müller, *Die Liebespoesie der Ägypter* (Leipzig: Hinrichs'sche, 1899) 8–9.

30. G. Dalman, *Palästinischer Diwan: Als Beitrag zur Volkskunde Palästinas gesammelt und mit Übersetzung und Melodie herausgegeben* (Leipzig: Hinrichs'sche, 1901) XI.

31. H.-P. Müller, "Die lyrische Reproduktion des Mythischen im Hohelied," *ZTK* 73 (1976) 23–41; idem, *Vergleich und Metapher.*

the poems of the Song properly. In my opinion, Krinetzki goes too far when he says:

Whoever wants to understand the message of the Song of Songs correctly must first seek to comprehend its "erotic psychology," an introduction to which I have written in "Die erotische Psychologie des Hohen Liedes" in *Theologische Quartalschrift* 150 (1970) 404–416, where I follow C. G. Jung and his methodology.... Fundamental is Jung's recognition that the Song of Songs is not about objective descriptions and experiences; rather it projects on another object one's own sensations of erection, of touch, of bodily organs. [To speak this way, one should say "sensations of orgasm" rather than "sensations of erection," because women, not only men, also sometimes wrote poetry in ancient Israel—Exod. 15:20–21; Judg. 5:1; 1 Sam. 18:7.] Thus what one encounters here are not primarily concrete partners and concrete love but some archetypal (i.e., superindividual), phylogenetically conditioned notions of male and female, of Eros and Sexus, which exist in the speakers' unconscious and which are transferred onto the partner. (39–40)

The problem with this approach is that even before the actual texts are studied the reader already knows they are meant to evoke Jungian notions of animus and anima, of inhibition and integration. Such an approach comes very close to an allegorical interpretation that has to know in advance that the Song is about God (or Christ) and Israel (or the church) so these can then be discovered like Easter eggs among the various shrubs and flowers of the Song.

Does a Comprehensive Plan Underlie the Song of Songs?

Viewing the Song allegorically as a portrayal of the relationship of Yahweh to Israel or Christ to the church leads to the temptation to read the book as a continuous story. For example, the Aramaic translation (the Targum of the sixth/seventh century A.D.) is a narrative interpretation that reads the Song as a presentation of the history of God with his people from the Exodus to the time of Solomon.[32]

Because the Song (with the exception of 3:9-10d) consists totally of direct speech, it would seem more appropriate to understand it as drama; Origen was the first to do so. The players are Christ and his angels as Solomon and his companions and the church and the believers as the bride and her playmates (see notes 10 and 11, above). The drama theory enjoyed great popularity again in the eighteenth and nineteenth centuries. The Song was occasionally interpreted in analogy to the pastoral plays and singspiels beloved at that time. A particularly popular version saw a human triangle in the Song— Solomon was trying to win a simple but very beautiful maiden for his harem, while she wanted to remain faithful to her shepherd boyfriend. A. Hazan published an interpretation of this kind as late as 1936 under the promising title, *Le Cantique des Cantiques enfin expliqué* (Paris). According to Rudolph's apt caricature of Hazan, "Every time the king thinks he will get what he desires, the

---

32. W. Riedel, *Die älteste Auslegung des Hohenliedes* (Naumburg: Lippert, 1898) 9–40.

shepherd boy appears out of nowhere and foils his intentions; yet the king accepts all this as calm as can be, persistently beginning again in the next act to idolize the girl anew. This happens three times in a row! The alleged triple parallelism, of which Hazan is very proud, is achieved only by the insertion of invented verses and invented characters" (97; see his note 10).

In order to find the cultic drama he seeks in the Song, Schmökel freehandedly rearranges the poems completely (45–47). For example:

Scene One

"Goddess, appear!"	(Men's chorus)	8:13
What is the goddess like?	(Women's chorus)	6:10, 5a
Ishtar's answer	(Priestess)	1:5-6

The result has little to do with the Song which has been demolished and its pieces put together in a new mosaic made to match a preconceived sketch. This seductive approach can produce surprising effects. It is a creative art (collage) but hardly exegesis.

In its traditional form, the Song itself offers no basis for a dramatic interpretation. Two or three poems are sometimes arranged in a kind of running continuity (e.g., 5:2-8; 5:9-16; 6:1-3), but the collector or redactor apparently has no interest in anything larger than such small units. This fact

puts an end to the whole phantom of a dramatic reading. A drama needs continuity and an ending. In a drama of love, like the Song of Songs, the only appropriate ending would be that, after all the intervening circumstances, the guy (using the vernacular) finally gets the girl. But in the Song, on the one hand, they come together much too quickly (even if one ignores earlier passages, the physical union is as clear as can be at the end of chapter 4); on the other hand, this union still seems far away in chapter 7 and at the beginning of chapter 8. (Rudolph, 97)

But even if the content of the Song is not continuous, might it not be possible to find a formal scheme of composition? It is evident to every reader of the Song that some elements turn up repeatedly—catchwords, striking similes and metaphors, even whole sentences and brief poetic units. Although some forms of address are concentrated in one part of the Song (e.g., "sister" and "bride" in 4:8—5:2), others are distributed more or less evenly throughout (e.g., "my love" [fem.] in 1:9, 15; 2:10, 13; 4:1, 7; 5:2; 6:4). Some phrases occur twice (e.g., "My beloved is mine and I am his; he pastures his flock among the lotus flowers"—2:16 and 6:3) or even three times (e.g., the entreaty to the daughters of Jerusalem not to stir up love—2:7; 3:5; 8:4). The latter formula is twice connected with another to make a brief poem (2:6-7 and 8:3-4). Even longer units are repeated—not verbatim but with clearly recognizable similarity—e.g., an experience in the night (3:1-5; 5:2-8) or the detailed description of the woman (4:1-7; 7:1-5 [2-6]). These factors have led to the division of the Song into two parts (1:2—5:1 and 5:2—8:14). J. Cheryl Exum subdivided these further, attempting to identify six units (1:2—2:2; 2:7—3:5; 3:6—5:1; 5:2—6:3; 6:4—8:3; 8:4-14).[33] W. H. Shea modified these six divisions slightly (1:2—2:2; 2:3-17; 3:1-4, 16; 5:1-7, 10; 7:10 [11]—8:5; 8:6-14), thinking he could identify a chiastic structure (see the commentary on 5:16cd).[34] For example, he points to the occurrence of "apple tree" at the beginning of his second section and at the end of the next-to-last section (2:3; 8:5). Unfortunately, this analysis requires breaking up a clear poetic unity (2:1-3); moreover, even though the two appearances of "apple tree" jump out at the reader, others of his so-called matches are much less clear or simply invented (e.g., he sees a connection between 1:8 and 8:11 because both flock and vineyard supposedly belong to Solomon, even though the text never claims that the flock is Solomon's). Chiasms may well have played a role in the structure of various parts of the Song, but I doubt that they played a role for the whole collection. Without claiming such a rigorous structure, Krinetzki (12–19) also finds six groups of songs, although he divides them somewhat differently than Shea (1:2—2:6; 2:7-16; 2:17—3:5; 3:6—6:3; 6:4—8:3; 8:4-14).

Along with Rudolph (97–98), Gerleman (who never considers overall composition), and Pope (40–54), I find no overall formal structure. Several smaller collections of poetry apparently preceded the Song in its present form (as with Psalms and Proverbs). I think this view best explains the existence of doublets in the book. Several different sayings are repeated in Proverbs (e.g., 22:13 and 26:13), as are several poems or parts of poems in Psalms (e.g., Ps. 14 = Ps. 53; 70 = 40:13-17 [14-18]). The collector or redactor of the Song appears to have drawn together poems that already existed, individually and in small groups, partly on the basis of a simple catchword principle and partly on the basis of content (see the introductions to the individual poems in the commentary). It is quite possible that he supplemented some poems with "appropriate" verses taken from others, a process that one can see in the Greek translation. (The words "I called him, but he gave no answer" from 5:6 are found in the Greek version, but not in the Hebrew, also after 3:1c.) Perhaps the composer or redactor took some songs directly from the oral tradition, where they might have circulated in different versions.

Thanks to its large number of repeated formulas and metaphors, the Song has seemed to many interpreters to be, if not a unified structure, at least the work of a single author.[35] But this impression of a unified pattern comes, I think, not so much from single authorship as from the secondary enrichment of the poems through formulas and verses from other songs (as just mentioned) and from the use of conventional language (for more on this point see pp. 25–30).

---

33. J. Cheryl Exum, "A Literary and Structural Analysis of the Song of Songs," *ZAW* 85 (1973) 47–79.
34. W. H. Shea, "The Chiastic Structure of the Song of Songs," *ZAW* 92 (1980) 378–96.
35. Cf., e.g., Rowley, "Interpretation," 358.

Formal Elements and Categories

Most recent major commentators (e.g., Rudolph, Gerleman, Pope, Krinetzki) agree that the Song consists of a collection of songs, even though Pope declines to delineate these songs and simply comments on the whole book, verse by verse.

The redactional work already described—enriching individual poems with elements from other poems and occasionally making artificial connections between two poems—makes it impossible to define the limits of the individual poems in every case. But this point dare not obscure the broad consensus that does exist among commentators. It is a cheap shot to use extreme positions or minor inevitable divergences to proclaim quickly the bankruptcy of biblical scholarship. True, the Masoretic division of the Hebrew Bible makes 19 poems of this material, while Herder has 20, Rudolph 30, Gerleman 34, Keel 42, and Krinetzki 52; but that discrepancy is because Krinetzki consciously proceeds from the smallest definable units, while Herder and, to a lesser degree, Rudolph accept the larger units created by the redactor. While all six systems do not have the same number of units, the divisions do, as a rule, come at the same places:

Masorah	Herder	Rudolph	Gerleman	Krinetzki	Keel
1:2-4	1:2-4	1:2-4	1:2-4	1:2-4	1:2-4
5-8	5-8	5-6	5-6	5-6	5-6
		7-8	7-8	7-8	7-8
9-14	9-14	9-17	9-11	9-11	9-11
			12-14	12	12
				13-14	13-14
1:15—2:7	1:15—2:7		15-17	15-17	15-17
etc.	etc.	2:1-3	2:1-3	2:1-3	2:1-3
		4-7	4-7	4-5	4-5
		etc.	etc.	6	6-7
				7	etc.
				etc.	

In 1935 F. Horst defined literary categories for the original songs, using criteria related to both form and content.[36] Horst distinguished among songs of admiration (e.g., 1:15-17; 7:6-9 [7-10]), comparisons and allegories (e.g., 1:13-14), descriptive songs—also named with the Arabic word *wazf* (e.g., 4:1-7), songs of desire (e.g., 2:14), and descriptions of an experience (e.g., 3:1-4); he also includes the less frequent categories of self-description (1:5-6; 8:8-10), vaunt song (6:8-9; 8:11-12), and jest (1:7-8). Pope, who includes the definitions of these eight categories (66–69)—as he includes so much else in the lengthy introduction to his com-

36. F. Horst, "Die Formen des althebräischen Liebesliedes," in *Orientalische Studien: Enno Littmann zu seinem 60. Geburtstag überreicht*, ed. R. Paret (Leiden: Brill, 1935) 43–54; reprint in Horst, *Gottes Recht: Studien zum Recht im Alten Testament*, TB 12 (Munich: C. Kaiser, 1961) 176–87.

mentary—notes somewhat ironically: "The application of form criticism to the Song of Songs has been attempted only rarely and without spectacular results." Krinetzki too reports these eight categories and adds three more: the song of entreaty (by which he means the refrain in 2:7; 3:5; 8:4), the call to joy (3:10e-11; 5:1ef), and the dialogue—"a creation of the redactor" (e.g., 4:16—5:1d). Krinetzki indicates the literary category of every single poem. This rather joyless task leads to an occasional inconsistency. For example, he calls Cant. 4:8 both a song of admiration (20) and a descriptive song (139). At best, one can scarcely differentiate between the two categories. Even the titles betray the use of criteria from different areas: admiration, like desire, is a state of mind, whereas description and self-description are formal processes. No one could argue that the descriptions in 4:1-7 or 7:1-5 (2-6) do not convey admiration. What is the difference between the song of admiration in 7:6-9 (7-10) and the descriptive song in 4:1-7? Horst identifies two parts of the song of admiration: the first part describes a person's beauty, the second the effects of such beauty, i.e., "either the wish or longing for union with the beloved or the joy over such union" (177). But a text that he clearly labels a descriptive song (4:1-7) contains these words:

> Until the day breathes
> > and the shadows flee,
> I will hasten to the mountain of myrrh
> > and the hill of frankincense. (4:6)

Here mere description has been left behind; here is precisely "the wish or longing for union with the beloved or the joy over such union" that is supposed to be specific to the song of admiration and ought not be found in a descriptive song.

Instead of labeling the poems with such questionable titles, I have as a rule preferred to begin the commentary on each song by stating the arguments from form and content that have led to its separation from the previous unit and by naming the elements of form and content that characterize the song thus delineated.

The following structure occurs frequently, in all possible variations: the woman (or less often the man) is described as beautiful and desirable (in nominal clauses or perfect verbs), and then the wish for contact with her (or him) is expressed (in nominal clauses, imperfect forms, imperatives, etc.). Sometimes the first (indicative) section is fully developed and the second only intimated; sometimes the first section is brief, the second developed at length. The order is occasionally reversed: a wish is expressed, using imperatives or imperfects (1:2a; 2:15ab; 8:6ab), and then reasons are given, in nominal clauses or similar forms (1:2b; 2:15d; 8:6cd).

This structure, which characterizes most songs in the book, leads to the conclusion that the basic mood of the songs is a wish for change, a longing for union with the beloved. This basic mood also gives rise to the fictitious experiences reported in the book (see the commentary on 3:1-5).

If one examines the songs for content rather than form, one would have to call almost all of them songs of desire. The peculiarity of the Song in this regard becomes clear only in contrast to Arab or classical poetry, where the primary element is the lover's lament, bemoaning the loss of the partner. Cant. 5:2-7 may once have been such a lament, but now the redactor has placed it in a new context, giving it a positive outcome. If only traces of the lover's lament remain in the Song, the repetitive litanies common to the ritual of the Sumerian sacred marriage are lacking altogether.[37]

In contrast, the love songs of the four ancient Egyptian collections take the same forms as the biblical love songs. Like the biblical songs, the Egyptian counterparts are consistently cast in direct speech. Again, like the biblical songs, the Egyptian ones often use the indicative to describe a condition that gives rise to a wish—although in the Egyptian songs the impetus is more often the speaker's own love rather than the beauty of the beloved, the latter being more typical of the Song. For example:

> My love for you is mixed throughout my body
> like [salt] dipped in water,
> like a medicine to which gum is added,
> like milk shot through [water] . . .
>
> So hurry to see your lady,
> like a stallion on the track.[38]

In addition, the ancient Egyptian love songs frequently include pure wishing songs, introduced with the formula "If only. . . ."[39]

Most important, the ancient Egyptian love songs also contain what I regard as the most notable element of the Song: the listing of different parts of the body, each described by an adjective, a simile, or a metaphor (cf. 4:1-7; 5:9-16; 7:1-5 [2-6]):

> One, the lady love without a duplicate,
> more perfect than the world,
> see, she is like the star rising
> at the start of an auspicious year.
>
> She whose excellence shines, whose body glistens,
> glorious her eyes when she stares,
> sweet her lips when she converses,
> she says not a word too much.

37. Kramer, *Sacred Marriage*, 68–69, 81–82, 99; cf. idem, "BM 23 631: Bread for Enlil, Sex for Inanna," *Or* 54 (1985) 117–32.
38. Papyrus Harris 500, group A, no. 2; tr. W. K. Simpson in *The Literature of Ancient Egypt: An Anthology of Stories, Instructions, and Poetry*, ed. W. K. Simpson, new ed. (New Haven and London: Yale Univ. Press, 1973) 298.
39. Cf. Cairo Love Songs, group B, nos. 21A-E; Papyrus Chester Beatty 1, group B, nos. 38–40; tr. M. V. Fox, *The Song of Songs and the Ancient Egyptian Love Songs* (Madison: Univ. of Wisconsin Press, 1985) 37–39, 66–67.

High her neck and glistening her nipples,
of true lapis her hair,
her arms finer than gold,
her fingers like lotus flowers unfolding.[40]

The portion of the similar song found on the relief in figure 121 is approximately contemporary with the previous song, dated in the twelfth century B.C.:

Your hair is lapis lazuli,
your eyebrows are *qaʿ*-stone,
your eyes are green malachite,
your mouth is red jasper.

A document from the Twenty-fifth Dynasty (712–664 B.C.)—when Egypt was ruled by the Nubian ruler with whom Hezekiah made an alliance against the Assyrians—shows that ancient Egyptian love poetry in general and this form of it in particular were still thoroughly alive in the eighth/seventh century B.C.:

Sweet, sweet of love,
      the priestess of Hathor, Mutirdis.
Sweet, sweet of love,
      says King Menkheperre.
Sweet, say men.
      Mistress of love, say women.
A princess is she,
      sweet of love,
most beautiful of women:
      a lass whose like has never been seen.
Blacker her hair than the black of night,
      than grapes of the riverbank.
[Whiter] her teeth
      than bits of plaster,
         than —— in a *hn*-plant.
Her breasts are set firm on her bosom.[41]

This form from ancient Egyptian love poetry, praising bodily features, may have survived up to Greek and Roman times. The Judeo-Hellenistic romance, *Joseph and Aseneth,* probably originating in Alexandria, contains a colorful description of Aseneth, perhaps combining Egyptian and Jewish material: "[Her face] was like the sun and her eyes (were) like a rising morning star, and her cheeks like fields of the Most High, and on her cheeks (there was) red (color) like a son of man's blood, and her lips (were) like a rose of life coming out of its foliage, and her teeth like fighting men lined up for a fight, and the hair of her head (was)

---

40. Papyrus Chester Beatty I, group A, no. 31; tr. Simpson, 315–16.
41. Tr. Fox, 349.

like a vine in the paradise of God prospering in its fruits, and her neck like an all-variegated cypress, and her breasts (were) like the mountains of the Most High God."[42] This description is much more magnificent than the brief *wazf* in the Qumran *Genesis Apocryphon* (20:1-8), which is the only residue of this form in postbiblical Jewish literature (Pope, 55).

Excursus: The Source of the Praise of Bodily Features in the Descriptive Songs

This unique way of presenting a person can be traced back to the Egyptian literature of the third millennium B.C. The oldest examples come from the Pyramid Texts, a large collection of utterances meant to assist the dead king's entrance into the world of the gods. It is not sufficient to make the king into *a* god; he is to become *the* god. In the most ancient form of this apotheosis, the king devours all the other gods, thereby appropriating for himself their powers. According to Pyramid Text 273–74 (§§ 400, 404):

> The king is one who eats men and lives on the gods . . .
> Their big ones are for his night meal,
> Their middle-sized ones are for his evening meal,
> Their little ones are for his night meal.

In contrast to this account, the deification of the various bodily features is a much more seemly form of the royal apotheosis. Pyramid Text 215 (§§ 148–49) reads:

> Your head is Horus of the Netherworld, O Imperishable . . .
> Your ears are the Twin Children of Atum, O Imperishable.
> Your nose is the Jackal (Wepwawet), O Imperishable . . .
> You demand that you ascend to the sky
> and you shall ascend.

Whereas nine parts of the body are mentioned in this text, Utterance 539 (§§ 1303–15) contains twenty-six. The comparisons are frequently based on the similar functions of the particular bodily features and the god with which they are identified; for example: "My tongue is the pilot in charge of the Bark of Righteousness," or: "My phallus is Apis (the bull)."[43]

Originally reserved for the king, these texts were democratized following the collapse of the Old Kingdom. The literary form deifying bodily features is then found in the *Book of the Dead* (which in principle is applicable to anyone); it was in use at the time of the New Kingdom (1540–1075 B.C.) and occasionally even later. In addition to the form

---

42. *Joseph and Aseneth* 18:9ff.; tr. C. Burchard in *OTP,* 2:232. For a description of Joseph, see *Joseph and Aseneth* 22:7; *OTP,* 2:238.
43. Translations of the three Pyramid Texts by R. O. Faulkner, *The Ancient Egyptian Pyramid Texts* (Oxford: Clarendon, 1969) 80–84, 42–43, 206–9. On the meaning of the texts, see E. Hornung, "Auf den Spuren der Sonne: Gang durch ein ägyptisches Königsgrab," *Eranos Jahrbuch* 50 (1981) (Frankfurt am Main: Insel, 1982) 446–49.

known in the Pyramid Texts, which also appears, for example, in Utterance 42 of the *Book of the Dead,* one also finds an utterance (no. 172) on a papyrus of the Eighteenth Dynasty (1540–1292 B.C.) in which some parts of the body are, according to the tradition, identified with a god, but others are identified with precious materials (the latter is also characteristic of the love poems): "Your beauty is that of a calm pool. . . . Your head, O my lord, is adorned with the tress of a woman of Asia; your face is brighter than the Mansion of the Moon; your upper part is lapis-lazuli; your hair is blacker than all the doors of the Netherworld on the day of darkness. . . . Your lungs are Nephthys; your face is Hapi and his flood. . . . Your gullet is Anubis; your body is extended with gold; your breasts are eggs of cornelian which Horus has inlaid with lapis-lazuli; your arms glitter with faience."[44]

As early as the Middle Kingdom, the form was used for the living as well as the dead. In an incantation for the protection of a small child, each of the child's members is identified with a deity:

> The crown of your head is Re [the sun-god], you healthy child,
> the back of your head is Osiris . . .
> Your eyes are the lord of humankind,
> your nose is the nourisher of the gods.[45]

If human beings can use this pattern to become divine, indeed to become *the* god, making them immortal or at least keeping them healthy, the gods can also use it to become the cosmos itself. A hymn to Amon proclaims:

> His heart is Sia (knowledge),
> his lips are Hu (word of power) . . .
> his right eye is the day,
> his left eye is the night . . .
> his body is the Nun (primal sea),
> its contents, the Nile . . .
> his wife is the field, when he fertilizes it,
> his seed is edible vegetation,
> his discharge is the grain.[46]

A rather isolated Akkadian hymn to Ninurta (after 1200 B.C.) uses this form to reconcile the claim of universal power by one single god and the existence of many gods:

> Lord, your face is the sun . . .
> your two eyes, lord, are Enlil and Ninlil . . .

44. Tr. R. O. Faulkner, *The Ancient Egyptian Book of the Dead,* ed. Carol Andrews, rev. ed. (New York: Macmillan, 1972) 170–71.
45. A. Erman, *Zaubersprüche für Mutter und Kind: Aus dem Papyrus 3027 des Berliner Museums,* AKPAW.PH (Berlin: Königliche Akademie der Wissenschaften, 1901) 48–49.
46. J. Assmann, *Ägyptische Hymnen und Gebete,* BAW (Zurich and Munich: Artemis, 1975) 320–21.

your eyelashes are the sun's rays . . .
The formation of your mouth is Ishtar of the stars . . .
your two ears are Ea and Damkina,
(you) spokesman of wisdom . . .
your neck is Marduk, the judge of heaven and earth.[47]

As with the deification of bodily features in Egyptian texts, here too one finds a correspondence between the particular part of the body and the specific power of the god with whom it is identified. For example, the ears, which hear, are equated with the wise and reserved Ea and his wife. Apart from this example, the form is scarcely found in Mesopotamia. As far as I can tell, it played no role in the cultic poetry or in the less frequent profane poetry (cf. Pope, 70).

Formal Elements and Categories: Conclusion

I have cited so many examples of this type of description (though many more Egyptian texts would be available) because it shows, first, that one of the forms typical of the Song is clearly of Egyptian origin. The biblical and Egyptian love songs are similar in more than content (see pp. 27–30). Second, one can see clearly that this form was originally used in the cult and then later employed for profane purposes. The secondary profane use does not imply that the Song contains disguised cultic texts (cf. pp. 12–15), but it does mean one has the right and the duty to seek a possible cultic-mythological origin behind its motifs, especially when these have a particularly lofty tone (e.g., 4:8). Third, the cultic origin of the form affords direct insight into its ability to mediate between the one and the many—a function that continues in the Song, even though there it is less clear and unambiguous. One of the central experiences of love is the lover's tendency to see all things beautiful and desirable as reminders of the beloved, finding in her or him their unity and meaning. The beloved gives the world not only a new radiance but also a meaningful center; yet, at the same time, the beloved becomes the lover's whole world. The very form of the *wazf,* which arises from the songs exalting the bodily features, is appropriate to take up this experience and give it shape. This appropriateness may well be the reason the form continues into modern times.

The form plays a prominent role in modern Arab love poetry. Each of the many collections contains dozens of examples; one must suffice here:

The eyebrows of my beloved
Are like the line of a stylus, drawn with ink,
And the hair of his forehead like the feathers of birds dyed with henna.
His nose is like a handle of an Indian sword glittering,
His teeth like pebbles of hail and more beautiful,
His cheeks like apples of Damascus,

47. A. Falkenstein and W. von Soden, *Sumerische und akkadische Hymnen und Gebete,* BAW (Zurich and Stuttgart: Artemis, 1953) 258–59; cf. ibid, 50–51, 385.

His breasts beautiful pomegranates,
His neck like the neck of the antelope,
His arms staffs of pure silver,
His finger golden pencils.[48]

Because of its richness the form has its adherents not only in the East, but also in Europe. Goethe ingeniously transforms it in his "West-Eastern Divan":

In thousand forms mayst thou attempt surprise,
    Yet, all-beloved one, straight know I thee;
Thou mayst with magic veils thy face disguise,
    And yet, all-present one, straight know I thee.
Upon the cypress' purest, youthful bud,
    All-beauteous-growing one, straight know I thee.[49]

R. M. Rilke used the same form, then almost five thousand years old, in his poem "Geburt der Venus"; the pattern provides a ready structure for the simple writer, while challenging the subtle poet to transform and enrich it.

    Fourth, and finally, this ancient structure teaches that the point of comparison between the receiver of meaning (the part of the body) and the lender of meaning (a divinity, a precious material, a plant, an animal, etc.) is only rarely a matter of shape or form (where modern Westerners generally seek such comparisons); more often the similarity has to do with color, value, or some dynamic quality. But that point leads to the next section.

Similes, Metaphors, Roles, and Situations

These descriptions of the beloved's body string together a variety of motifs. By "motif" here I mean primarily similes ("Your eyes are like doves"), metaphors ("Your eyes are doves"—without the connecting particle), and the description of the beloved in various guises, roles, and caricatures (as king, shepherd, sister) and in typical situations (all admire the beloved, love under the trees). The proper understanding of these motifs remains one of the chief difficulties in dealing with the Song. Modern Westerners do not immediately grasp what the poet had in mind when he compares the hair with a flock of goats or with grapes or lapis lazuli. Having devoted a preliminary study to this problem,[50] I can briefly summarize the results here.

48. The English translation (quoted by Pope, 56) is by M. Jastrow, Jr., *The Songs of Songs, Being a Collection of Love Lyrics of Ancient Palestine: A New Translation Based on a Revised Text, together with the Origin, Growth, and Interpretation of the Songs* (1921) 246; the poem is taken from Dalman, *Diwan,* 100–101; cf. ibid., 110ff., 120ff., 130ff., 245ff., 251ff. Other translations of modern Arabic love poetry include E. Littmann, *Neuarabische Volkspoesie,* Abhandlungen der Königlichen Gesellschaft der Wissenschaften 5/3 (Göttingen: Weidmann, 1902); and S. H. Stephan, "Modern Palestinian Parallels to the Song of Songs," *JPOS* 2 (1922) 199–278.
49. *The Poems of Goethe,* tr. E. A. Bowring et al. (Boston: Cassino, 1882) 406.
50. O. Keel, *Deine Blicke sind Tauben: Zur Metaphorik des Hohen Liedes,* SB 114/115 (Stuttgart: Katholisches Bibelwerk, 1984).

Introduction

Many words have a metaphorical sense in addition to their primary meaning. When one says, "The hunter shot a fox," the word "fox" simply means a particular animal; but when one says of another person, "He's a fox!" one singles out just one (alleged) aspect of the fox: a slyness or cunning that engenders mistrust. The (sly) person is the receiver of meaning in this metaphor. Qualifying that person as "fox" makes him understood in a particular way. The metaphorical fox is the lender of meaning. The aspect (of the fox) envisaged by the metaphor is the third element (the *tertium comparationis*), the point of comparison. The point of comparison in the fox metaphor is clear today. But can one assume without question that the fox metaphor means the same thing in Cant. 2:15 that it means to modern Westerners? "Fox" is a complex notion (color, shape, behavior) from which different cultures may select different aspects. Ancient Egyptian portrayals suggest that the foxes in Cant. 2:15 have more to do with a never-satisfied sexual appetite than with slyness (Luke 13:32?). One must also recognize that a simile or metaphor, functioning as a model, can evoke several aspects at the same time. Thus the palm, as a model of a desirable woman (Cant. 7:7 [8]), may signify at the same time the aspects of magnificent appearance, tall and slender growth, abundant fruit, and sweetness.

One can determine which aspects a particular culture perceives in a given phenomenon only by examining as fully as possible the pertinent documents from that culture. The process is easier the more a culture lives from conventions and traditions, which was much more the case in the ancient Near East than it is today. Whereas today every would-be poet seeks as quickly as possible to develop a unique, original, and unmistakable style, using his or her own similes and metaphors (which often remain indecipherable in this private usage), writers in the ancient Near East often used the same figurative language over millennia; the art was to employ this language in new ways, to enrich it with additions, and to renew and keep alive the traditional material without drawing great attention to oneself.

Before I begin to shed light on the *lender* of meaning in these similes or metaphors—which is generally seen as the only task of the exegete in this regard—it is always advantageous first to determine which aspects of the *receiver* of meaning were important in OT culture.

Three times the Song compares eyes to doves. Interpreters have frequently found the point of comparison in the form of the eyes (Gerleman). Western languages often use parts of the body in connection with shapes: the "arm" of the sea, the "nose" of a ship, or the "neck" of the bottle. Hebrew, however, uses "arm" in connection with strength, "nose" with snorting or anger, "neck" with stretching or pride (cf. Ps. 75:5 [6]; Job 15:25–26), "eye" with twinkling or sparkling, "heart" with reflection or thought, etc. This characteristic is of fundamental importance when interpreting the descriptions of bodily features. To operate unreflectively with the notion that the same aspects are important in Hebrew usage that would be important in modern English when referring to a bodily feature is to risk failure from the outset (see, e.g., the commentary on Cant. 4:5).

26

A concentric circle model is useful in seeking which aspects of a phenomenon are important to a particular culture, both for the lender of meaning and for the receiver of meaning in comparative speech. The first and smallest circle is the immediate literary context. When Cant. 5:11 refers to the beloved's locks as "black as a raven," the envisaged aspect is clearly described by the adjective "black." But such unequivocal references occur only rarely in the Song; most often they are lacking, as in 4:4a: "Your neck is like the tower of David." The amplification, "on it hang a thousand bucklers," implies strength, an interpretation that is confirmed when one expands to the next concentric circle, the whole Song. In 8:10 the tower analogy occurs again: "I was a wall, and my breasts were like towers." The context makes clear that "towers" do not signify something tall and slender (which was seldom the case in the ancient Near East) but something strong, unapproachable, proud. This idea is shared also by the receiver of meaning in the comparison, the neck. To "speak with neck" in Hebrew is to speak with pride (p. 26).

After using this method to establish the meaning of a simile or metaphor in a particular place, one must guard against the notion that this meaning can mechanically be plugged in anywhere the same catchword appears. When 5:13 equates the beloved's cheeks with "towers" of ointments (see the commentary), the new context emphasizes a different aspect of tower than strength or valor.

If neither the immediate context nor the larger circle of the Song offers clues to the understanding of a particular motif, the next move (with the aid of a concordance or lexicon) is to the whole OT. Most productive are texts that, like the Song, speak of things like the relations between men and women and the joys of love—and not only those texts that do so positively (e.g., Genesis 2; Psalm 45; Prov. 5:18-20) but also those that view such things critically and with mistrust (cf., e.g., Prov. 7:17 with Cant. 4:14 and 1:13; Isa. 3:16 with Cant. 4:9; Hos. 4:13 with Cant. 1:16-17). The wisdom teachers and prophets often viewed the erotic realm differently than the poets of the Song.

When one can find no further help from the OT—as in the case of eyes as doves, or breasts as "twins of a gazelle that feed among the [lotuses]," or the beloved as one who lingers in Lebanon among lions and leopards—then one draws a wider circle, encompassing the land where the Song originated (see the map on p. 36). But another trap awaits here. The natural world has innumerable aspects, but culture is interested in only a few of them. The Song is a cultural product; its interpretation depends more on an understanding of culture than of nature. The dependence of culture on natural surroundings is usually much less than the layperson would be inclined to believe. To understand the Song it is much more important to study archaeological findings than to study the landscape—above all, one should study the pictorial images in seals, amulets, ivories, and other valuables with which the well-to-do people who wrote the Song were daily surrounded. Here one finds gazelles and lotus flowers, doves and lions in the context of art and luxury for which erotica has always had a special affinity.

27

Introduction

Because Israel/Palestine was small and hardly well-off, the examples of skilled craftsmanship found there are often foreign, imported more or less equally from Egypt and from Syria/Mesopotamia (but sometimes also from the west, e.g., Cypress). When Gerleman limits his search for parallels to the Song's motifs to Egypt, and Pope looks chiefly toward Syria and Mesopotamia (or even India), and Kramer consults only Sumerian texts, none of these does justice either to Palestine/Israel's physical situation (between the two cultural spheres of Egypt and Mesopotamia) or to its openness to the Mediterranean islands.

Images uncovered by archaeology in Palestine/Israel show that its iconography portrayed, for example, the regenerative aspect of the lotus or the distancing effect created by a lion escort. At the same time, the existence of these pictorial records makes it seem likely that not only foreign iconography but also foreign love poems were imported, thus influencing Hebrew love songs—even though up to now archaeology has found no trace of such songs. "Foreign women," especially at court, may have played a key role in this enterprise. As previously demonstrated in the discussion of the Song's origins and forms (recall especially the descriptions of the body), the similarities to Egyptian love lyrics are often astonishing, at least for the period 1300–700 B.C. The role of metaphors and similes referring to lotuses (see the commentary on 2:1ff.; 4:5; 5:13; 7:2 [3]), pomegranates (commentary on 7:13 [14]), gazelles (2:9), amulets (1:13-14), and seals (8:6) in the Egyptian lyrics is similar to their role in the Song. One also finds situations like love under the trees (see the commentary on 2:4-5) and the roles of shepherd, sister, and mother in the Egyptian material.

Comparisons with the Near East are made difficult by the fact that no collection of love songs comparable to the Song or to the Egyptian collections has been found in Phoenicia, Canaan, or Assyria. The only large collection from Mesopotamia—the Sumerian love songs of the third or early second millennium B.C.—is not only separated by great time and distance but also differentiated from the Song by a sometimes clearly marked *Sitz im Leben* (sacred marriage) and by form (addresses in litany style).

Most significantly, the Sumerian love songs use a totally different style. Instead of the rich and colorful images of the Song, the Sumerian poems employ a limited number of stereotypical metaphors (erotic pleasure as a mixed drink or honey, the pubic area as a field, coitus as plowing, etc.).[51] Moreover, these poems include many explicit references (tongue kissing, vulva, ejaculation, etc.)[52] of a kind lacking in the Song. Ceremonial intercourse in the Sumerian texts has a clear purpose: to promote prosperity in all realms of natural and political life.[53] The Song knows no such thing. The whole atmosphere is therefore very different

---

51. Kramer, *Sacred Marriage*, 94, 96; B. Alster, "Sumerian Love Songs," *RA* 79 (1985) 127ff.
52. Kramer, *Sacred Marriage*, 94, 98, 103–5.
53. Ibid., 49–66, 81, 83, 102.

(though they have some commonalities; see the commentary on 2:3). A direct connection between the Song and these Sumerian texts is out of the question. But Sumerian literature had a strong, demonstrable influence on Akkadian and ancient Syrian literature. No collection of love songs has survived from this area, but that does not mean that none existed. That many of the Song's motifs come from the Near East is clear from the pictorial evidence, if not from written sources. For example, the dove as a messenger of love is never found in Egypt, but it appears frequently in Near Eastern iconography. The same can be said for the goddess on the mountain accompanied by lions and leopards (see the commentary on 4:8).

Given the lack of a significant collection of Northwest Semitic love songs to compare to the Song, one might decide to turn to the early Greek loves songs (e.g., by Sappho); important cultural contacts existed between Greece and the Levant from the eighth/seventh century B.C.[54] Likewise, the Arab love songs of nineteenth-century Palestine may have some connection (though certainly difficult to determine) to the metaphorical language of the ancient Near East (see note 48 for the texts). But to use these late sources to try to prove a secular origin for one of the Song's motifs would be to put the cart before the horse (see the commentary on 7:7 [8]).

This issue serves to introduce the final point of this section. The discussion of "Form" (pp. 18–22) showed how the description of bodily features was taken over from the realm of cult and ritual (deification of the dead, hymns) into the realm of love songs. Similarly, several of the book's motifs—for example, those used to represent and make tangible such characteristics as the beloved's distant majesty or regenerative power or value—seem to originate in the sphere of the gods. In all ages and all places, lovers have experienced the value and significance of the beloved as divine and have attempted to express the partner's value by portraying him or her as a god or goddess. This portrayal has been labeled *"Götterverkleidung," "Göttertravestie,"* "theomorphism," or "divine fiction." This tendency caused little trouble for polytheistic religions, where the border between the divine and the human is less clear than in monotheistic religions. In one Egyptian love song, the beloved is addressed simply as "My god, my lotus."[55] The poem by Ricarda Huch, quoted in the commentary to 5:1cd, shows that this view is still possible in a monotheistic milieu (cf. also Psalm 45). Otherwise, in Christian areas the beloved is often called an "angel," and in Muslim areas a "virgin of paradise." The Song never directly relates the man or woman to the divine sphere in this way; whatever numinous aura they are given comes only through the attributes with which they are described. In the concluding section I consider the relationship between the characters of the

---

54. Cf. W. Burkert, *Die orientalisierende Epoche in der griechischen Religion und Literatur,* Sitzungsbericht der Heidelberger Akademie der Wissenschaften. Phil.-hist. Klasse 1984/1 (Heidelberg: C. Winter, 1984).
55. Cairo Love Songs, group A, no. 20C; tr. Fox, 32.

Song (provided with numinous splendor) and the God of Israel, and the theological relevance of this relationship for the Song.

The Song of Songs and Yahwism

A theological interpretation of the Song requires delicate balance. This point is already obvious from the fact that many situations that the Song views as expressions of heavenly bliss for the lovers are seen quite differently by the wisdom teachers and prophets; with just a slight shift in accent and nuance, they condemn the same situations.

Love as an Elemental Power

While 1:16-17 announces the desire to express love under cedars and pines (cf. also 7:11-12 [12-13]), Hosea polemicizes against the daughters who "play the whore" in the shadow of oaks and terebinths and against the brides who commit adultery there; Yahweh declines to punish them only because the men are doing the same thing (thereby demonstrating an impartiality that is remarkable even today—Hos. 4:13-14). One might object that the one case involves the innocent love of a bridal couple while the other is part of the Baal cult, but such distinctions arise only from a tendentious interpretation of both texts. The prophetic text is already polemical, rigorously interpreting the practice it condemns from only one perspective; but one is left to wonder whether the practice intended in Cant. 1:16-17 would not also have fallen under the prophetic verdict.

The Song speaks of the woman as one who holds her head high (4:4; 7:4a [5a]), who throws seductive glances (1:15; 4:1, 9; 5:12; 6:5), and who is richly bejeweled (1:10-11). Isaiah polemicizes against the haughty daughters of Zion who walk with outstretched necks, glancing wantonly with their eyes, their jewelry jingling (Isa. 3:16).

The woman in the Song wanders through the streets by night, seeking her lover (3:1-5; 5:2-8); she imagines kissing him when they meet. The wisdom teacher grimly describes how the adulteress seeks a lover on the streets at night and how she seizes and kisses him when she finds him (Prov. 7:6-13). Again, one might object that the one case involves a bride with the purest of intentions seeking her bridegroom with all her heart and soul, while the other involves a common adulteress. But the night watchmen of Cant. 5:7 apparently have trouble making such clean distinctions; they beat and wound the poor "bride."

Thus it is no surprise that the legally rigorous rabbis had trouble with the Song. According to a gloss to the Mishnah tractate *Pirqe 'Abot,* which has been handed down anonymously and may therefore be quite old: "Originally, it is said, Proverbs, Song and Songs, and Ecclesiastes were suppressed; for since they were held to be mere parables and not part of the Holy Writings, (the religious authorities) arose and suppressed them; (and so they remained) until the men of Hezekiah [or 'the men of the Great Assembly'] came and interpreted them."[56] The "men of the

56. *'Aboth de Rabbi Nathan* A1:5; tr. J. Goldin, *The Fathers according to Rabbi Nathan*

Great Assembly" are a fiction of Pharisaic erudition, invented to bridge the gap between prophecy and Pharisaic Judaism. This invention gives insight into the beginnings of that movement, and the tradition shows that there was a problem regarding the public use of the Song and its place among the Holy Writings (which were read in public). The well-known discussion in the Mishnah tractate *Yadayim,* whether the Song "imparts uncleanness to the hands,"[57] does not appear to be a question about canonicity but about public reading (cf. Rudolph, 78). In a community more and more defined by its liturgical life, no one knew what to do with the Song—at least not until the advent of the escape into allegory, which made a book of questionable content into the holiest of all holy books. The latter was the judgment of Rabbi Aqiba (died 135 A.D.) in the section of the Mishnah tractate *Yadayim* just cited. Yet allegorizing is nothing other than an elegant way of despising the text; like a pack mule, the book is laden with every conceivable meaning, but in the process its own voice and its own meaning are suppressed. Nevertheless, as the history of the allegorical interpretation demonstrated (see pp. 5–11), even such a radical immunization strategy could not prevent the virulent original sense of the Song from breaking out again and again.

Neither the totalitarian alteration of the Song's theological personality imposed by an allegorical reading nor the moralistic attempt to domesticate and limit its interest to ordinary courtship and marriage has finally been able to obscure the fact that the Song describes love as an elemental power, comparable to death (8:6-7), and having little to do with morality and theology.

When I say "love," I do not mean a relationship limited to sexual gratification. The basis of love in the Song is not a vague genital lust but great admiration of the beloved partner, who seems inapproachable in his or her radiance—distant on inaccessible mountains, hidden in locked gardens, painfully longed for and sought. The lovers mutually experience one another as so beautiful, so radiant, so magnificent that every discovery, every approach, every possession of the other can be experienced only as unfathomable gift, never taken for granted.

The wisdom literature gave an explicitly theological interpretation to this experience: "House and wealth are inherited from parents, / but a prudent wife is from the Lord" (Prov. 19:14; cf. 18:22). The loving encounter in Genesis 2 is described quite similarly to the Song. The encounter with the woman, whom the man recognizes as one profoundly like himself, emphasizes his distress and limitation in being alone. Adam greets Eve with a formula stating the relationship: "This at last is bone of my bones and flesh of my flesh; / this one shall be called Woman [אִשָּׁה], for out of Man [אִישׁ] this one was taken" (Gen. 2:23). The happy experience of finding another person whom one admires and to whom one also feels profoundly related ("bone of my bones") is expressed in the love songs through the address "sister" or "brother" (see the commentary on 4:9).

(New Haven: Yale Univ. Press, 1955) 5.
57. Mishnah, *Yad.* 3:5; tr. Neusner, *Mishnah, 1127.*

The feeling of belonging and the happiness that each gives the other push the existing social barriers and differences in rank between man and woman into the background. Love presses toward paradise. Nowhere in the OT is the equality of the sexes—a precondition for overcoming loneliness and the basis for mutual solidarity—as real as in the Song. Nowhere is the value of the single human being (the proverbial "individual") so convincingly celebrated.

When a man and woman come into this kind of relationship, it pushes them together with elemental force. They feel safe (2:3), functioning as amulets or talismans for one another (1:13-14); their union is seen as providential and dare not be disturbed (2:6-7; 8:3-4). The Song assumes that only one person can be this kind of partner for the other (2:1—3:6, 8-9), even though this conviction, expounded with great enthusiasm, is ironically challenged by the "daughters of Jerusalem" (cf. 5:9). Yet the Song does not say that such a relationship will last forever.

If love is not a mere animal impulse in the Song, it is even less a nonphysical spiritual behavior, which regards human beings as pseudo-angels and arrogantly denigrates all the good things we have in common with the animals as mere "fleshly lust." Every human pleasure combines physical, emotional, and spiritual powers, stimulating each of these equally. The Song simply takes such a view for granted; it does not seem to enter into a deliberate argument with Platonic or Hellenistic tendencies (contra Krinetzki, 29).

Astonishingly, just as the Song sovereignly ignores any tendency to deny the body, it also ignores the claims of society that often come into conflict with spontaneous expressions of love. In the OT world, society's interests are expressed primarily in the patriarchal family, the institution of marriage, and the production of offspring. But the Song simply has nothing to do with such things. Its partiality toward journeys into uninhabited areas (cf., e.g., 7:11-12 [12-13]) derives from the difficulties it encounters when it tries to find room within society for spontaneity and individuality. Krinetzki betrays an idealistic notion of "law": "Wherever two people truly love one another, even without the law they fulfill its demands by their inner urgency" (43). This unrealistic perspective has little to do with the OT.

The Theological Relevance of Love as an Elemental Force

The ancient world often regarded love—an elemental force as strong as death—as a divine power in the midst of other conflicting divine powers. At first glance, one finds no such exaggerated notions in the Song. Gerleman perceives this lack as its great theological achievement:

What is so astonishing is that the figures in the Song of Songs live in a completely desacralized and demythicized secular world and that the events are thoroughly characterized by what is uniquely human. Any theological evaluation must take this fact seriously rather than trying somehow to detour around it. There is great theological relevance precisely in this purely negative reality, in the lack of any deification of sexuality. Israel's opposition to the mythically satiated atmosphere

32

of its environment is nowhere more clearly and simply expressed. To portray an area of life that the neighboring religions regarded as a sacral mystery and a divine event in a fully demythologized form is a theological achievement of greatest significance. The love poems of the Song of Songs confidently presuppose that Yahwism is incompatible with a divinization of sex. Yahweh stood "beyond the polarity of sex."[58] In Israel, sexual love could be described only in an atmosphere of spiritualized secularity, as one finds it in the Song of Songs.

This desacralized and demythicized view of erotic love is strongly reminiscent of the Old Testament's understanding of death. Yahwism has very little to say about the phenomenon of death itself. Israel never tried "to make herself ideologically or mythologically lord of death."[59] It is noteworthy that in Israel there was no attempt to portray sexuality and death mythologically, to objectify or give autonomy to the great primal powers of nature. (84-85)

But is it appropriate to ascribe such a passionately antimythological role to the Song? Does not this ascription give a prophetic edge to a book from the wisdom tradition, when wisdom's rational perspective has no use for the kind of mythology the prophets opposed? The distinction between the profane and the holy certainly plays an important role in the Israelite cult (Ezek. 22:26). The cult distinguishes between that which is appropriate to and belongs to Yahweh and that which remains for human use. But that distinction has no meaning in the wisdom literature. Wisdom is interested in the whole world as the work of God, as God's creation; and "All the works of the Lord are very good" (Sir. 39:16). There is neither holy nor profane. When Gerleman describes the Song as "profane," he can only mean to separate it from things like sacred marriages observed cultically in temples or sacred prostitution. Yahweh would have nothing to do with sexuality in such arenas. But simply as part of the wisdom literature the Song has nothing in common with this world of thought.

Or perhaps Gerleman uses "profane" to mean primarily "not pious." After all, the literature most like the Hebrew love songs—the ancient Egyptian love songs—also show scarcely a trace of a mythologizing of love; but they do introduce Hathor ("the Golden One") as the protector and patron of love. The woman wishes to be commended to her beloved by "the Golden One of women" (the goddess). The man begs Hathor to deliver his beloved to him, and he makes vows to the goddess. Whoever seeks the love of a beloved does so at the bidding of "the Golden One."[60] Another deity is occasionally chosen to be the patron of love, as in the petition, "may Amun give me what I have found for all eternity."[61]

Such petitions and prayers, if addressed to Yahweh, would seem quite appropriate in the OT. Yahweh ordained that the man cleave more firmly to his wife than to his parents (Gen. 2:24). A prudent wife is

58. *G. von Rad, Old Testament Theology,* tr. D. M. G. Stalker, 2 vols. (New York: Harper & Row, 1962, 1965) 1:27.
59. Ibid., 390.
60. Cf., e.g., Papyrus Chester Beatty I, group A, nos. 32, 35, 36; group B, no. 40; group C, no. 42; tr. Fox, 52–55, 67, 71.
61. Papyrus Harris 500, group B, no. 12; tr. Simpson, 304.

Yahweh's gift (Prov. 18:22; 19:14). But it would be clearly contrary to the direction of the OT to pray to Yahweh (as one would to Hathor) for success in love without specific reference to marriage and to the blessing of offspring (Tob. 8:7). Thus, one is inclined to agree at least in part with Gerleman.

The Song is in fact less pious than the Egyptian poems. It does not mention God at all (see the commentary on 8:6). It has been compared in this regard to the little book of Esther and to 1 Maccabees, which at first glance seem to do the same. But at decisive moments, Esther uses a passive construction that clearly refers to God (4:14), and 1 Maccabees simply paraphrases God with "Heaven"—e.g., "strength comes from Heaven" (3:18-19, 50, 60, etc.). Do the lovers in the Song also have a secret relationship with Yahweh, or are they really left totally to themselves?

In Cant. 2:7 and 3:5 the women of Jerusalem are adjured not to disturb love and its pleasures. Such admonitions are generally made in the name of a deity; the Song refers instead to gazelles and does—animals related to the goddess (see the commentary on 2:7 and 3:5). The omission of the animals in the third occurrence of this exhortation (8:4) indicates some discomfort with their presence. But Yahweh's antipathy to sexuality in the cultic-mythic arena was apparently so strong that it was not possible to call on him as love's protector even in this non-mythical context.

In addition to the hidden reference to taking refuge in the goddess found in this oath taken in the name of gazelles and does, the Song includes texts that move toward a personification of "Love" (cf. 2:4b; 8:6c). According to Prov. 8:30-31,[62] "Wisdom," Yahweh's delight, is his semiautonomous helper in the formation of the world, just as the chaos monsters are his semiautonomous opponents (cf. Job 40–41). Similarly, Christians in the Middle Ages could not comprehend the world without reference to a somewhat autonomous "Love"; they created the iridescent figure of the medieval "Venus" for that purpose.

Finally one must look at the figure of Solomon. His portrayal is the reason Krinetzki says it would be wrong "to speak of the Song of Songs as a profane love song in the modern sense. It is simply impossible in Israel to conjure up David (4:4) or Solomon (1:5; 3:7, 9, 11; 8:11, 12) or to call to mind the "mighty men of Israel" (3:7) or Israel's hosts (6:4, 10) or Jerusalem (1:5; 2:7; 3:5, 10; 5:8, 16; 6:4; 8:4) or Tirzah (6:4), without at least indirectly calling to mind the One who availed himself of a David or a Solomon to pursue his own objectives" (28). But it seems highly questionable that the missing explicit references to Yahweh can be replaced by a tower named for David (4:4), the "mighty men of Israel" (3:7), Tirzah and Jerusalem, or the "daughters of Jerusalem" (1:5; 2:7; 3:5, 10;

---

62. For more on "Wisdom" in Prov. 8:30–31 as a mediator between Maat (world order) and Hathor, see O. Keel, *Die Weisheit spielt vor Gott: Ein ikonographischer Beitrag zur Deutung des $m^e.sah\ddot{a}q\ddot{a}t$ in Spr. 8,30f.* (Fribourg: Universitätsverlag; Göttingen: Vandenhoeck & Ruprecht, 1974); also reprinted in *Freiburger Zeitschrift für Philosophie und Theologie* 21 (1974) 1–66.

5:8, 16; 8:4). (Israel's "hosts" are not mentioned at all; see the commentary on 6:4, 10.) Solomon is the only figure that enjoys a particular prominence in the Song. True, 1:5 mentions only the curtains in his palace, while 8:11-12 ridicules his harem with its many keepers; but in 3:7, 9, 11 he is the hero of the fictitious(?) marriage, and the superscript (1:1) regards him as the author or at least the patron of the whole collection. Thus, along with the "gazelles" and "wild does," along with "Love" as a personified power, one can see Solomon as a third entity bringing honor and significance to the "love" celebrated in the Song.

Solomon ruled during the period that went down in Israel's history as the best and most successful, when all sat under their vines and fig trees enjoying life (1 Kgs 4:25 [5:5]; cf. Mic. 4:4).[63] But even with all its glow and glitter, the period was not free of conflict, occasioned precisely by Solomon's splendor and uninhibited love affairs (cf. 1 Kgs 11:1-10; 12:4). These conflicts scarcely show up in the Song (though cf. 5:7), because the love described there takes place in the realm of fantasy, quite apart from the narrow limitations of everyday reality. Its favorite place is the inner chamber (1:4; 3:4) or, as already mentioned, out of doors, far from the normal hustle and bustle of daily life (1:5-6, 15-17; 2:10-13; 4:12—5:1; 6:11; 7:11-12 [12-13]). In contrast, the wisdom of the schools is at home in the busiest parts of the city, in the midst of everyday affairs (cf. Prov. 8:1-3). Whereas the night is the time for love (Cant. 2:7; 3:1; 4:6), the time of regular human labors is the day (Ps. 104:22-23).

Like Ecclesiastes, the Song presents experiences and insights that endanger the everyday life ruled by justice and law, faithfulness and rewards. Both books are ascribed to Solomon, whose knowledge and wisdom were greater than those of all other people (cf. 1 Kgs 4:29-30 [5:9-10]) and who could do virtually whatever he pleased. He was surely the right man to point out convincingly the limits of human life and its rules. Ecclesiastes calls into question an understanding of justice that expects a meaningful correspondence between acts and consequences and that, as such, was the foundation for both the prophetic oracles of judgment and for traditional wisdom.

More than anything, it is death that destroys a meaningful correspondence between act and consequence. Cant. 8:6-7 compares death to love. Love appears in the Song as a natural force, a mountain stream whose waters sometimes nourish and sometimes destroy. Its energies have not yet been channeled by human ethos into the garden of faithful and fruitful marriage, much less allegorized into a navigable canal carrying colorful—but foreign—ships that then, in gratitude, pollute its water with their refuse. Courageous love and unrelenting death determine the rhythm of life. Love builds up a world that death tears down again.

63. But the paradise story does not appear to work well as a point of reference for the Song, at least at the literary level; contra F. Landy, "The Song of Songs and the Garden of Eden," *JBL* 98 (1979) 513–28; idem, *Paradoxes of Paradise: Identity and Difference in the Song of Songs,* Bible and Literature Series 7 (Sheffield: Almond, 1983). In terms of content, of course, the garden motif does provide a connection between the song and the paradise story. See the commentary on 4:12.

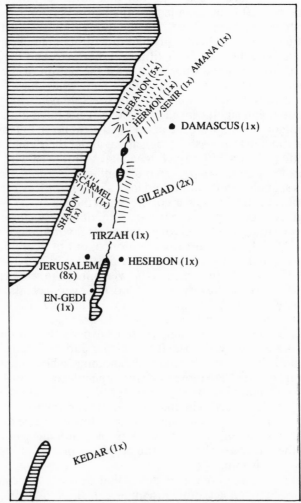

This map shows the towns and regions named in the Song. The numbers in parentheses indicate how often each name occurs. Jerusalem appears with by far the greatest frequency (1:5; 2:7; 3:5, 10; 5:8, 16; 6:4; 8:4), although many of these references seem to be editorial additions. The second most frequent name is Lebanon (3:9; 4:8, 11; 5:15; 7:4 [5]), whose trees play an important role in describing the splendor of Solomon (1 Kgs 5:6, 9, 14 [20, 23, 28]; 7:2). The three different terms used for Anti-Lebanon or parts thereof—Hermon, Senir, and Amana (Cant. 4:8)—were surely better known in the Northern Kingdom than in the Southern Kingdom. Damascus (7:4 [5]) had a close relation with the Northern Kingdom, and the latter included the Plain of Sharon (2:1), Mt. Carmel (7:5 [6]), the slopes of Gilead (4:1; 6:5), Heshbon (7:4 [5]), and Tirzah (6:4). Other than Jerusalem, only En-gedi (1:14) is in Judah. Kedar (1:5) is far from either kingdom. Note that, seen from the perspective of Samaria (the center of the

Knowing this situation, the wisdom teachers could not absolutize the traffic laws needed for daily life. It goes without saying that both synagogue and church have had trouble with the Song and with Ecclesiastes. Both little books contain a measure of anarchy. When our hearts condemn us for doing wrong (and rightly so, according to church and synagogue), these books give us a glimpse of a God who is greater than our hearts and who knows everything (1 John 3:20)—both the despairing nihilism suggested by death (Matt. 27:46) and the vibrant bliss granted by an unexpected experience of love (Luke 7:44-47).

Northern Kingdom), the towns and regions mentioned in the Song are primarily peripheral and "exotic."

Title

Text

1:1 a The Song of Songs,
    b which is Solomon's.

Commentary

[1:1a] The Hebrew term שִׁיר, like the more or less equivalent English
"song" (or German *Lied*), can refer equally to cultic/liturgical songs like
pilgrimage songs (Psalm 120), Zion songs (Ps. 137:3), and songs for the
Sabbath (Psalm 92) or to drinking songs (Isa. 24:9; Amos 6:5-6) and—of
special interest here—love songs (Psalm 45; Isa. 5:1; Ezek. 33:32). When
a forgotten prostitute is challenged to sing so that she "may be remem-
bered" (Isa. 23:15-16), the reference is obviously to songs with explicit
erotic content. In contrast to German or English usage, שִׁיר normally
refers only to joyful songs, not songs of lamentation; Hebrew employs
other terminology for laments. Appropriate to its joyful content, a שִׁיר is
normally accompanied by one or more instruments, including lyre, flute,
and tambourine. Sometimes שִׁיר apparently means simply "music" (Neh.
12:27).

The expression "Song of Songs" is a superlative, like "king of
kings" (Dan. 2:37), "holy of holies" (the "most holy" of Exod. 26:33), or
"ornament of ornaments" (the "full womanhood" of Ezek. 16:7). The
"Song of Songs" is simply *the* song—incomparable and most beautiful.
Luther invented the rather ceremonial title *"Das Hohe Lied"* (the high
song).

The singular does not necessarily imply a single song. The term שִׁיר
is frequently used collectively for a group of songs (e.g., Ps. 137:3: "Sing
us one of the songs of Zion [שִׁיר צִיּוֹן]"; 1 Chron. 6:31 [16]). Two collections
of Egyptian love songs from the thirteenth/twelfth century B.C.—in-

38

cluded in the London Papyrus Harris 500—bear these titles: "The beginning of the songs [singular in the original] of excellent enjoyment for your sister, beloved in your heart, when she returns from the fields" and "Beginning of the songs [singular in the original] of entertainment" (Papyrus Harris 500, group B, no. 9; group C, no. 17; tr. Simpson, 302, 308). Even though the individual songs in the collection are clearly separated from one another by notations like *gerech* (pause), the title refers to "song" in the singular. The title "Song of Songs" cannot be used to prove that the collector meant his collection to be understood as a single composition.

[1:1b] The title, "The Song of Songs," is supplemented by a relative clause: "which is Solomon's." Even if the clause means to identify the author, one cannot read it as strictly as a similar modern statement. The love songs collected here in the Song are understood to be related to Solomon in the same way the proverbs that were gathered and published by the officials of King Hezekiah (Prov. 25:1) were related to him. There was sufficient reason to assume that love songs circulating in Israel would be by Solomon. First, Solomon was renowned for his strong bent toward riches (cf. Cant. 3:9-10 and 1 Kgs 10:14-29), and there is a marked connection between luxury and erotica. Second, Solomon was famous for his many relationships with women (recall Abishag the Shunammite, 1 Kgs 1:17-22; pharaoh's daughter, 3:1; the queen of Sheba, 10:1-10; Solomon's huge harem, 11:1-3). Third, he was known as a gifted songwriter: "His songs numbered a thousand and five" (4:32 [5:12])—meaning, even more than a thousand (cf. the Thousand and One Arabian Nights). It is no wonder that anonymous Israelite love songs of all kinds were eventually ascribed more and more to Solomon, the great patron of both love and songs. Just as the title "for/of David" marked a song belonging to the liturgy (the Psalms), the notation "for/of Solomon" was used for a song or proverb belonging to the joys and the wisdom of life.

Longing for
the Greatest Pleasure

Text

1:2 a Let him kiss me with the kisses of his mouth!
   b For your love is better than wine,
  3 a [and better than the scent of your anointing oils.]
   b Your name is perfume poured out;
   c therefore the maidens love you.
  4 a Draw me after you, let us make haste.
   b The king has brought me into his chambers.
   c [We want to be unrestrained, to enjoy ourselves with you;]
   d we will extol your love more than wine;
   e rightly do they love you.

Analysis

Love, which offers more joy than wine (vv. 2b and 4d), and the young women, who gush over the royal lover (vv. 3c and 4e), define the boundaries of this poem, separating its content clearly from what follows. The wish in v. 2a to be kissed by "him" (by whom?) puts the whole song in the context of longing desire and impetuous wishful thinking (see pp. 11–15, 18–22). With this point in mind, the interpreter must try to distinguish among the rapidly changing addressees, who are very hard to identify. Translators have often glossed over these difficulties. Gerleman points out that such fluctuations are also found in Egyptian love songs and are consciously employed here as a literary device. The sudden changes of address allow infatuation and desire to be described with all their openness and chance—a particularly significant notion, especially here in the first poem.

40

Commentary

[1:2a] Attention is drawn first to the infatuated woman, desiring to be kissed and expressing her passion without inhibition (cf. 8:1-2). The use of "kiss" as both verb and object shows the exuberance of her wish. "The kisses of his mouth" is a literal rendering of the Hebrew, although "mouth" is included only to strengthen the personal pronoun ("his"; cf. 1:7; 3:1; etc.). In ancient Egypt tender contact was made primarily by touching noses, which had more to do with smell than with touch. But in the Near East, as far back as the sources go, lovers kissed on the lips. In the Sumerian Myth of Enlil and Ninlil, the virgin Ninlil complains, "My lips are too narrow and have never been kissed."[1] The head of a Sumerian pin shows an embracing couple kissing on the lips (fig. 1). The Ugaritic myth Shachar and Shalim tells of El bending over two women:

> He stooped (and) kissed their lips;
> behold! their lips were sweet,
> sweet as pomegranate[s].
> In the kissing (there was) conception,
> in the embracing (there was) pregnancy.[2]

Both the pin and the Ugaritic text demonstrate that kissing can stand for lovemaking in the fullest sense.

By the second half of the second millennium B.C., kissing on the lips seems to have become widespread also in Egypt (perhaps from Near Eastern influence). A relief from Tell el-Amarna shows Nefertiti kissing her oldest daughter on the lips (fig. 2), and an unfinished plaque portrays Nefertiti and her husband kissing (fig. 3). A short Egyptian love song from around 1300 B.C. says:

> I kiss her,
> her lips open,
> and I am drunk
> without a beer.[3]

The final line of the Egyptian song celebrates the intoxicating power of love, which is also envisioned by the comparison with wine in v. 2b.

[1:2b] The woman now addresses her husband in the second person (vv. 2b-4a). The change from third to second person is also frequent in the Egyptian love songs. For example:

1. H. Behrens, *Enlil and Ninlil*, Studia Pohl, Series Maior 8 (Rome: Biblical Institute Press, 1978) 30.
2. Shachar and Shalim 49–51; tr. J. C. L. Gibson, *Canaanite Myths and Legends*, 2d ed. (Edinburgh: T. & T. Clark, 1978) 125–26.
3. Cairo Love Songs, group A, no. 20G; tr. W. K. Simpson in *The Literature of Ancient Egypt: An Anthology of Stories, Instructions, and Poetry*, ed. W. K. Simpson, new ed. (New Haven and London: Yale Univ. Press, 1973) 311.

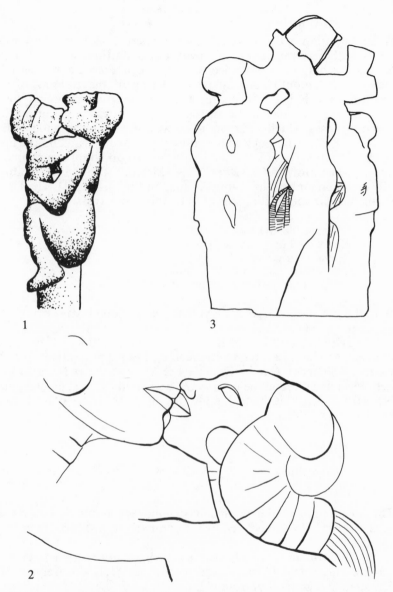

Fig. 1. A naked man (*left*) and a naked woman in close embrace kiss on the lips. (Head of a 5-inch [13-cm.] copper pin from southern Mesopotamia; first half of third millennium B.C.)

Fig. 2. The Egyptian queen Nefertiti (Nefertiri), wife of Akhenaton, kisses one of her daughters on the mouth. (Remnant of a limestone relief from Tell el-Amarna; ca. 1340 B.C.)

Fig. 3. King Akhenaton kisses his wife Nefertiti on the lips. (Unfinished carnelian plaque; ca. 1340 B.C.)

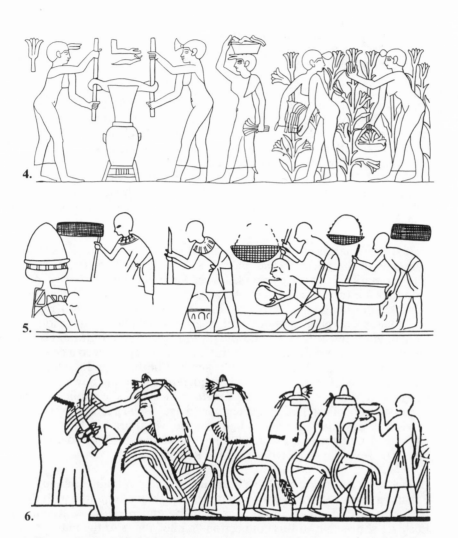

Fig. 4. Women pick lilies and press out the flowers using a sack and two wooden rods. The extract was used for perfume or ointment. (Limestone relief from the Saite period, seventh/sixth century B.C.)

Fig. 5. Three men crush oil fruits in truncated conical mortars. A worker grinds resin (*lower left*); on the table above him stands a vessel of finished ointment that has been prepared by the cook (*right*) and formed into balls by the worker kneeling (*middle*). (Wall painting from West Thebes, tomb no. 175; ca. 1400 B.C.)

Fig. 6. Men and women sit apart at an Egyptian drinking bout. A servant (*right*) brings a bowl of wine to a woman. A woman who has had too much to drink is vomiting (*far left*). All the women wear cones of ointment on their heads; three (*to the left*) also wear lotus flowers. (Painting in the tomb of Neferhotep, West Thebes, no. 49; ca. 1320 B.C.)

43

> He does not know my lust to embrace him,
> or that he could write my mother.
> Lover, I am given over to you
> by the Golden Goddess of womankind.[4]

In v. 2b she is no longer calling on a longed-for lover but one who is actually present. Foreplay and sexual intercourse are touched on directly, because these pleasures are what is meant by the Hebrew term for "love" used here, דּדִים (cf. Ezek. 16:8; 23:17; Prov. 7:18; Cant. 7:12 [13]). The comparison with wine also demonstrates that the greatest pleasures are envisioned. Wine was created to bring joy to gods and human beings (Judg. 9:13; Ps. 104:15). "What is life to one who is without wine?" (Sir. 31:27). "Wine and music gladden the heart, / but the love of [lovers] is better than either" (Sir. 40:20). Love intoxicates more than wine (Cant. 5:1).

[1:3a] Like wine, anointing oils were an integral ingredient of life's festive moments in the ancient Near East (Eccl. 9:7-8; Ps. 23:5; Prov. 21:17). The aromatic products of pressed sweet-smelling blossoms (fig. 4) or ground resins (cf. Cant. 1:13; 4:10c) were mixed with oil and boiled down to make ointments (fig. 5). No banquet of the Egyptian New Kingdom (fig. 6) was complete without both readily available drinks (note the woman vomiting at far left) and the perfumed cones of ointment on the head. As the cones melted in the warm climate they produced a charming scent (Ps. 133:1-2). But even the pleasures of perfume and wine cannot match the joys of love. This song is echoed by the young nun in the first story of day three of Boccaccio's *Decameron,* when she confides rather openly to her colleague: "I have again and again heard ladies, who come to visit us, say that all other delights in the world are but toys in comparison with that which a woman enjoyeth, whenas she hath to do with a man" (tr. John Payne [New York: Blue Ribbon, 1931] 131).

[1:3bc] After anointing oils have been declared less valuable than love (v. 3a), it is a surprise here to find the name of the beloved equated with these perfumes. The comparison of a good name and precious ointment in Eccl. 7:1 shows that in this connection "name" refers to the man's reputation, which spreads like the aroma of spilled perfume and stimulates the young woman's love. By mentioning her comrades, the young woman who had called attention to herself with her passionate wish to be kissed now blends back into their number. Her passion is seen to be normal; her friends react in the same way.

[1:4ab] But she quickly reemerges, this time not only with a wish (like "Let him kiss me") but with a command and a call to common action. It is not enough for her to hear reports about the beloved (cf. in 1 Kings 10:7; Job 42:5). Neither his legendary fame nor the adoring repetition of

---

4. Papyrus Chester Beatty I, group A, no. 32; tr. Simpson, 317.

his name is sufficient now; she wants the man himself. Then she proudly announces that the king has brought her into his (bed)chamber (cf. Cant. 2:4; 3:4). The prototype of Sumerian women, the goddess Inanna, wanted the same thing: "Lion, I would be carried off by you to the bedchamber."[5] She reported proudly: "The brother brought me into his house, / Laid me down on a fragrant honey-bed."[6] This proud announcement is the high point of 1:2-4; it is marked by the woman labeling her lover a triumphant king. The expression translated "Draw me after you" can also be rendered "Drag me after you" (Ps. 28:3; Job 24:22; 41:1 [40:25]). In the Sumerian poem just mentioned the woman refers to her lover as a beast of prey (a lion) dragging away his plunder.

[1:4cd] In what follows, the woman again reflects Inanna in the Sumerian song as the latter continues, "You have captivated me, I stand trembling before you."[7] No sooner has the singer in the Song announced her triumph than she retreats again into the chorus of her friends (as in v. 3c), wanting to enjoy the pleasures of love along with them, to extol love more than wine—although for now this all remains in the unreal world of fantasy. It seems that she can tolerate his direct presence ("your love") only when surrounded by her friends.

[1:4e] This line returns fully to the world of calm reflection. As in v. 3c, the Hebrew words are characterized by long *a* vowels, producing a calm, dark sound. As before, this sentence affirms that the young women, who have apparently aroused the erotic desires of the singer, are rightly enthusiastic about love. In her fantasy the singer has experienced it herself.

5. S. N. Kramer, *The Sacred Marriage Rite: Aspects of Faith, Myth, and Ritual in Ancient Sumer* (Bloomington: Indiana Univ. Press, 1969) 92.
6. Ibid., 104.
7. Ibid., 92.

Different from the Others

Text

1:5 a I am black and beautiful,
   b O daughters of Jerusalem,
   c like the tents of Kedar,
   d like the curtains of Solomon.
  6 a Do not gaze at me because I am dark,
   b because the sun has gazed on me.
   c My mother's sons were angry with me;
   d they made me keeper of the vineyards,
   e but my own vineyard
   f I have not kept!

Analysis

These two verses have usually—and correctly—been accepted without question as a unit. They are held together thematically by the motif of the young woman's dark complexion, a motif that distinguishes this poem from the material that precedes and follows it. It is also formally distinct from the preceding verses; their action and excitement, their wishes, commands, and changes of voice are replaced by a calm and unified self-portrayal (note the several occurrences of "I" and "me").

Verses 5-6 are loosely connected with vv. 2-4 by two pairs of catchwords: Solomon and king, vineyards and wine. These catchwords probably explain why the redactor inserted the verses at this point in the collection.

Commentary

[1:5] Jerome already translated "I am black and beautiful" (cf. 2:14; 6:4) as "I am black *but nevertheless* beautiful." Although this translation is possible, it is neither necessary nor probable. The Arab love songs of

46

Palestine do record a controversy between brown and white women, where the brown are the bedouin girls and the white are the spoiled city dwellers.[1] But the OT has no such antithesis. Blackness can be a sign of sickness (Job 30:30; Lam. 4:8), but, especially in reference to hair, it can also signify health, youth, and vitality (Lev. 13:31, 37; Eccl. 11:10; Ps. 110:3; Cant. 5:11; cf. 4:1; 6:5). The meaning of "black" in this verse is explained by two similes.

The "tents of Kedar" are nomads' tents, made of black goat hair. The simile takes its nuances from the associations that come with "Kedar." Kedar's forefather was Ishmael, the "wild ass of a man" who lived "at odds with all his kin" (Gen. 16:12; 25:13). The children of Kedar lived alone, far out in the desert, as warlike as their forefather but blessed with immeasurably large flocks (Isa. 21:16-17; 42:11; 60:7; Jer. 49:28-33; Ps. 120:5). Geographically, Kedar is the most distant area from Jerusalem in the Song. In Jer. 2:10 Kedar stands for the farthest east.

The second simile evokes a totally different picture. Whether the black יריעות are tapestries, curtains, or wall hangings, since they are connected to Solomon one should understand them as artistic and precious palace furnishings. The tradition remembers that Solomon spared as little in furnishing his palace as he did in building the temple (cf. 1 Kgs 7:1-12; 10:14-29). Like many other items in the Song, curtains play an important role in the cult (Exodus 26 and 36).

This combination of the poor, exotic, and terrifying world of Kedar with the equally exotic and fascinating luxury of Solomon makes the blackness of the speaker at once frightening and fascinating; she is mysteriously different. The study of religions introduces many goddesses and other numinous beings who are portrayed as black. A Hittite ritual (near present-day Turkey) is an order to move the "black goddess" from one temple to another.[2] Another example is Ahmes Nefertari, the wife of Ahmose I, founder of the glorious Eighteenth Egyptian Dynasty. After their deaths, this couple became the patron saints of the mighty necropolis at Thebes. It is no longer certain why she is portrayed as black, but we know she was not of Negroid origin. Like the green color of Osiris and the blue color of Amon ("king of the gods"), her blackness signifies that she belongs to the realm of the other, the divine. It is no longer the mortal Ahmes Nefertari who appears before us; it is a goddess, black as ebony, even though she still wears the costume of an Egyptian queen (fig. 7). Greek and Roman authors speak of black statues depicting the goddesses Isis, Cybele, Demeter, Diana, and Aphrodite (or Venus). Many of these seem to derive from a black stone fallen from heaven (a meteorite). Finally, one can point to the several black madonnas in Europe (Montserrat, Altötting, Einsiedeln). Whether these madonnas owe their origin

1. G. Dalman, *Palästinischer Diwan: Als Beitrag zur Volkskunde Palästinas gesammelt und mit Übersetzung und Melodie herausgegeben* (Leipzig: Hinrichs'sche, 1901) 250–51, 285–86, 294, etc.
2. H. Kronasser, *Die Umsiedlung der schwarzen Gottheit: Das hethitische Ritual KUB XXIX 4 (des Ulippi)*, Sitzungsberichte der Österreichischen Akademie der Wissenschaften. Phil.-hist. Klasse 241/3 (Vienna: Böhlau in Komm., 1963) 38–39.

7.

Fig. 7. The transfigured Queen Ahmes Nefertari is regularly portrayed as black. "Black" evokes something "totally other" (see also fig. 143). (Wall painting from an unidentified Theban tomb; fourteenth/thirteenth century B.C.)

to pagan goddesses, to this passage in the Song, or to banal natural causes (soot from candles), their blackness has a numinous effect.

This mysterious self-portrayal is addressed to the "daughters of Jerusalem." "Daughters" is used here to imply belonging; they are "residents of Jerusalem." The "daughters of Shiloh" are the young, marriageable woman of that city (Judg. 21:21). The women of Jerusalem are probably used in the Song as the stereotypical public (2:7; 3:5, 10, 11; 5:8, 16; 8:4) because these spoiled, idle, and curious women of the capital city were said to be especially versed in matters of beauty and love (like the Parisiennes in nineteenth-century fiction). The prophetic tradition judges the "daughters of Zion" (3:11b) by a very different standard from that of the Song, condemning those who throw their seductive glances and jingle their ankle bracelets as they walk (Isa. 3:16-26).

[1:6] The numinous effect of her black skin is only underscored by the demand that the women of Jerusalem pay no attention to it. The demand repeats the description and gives it, for the time being, an enigmatic explanation: "the sun has gazed on me." The verb here שׁזף means literally "to gaze on" (Job 20:9; 28:7). The common translation, "to burn, scorch," is taken from the context ("I am black"). Why has the sun looked so harshly on this young woman? Throughout the ancient Near East the sun was a manifestation of important deities, and Israel too could never completely escape its religious attraction (cf. Job 31:26; 2 Kgs 23:11). One of the most important functions of the sun-god was to be judge and vindicator, especially of hidden injustices.

Finally, v. 6cd gives the reason for the punishing glare of the sun on the speaker. Her brothers, who were angry with her (for reasons not given here), sent her off to watch over the vineyards. This job was normally for men (8:11-12; Isa. 27:2-3), who were thought more fit than young women to drive away thieves, wild boars (Ps. 80:13 [14]), and foxes (cf. Cant. 2:15). According to the tradition, young women hang around vineyards for other reasons! Even though he may be right about their intent, Krinetzki apparently does not think the brothers very smart when he assumes they sent her to the vineyards so that hard work would drive out her precocious thoughts about young men. Vineyards are full of erotic associations; whenever a girl found a chance to be with her lover in the ancient Near East, it was in a vineyard (7:12 [13]). An Egyptian letter from the thirteenth century B.C. scolds a messenger: "Thou art come into Joppa, and . . . findest the fair maiden who is watching over the [wine] gardens. She takes thee to herself as a companion and gives thee the color of her lap"[3] (see the commentary on 2:10-13).

Purpose and Thrust

In this poem, the task of keeping the vineyard serves only as background for her revealing comment: "My own vineyard I have not kept!" Here "vineyard" can refer only to her feminine charms. In the love song that

3. *ANET*, 478; cf. Cant. 2:10-15.

lies behind Isa. 5:1ff. (cf. Isa. 27:2), the vineyard is a metaphor for the beloved woman. She also appears as a vineyard in Cant. 8:12. This metaphor is a variation of the garden metaphor (cf. 4:12). By admitting that she has not kept her own vineyard and that a judging sun has therefore gazed upon her in punishment, she gives herself an air of infamy; like her dark complexion, this infamy only heightens her attractiveness. That attractiveness is the whole purpose of this self-portrayal; even in its literary form it can be seen only as an expression of pride and self-worth.

If You Want to Find Him

Text

1:7 a Tell me, you whom [I fervently love],
　　b where you pasture your flock,
　　c where you make it lie down at noon.
　　d [For why should I (appear) like one wandering in confusion
　　e among] the flocks of your companions?
　 8 a If you do not know,
　　b O fairest among women,
　　c follow the tracks of the flock,
　　d and pasture your kids
　　e beside the shepherds' tents.

Form and Structure

Verses 7-8 form a unit characterized by references to the milieu of the shepherd. Along with the royal court (1:2-4) and the vineyard (1:5-6), this setting is a favorite for love poetry. Pastoral images play an important role in descriptions of the prototypical Sumerian lover Dumuzi. Shepherd scenes are undoubtedly popular not only because of this mythical background but also because they are a good place for lovers to meet in real life (cf. Gen. 29:9-14; Exod. 2:15-22).

The question-and-answer form produces the song's unity. The questions are obviously addressed by the woman to her lover, and one expects to hear an answer from him. But the relative clause used to describe the lover in 1:7 ("whom I fervently love") is used three times in 3:1-3 to speak of him precisely when he is absent. Verses 1:2-4 have already addressed the absent lover. Both other times the young woman is addressed as "O fairest among women" (5:9; 6:1) the speakers are the female companions. In both instances the phrase has a slightly ironic tone. This tone seems to apply here as well, whether the answer comes

51

from her lover or from her companions (which seems much more likely). In any case, it cannot come from the lover's fellow shepherds (versus Krinetzki) because v. 8 speaks of them in the third person.

Commentary

[1:7a] The girl describes her lover in a relative clause that is normally translated "whom my soul loves." The Hebrew word נפש, translated as "soul," actually means "throat," although it includes related dynamic qualities like heavy breathing, longing, and desire. When the term is used, as it is here, to stand for the whole person, it describes someone in need, a creature thirsty for life, full of yearning. The relative clause "whom my נפש loves" does not mean the lover is her soul mate but a man who is the focus of all her desire and passionate longing. This same description of the man occurs four times in 3:1-5, another poem whose theme is the woman seeking her lover.

[1:7bc] The woman asks the man she loves so much where he will be pasturing his flock: Where will he let them rest under the hot midday sun? At which spring or under which tree? Her question is virtually identical to that of the stay-at-home Joseph, asking about the whereabouts of his less-coddled brothers (Gen. 37:16).

[1:7de] She wants this information to spare herself the unpleasantness of being found wandering around among the flocks of her friend's companions (cf. 8:13), as though she did not know where her lover was. She does not want to have to reproach herself: "It was a mistake on my part that I did not ask."[1] All of this analysis seems reasonable—perhaps too reasonable for a woman who is ostensibly head over heels in love, or too reasonable for a world that included the traditional motif of women pursuing their lovers with everything they had, taking no regard for themselves. The most impressive examples are mythological: Anat, seeking Baal when he has disappeared, or Isis, wandering through the whole country to find the kidnapped Osiris (see the commentary on 3:1ab). In one Egyptian love song, the woman asserts:

> Yet I will not leave it unless sticks beat me off
> to dally in the Delta marshes
> or ⟨driven⟩ to the land of Khor with cudgels and maces
> to the land of Kush with palm switches
> to the highground with staves
> to the lowland with rushes.[2]

In the parallel poems (3:1-5 and 5:2-7), the woman, who seems at first to want to avoid any inconvenience to herself (5:3), wanders the whole city, seeking her lover, not even giving up when beaten by the sentinels.

1. Babylonian Talmud, *Nid.* 68b; tr. I. Epstein (London: Soncino, 1948) 478.
2. Papyrus Harris 500 group A, no. 4; tr. Simpson, 299.

[1:8ab] The answer begins with a reproachful or mocking tone. This answer fits better in the mouths of her companions than that of her lover (see p. 51). The reproach ("You surely ought to know") and the challenge ("Otherwise, you are just going to have to look") would sound quite unpleasant coming from her lover. But coming from her companions it fits perfectly. In other places too the companions bring the woman back to the realities of love (cf. 5:9). A woman who wants to find her lover dare not shy away from this role of the amorous seeker.

[1:8cd] It is not clear whether the advice to follow the tracks of the flock means that she should literally follow the tracks of her lover's flock and those of his friends or that she should follow her own flocks, i.e., seek her lover by disguising herself as a shepherdess. The parallel command to pasture her kids seems to suggest the latter.

   The command to pasture her kids may be a way to say that she should not be ashamed of her lust for life. In the ancient Near East, grazing goats symbolized an intense hunger for and almost mystical appropriation of life. The well-known goats from the royal cemetery of Ur are shown feeding on a blooming tree that belongs to the domain of Inanna/Ishtar (fig. 8). A feeding goat was often found on Israelite seals two thousand years later. Figure 9 shows examples from Megiddo, Beth-shan, Taanach, and Tell el-Farah (South). The impression from a cylinder seal found in Mitanni portrays two reclining goats flanking a stylized tree or a naked goddess (fig. 10). On a more-or-less contemporary small ivory box from Ugarit, a goddess, bare from the waist up, is feeding two goats (fig. 11). (See the commentary on 2:7b for more on goats and other animals used to accompany or characterize Mesopotamian and Egyptian goddesses.)[3] Note also that 4:5 (cf. 7:3 [4]) compares the woman's breasts to grazing kids. Perhaps the ancient goddess of love with her prominent breasts and her goats lives again—though in a more ordinary form—in the young woman pasturing her kids in this verse.

[1:8e] The closing line ("beside the shepherds' tents") is a variation of v. 7e ("beside the flocks of your companions"). Finally, in search of her lover, she has to go where she did not want to go. If her desire is as great as she claims, she cannot avoid this consequence.

3. Cf. also B. A. van Prosdij, "Aphrodite met den Bok," *JEOL* 8 (1942) 621–23.

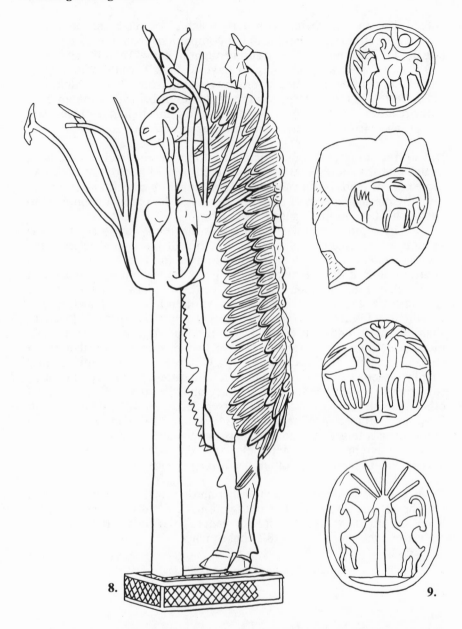

Fig. 8. He-goat stretched out on a rosette tree, from the domain of Inanna/Ishtar. (Composite figure of gold, lapis lazuli, shell, etc., from the royal cemetery of Ur; ca. 2650 B.C.)

Fig. 9. Individual goats with a stylized tree or two goats flanking a tree. (*From top down:* scarab from Megiddo, seal impression from Beth-shan, conical seal from Taanach, scarab from Tell el-Farah [South]; tenth–eighth centuries B.C.)

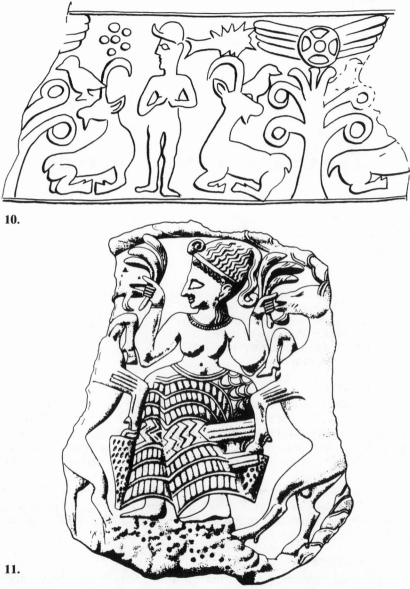

10.

11.

Fig. 10. Two reclining goats, flanking both a stylized tree and a naked goddess touching her breasts. Like the goats, the scorpion (to the right of the goddess's head) also belongs to the domain of the goddess (cf. figs. 24 and 48). (Mitanni cylinder seal impression from Kirkuk; fourteenth century B.C.)

Fig. 11. A goddess with naked upper body, whose hairstyle betrays western influence, feeding two goats. She is seated on a mountain. (Carving on a small ivory box from Ugarit; fourteenth/thirteenth century B.C.)

The Charms of the Beloved

Text

1:9 a [To a mare among the battle horses of pharaoh's chariots
   b I compare you, my love.]
10 a Your cheeks are comely with ornaments,
   b your neck with strings of jewels.
11 a We will make you ornaments of gold,
   b studded with silver.

Structure

In v. 9 the scene shifts from the simple world of the shepherds to the magnificent world of the horse-loving pharaoh. Although v. 10 does not connect very closely with v. 9, it fits at least insofar as the cheeks and neck of royal horses were always decorated with particular care (see figs. 12–13 and 17). Verse 11 is directly related to v. 10 by the repetition of "ornaments."

It is not only the setting of vv. 9-11 that differs from 1:7-8; the action is also totally different. Verses 7-8 are about longing and searching; vv. 9-11 are the praise of a proud loved one. I shall describe the special function of v. 11 below.

Commentary

[1:9] The usual translation, "To a mare among pharaoh's chariots," does not do justice to the Hebrew text, which does not speak of a single chariot but of the chariot corps (plural in Hebrew). Even if one tries to force something like a majestic plural out of this plural form of an already collective term (a corps already consists of several chariots), one is still left with the difficulty that, according to all the texts and pictures, pharaoh's chariots were pulled by stallions, not mares. Whether he is driving his team into the midst of the tumultuous and chaotic hordes of the

56

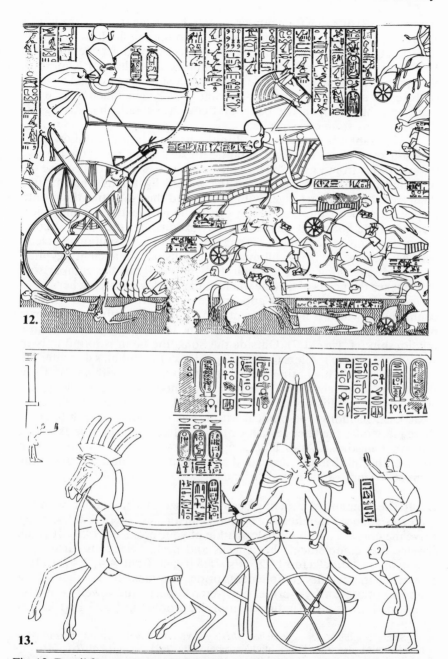

Fig. 12. Detail from a portrayal of the Battle of Kadesh at the mortuary temple of Ramses II in West Thebes (ca. 1250 B.C.)

Fig. 13. Akhenaton with his wife Nefertiti and daughter in a chariot. (Relief on the tomb of Mahu near Tell el-Amarna; ca. 1340 B.C.)

enemy (fig. 12) or going for a quiet ride with his queen (fig. 13), the horses are always stallions. Pope found a solution to both difficulties by calling attention to a monument to an Egyptian officer named Amenemheb (ca. 1450 B.C.), who tells how, on the occasion of a battle near Kadesh in Syria, the enemy had sent a mare into the midst of the Egyptian army to confuse the stallions pulling the chariots. But Amenemheb chased the mare on foot, slit open her belly, and cut off her tail, thus saving the Egyptian army from catastrophe.[1]

The rabbinic exegesis of 1:9 in the first centuries A.D. shows that they still knew about this kind of battle trickery. They relate the passage to the Exodus from Egypt: "[The expression 'mares' is used] because the Israelites appeared like mares and the wicked Egyptians who pursued them were like stallions eager with desire, and they ran after them until they were sunk in the sea."[2] One can no longer justify an allegorical reading of the Song that relates it to the exodus, but the point of comparing the woman to a mare among pharaoh's battle stallions is clear: with her beauty, she brings all men into confusion. An ancient Egyptian love song says, somewhat less colorfully and without the comparison: "She makes the heads of all (the) men/ turn about when seeing her."[3]

Verse 9 marks the first appearance of the term "my love" (friend, companion), which is used frequently in the Song to address the female partner (1:15; 2:2,10, 13; 4:1, 7; 5:2; 6:4). The Hebrew root implies a close relationship (cf. Isa. 11:7). Outside the Song, the noun is found only in Judg. 11:37, where it refers to the companions of Jephthah's daughter (cf. Ps. 45:14 [15]). In his Latin version, Jerome translated with *amica*. Even though the term "girlfriend" sounds all too modern, the etymology, linguistic usage, and history of translation would justify its use. The ancient Near East, including the biblical world, was not nearly so inhibited in these matters as the later Jewish-Christian-Muslim world. For example, modern Palestinian Arab love songs only rarely allow themselves to speak of the "girlfriend"; instead, they conceal her behind the masculine form of "friend" or the plural "friends."[4]

[1:10] The woman's distracting beauty, praised by comparison with the mare, is enhanced significantly by her sophisticated use of jewelry. "You drive me crazy . . . with a single sparkle of your necklace" (4:9). It is the jewelry that complements her cheeks and neck. "Neck" is virtually a synonym for "pride" (Job 15:26; Ps. 75:5 [6]; cf. Cant. 4:4; 7:4 [5]). It is interesting that jewelry complements pride. The constellation that is here found so praiseworthy—pride, outstretched neck, and jewelry—is precisely what arouses the indignation of the prophet in Isa. 3:16-17. This

1. K. Sethe, *Urkunden des ägyptischen Altertums,* vol. 4/3 (1930; reprint, Berlin: Akademie; Graz: Akademische Druck- und Verlagsanstalt, 1961) 894, 5–12; *ANET,* 241.
2. *Midrash Rabbah,* Song of Songs I.9:6; tr. Maurice Simon (London: Soncino, 1939) 71.
3. Papyrus Chester Beatty I, group A, no. 31; tr. M. V. Fox, *The Song of Songs and the Ancient Egyptian Love Songs* (Madison: University of Wisconsin Press, 1985) 52.
4. Cf. Dalman, *Diwan,* XIII.

phenomenon recurs: what the Song celebrates, the prophets criticize (see the commentary on 1:5, and pp. 30–32).

The Hebrew word תּוֹרִים, translated in the NRSV as "ornaments," literally means "rows" (Esth. 2:12, 15), "bands" (Akkadian), or "borders" (Aramaic). One must think of a kind of jewelry that sets off the cheeks, similar to the cheek bands on a horse's bridle. Possibilities include dangling earrings, ribbons on a headdress, or the locks of a wig. The strings of jewels on the neck refer to a kind of collar or necklace made up of several vertical rows of decorative pearls. Near Eastern frit masks (fig. 14) and ivory busts (fig. 15) show such collars worn tightly around the neck, especially in Syria. More typical in Egypt, other than the well-known wide chain collars (cf. fig. 7), were necklaces like the one shown on the wooden carving in figure 16. In all three cases, the jewelry emphasizes the proudly outstretched neck (cf. also Cant. 4:4).

The similarities between these pieces of jewelry and horse bridles and ornamentation is evident; yet one dare not push this comparison too far. Cheek straps and a hood covering the area where the head joins the neck are common on Egyptian horses. A rein attached to the bridle forces the horse to keep its head close to the neck and creates the proud curve of the neck characteristic of Egyptian horses (cf. figs. 12–13). Actual ornamental collars are not found on Egyptian horses, although they occasionally appear in Assyria (fig. 17).

[1:11] The songs of admiration and descriptive songs generally close with an indication of the future development of the relationship (1:16b-17; 4:6). In this case, one hears the resolve to fashion this proud and beautiful woman's striking jewelry from the most precious materials in order to match and radically intensify her own attractiveness. The jewelry is "studded with silver," reminiscent of the decorative studs on Assyrian and Egyptian bridles.

In the plural subject ("We will make") one meets for a second time the admirers, who were previously portrayed as pharaoh's confused stallions. But now they have suddenly exchanged that passive role for an active one. They are "horse" lovers; and their pampering threatens to turn the proud "mare," who had confused the "stallions," into a docile, if luxurious, pet—one that would prance before pharaoh and allow him to feed her (fig. 18) or that could be brought before the king of Assyria standing on her hind legs (fig. 19). Verse 9 is one of the few passages in the OT that mentions horses positively. The prophets always rejected them because they are symbols of luxury and power that lead to arrogance (Isa. 30:16; 31:1, 3; Zech. 9:10). The horse typifies the presumptuous enemies of Israel, the Egyptians and Assyrians.

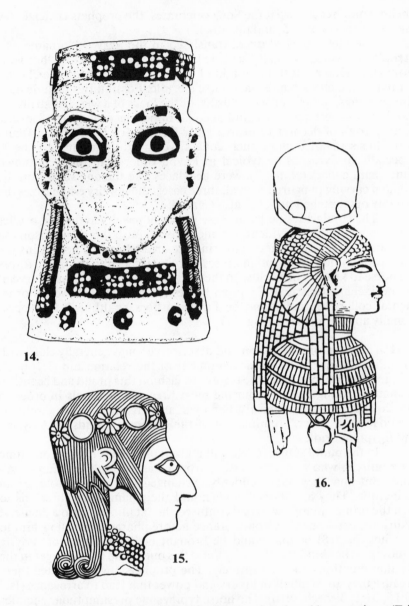

Fig. 14. Woman's face with bejeweled forehead and neck and long earrings. (Frit mask from Tell al-Rimah, northwestern Iraq; thirteenth century B.C.)

Fig. 15. Woman's head with jeweled headdress and a necklace consisting of several vertical rows. (North Syrian ivory carving, found in Calah [modern Nimrud]; ninth/eighth century B.C.)

Fig. 16. Portrayal of the goddess Hathor, whose opulent neck jewelry emphasizes her proud bearing. (Wood carving from Gurob in Middle Egypt; ca. 1300 B.C.)

60

17.

18.   19.

Fig. 17. Two Assyrian battle chariots, each with a team of three horses. The horses are wearing neck chains composed of round links. The standard on the first chariot pictures the belligerent weather-god, Adad, upon his bull; the second standard carries his symbol, lightning, between two bulls leaping in opposite directions. (Alabaster relief of Ashurnasirpal II, from Calah [Nimrud]; ca. 850 B.C.)

Fig. 18. Pharaoh Amenophis II, feeding a horse. (Carnelian placard in the British Museum; ca. 1420 B.C.)

Fig. 19. The king of Assyria training a horse; an official stands in front of him. (Seal impression from Calah [Nimrud]; seventh century B.C.)

61

The Fragrance of Nard

Text

1:12 a [Unto the place where the king (rests) with his table guests,
   b penetrated the fragrance of my nard.]
or
   12 a While the king was [tarrying at his table]
   b my nard gave forth its fragrance.

Form and Structure

This little song again moves in the world of intoxicating beverages, fragrances, and the king (like 1:2-4). Formally, it is self-praise, like 1:5-6, or perhaps—if one prefers the second translation—a formula of solidarity (cf. 7:10 [11]). Thus the little song is clearly distinguished from what precedes it in two ways.

Commentary

The introductory preposition עד is most often translated here as an expression of duration: "while,". "as long as," "during" (cf. NRSV). But the term normally introduces a spatial or temporal boundary. It always does so in its other uses in the Song (2:7, 17; 3:4-5; 4:6; 8:4). If one translates the preposition here as "unto . . . where," instead of "while," it is no longer necessary to correct the verb (participle instead of perfect) as most commentators feel compelled to do.

The king's table represents the highest society. Nard *(Nardostachys jatamansi* [Wallmann] de Candolle) is a precious fragrance extracted from a perennial plant of the valerian family. It came originally from the Himalayas and was regarded as an aphrodisiac in India (cf. 4:13-14). As in 1:3b, a person's fragrance stands for their name or reputation (cf. also Eccl. 7:1; Exod. 5:21). The young woman claims that the reputation of her beauty (her sex appeal) has reached the king (recall how

62

the courtiers reported Sarai's beauty to pharaoh in Gen. 12:15). The term "king" needs to be taken no more literally here than in 1:2-4.

Thrust and Purpose

The usual interpretation understands the preposition differently, in the sense of "while" or "as long as." The term translated "table guests" is taken to signify a gathering for erotic purposes (cf. 2:4: "He brought me to the banqueting house, and his intention toward me was love"). The odor of her nard signals her erotic presence (cf. 4:10; 7:13 [14]; Prov. 7:17). As long as her lover pours out wine with royal generosity, she pours out herself. As long as it pleases him, it pleases her as well. Drinking and anointing symbolize a festive existence, as in an Egyptian love song where the two lovers are "drunk with wine of grape and pomegranate, / and bathed in moringa oil and balm."[1] In contrast to 1:2-4, where erotic pleasures are not identified with the wine and oil, in 1:12 wine and oil are metaphors for the royal love feast to which both the man and the woman make their contribution.

1. Turin Love Song 28; tr. Fox, 44.

What He Means to Me

Text

1:13 a My beloved is to me a bag of myrrh
    b that lies between my breasts.
  14 a My beloved is to me a cluster of henna blossoms
    b [from] the vineyards of En-gedi.

Analysis

Gerleman views 1:12-14 as a single poem: "The three verses have a common unifying theme . . . : 'The fragrance of the beloved.'" That point is true, but the verses have thematic differences as well. The traditional elements in 1:12 are the banquet, the perfumed ointments, and the king (cf. 1:2-4; 4:10), but the king and banquet are absent from vv. 13 and 14 (which are verses in strict parallelism). Instead, these verses employ the conventional motif of fragrant plants.

Form

In form, 1:13-14 is neither self-praise (the first option for 1:12) nor a formula of solidarity (second option) but rather a descriptive song. Instead of praising the beloved's beauty as such songs usually do, however, this one tells what the beloved means to the woman.

Commentary

[1:13] The term "beloved" (דּוֹד), which is used thirty-one times in the Song to describe the male partner, occurs here for the first time. The original sense of the word, which is still frequently found in the OT, is "father's brother" or "uncle" (Lev. 10:4; 1 Sam. 10:14-16). The term was then extended to include the uncle's son (the cousin), although as a rule he is described in the OT as the "son of the דּוֹד" (Jer. 32:7-8). The cousin was a common marriage partner (recall how Jacob married his cousins

64

Leah and Rachel), hence the term naturally came to designate the lover or the beloved. Further, in Ugaritic *dd* describes "love" or "sexual pleasure," a meaning that is connected in Hebrew with דּוֹדִים, the plural of דּוֹד (1:2, 4, etc.).

In v. 13, the woman celebrates her דּוֹד as a bag between her breasts. Since the third millennium B.C., such a bag was used in Egypt as an amulet. The old form of the hieroglyph read as *demedh* consists of a small bag made of one or two cloth strips. The bag is not sewn but is formed when the cloth is wrapped around one or more objects, which it then holds. It is held together by a pin (fig. 20). The dancing girl in figure 21 is wearing this kind of bag. According to written documents from the time of the New Kingdom through the Greco-Roman period, these bags contained a great variety of objects, including mouse bones and cloth heads of Ibis. Spell 13 of the *Book of the Dead* speaks of a pellet of the "plant of life" (henna) in a band of fine linen, and the Leiden Papyrus (dealing with magic) speaks of a pellet formed from the blossoms of a small tree (v. 2).[1] Similar neckware is found on bronze figures from Cyprus (fig. 22) and terra-cotta figures from Palestine/Israel. These are the kind of amulets Isa. 3:20 mentions (literally, "houses of life" in Hebrew). The mix of fashionable clothing, jewelry, and magical objects in Isa. 3:18-23 shows there was no clear distinction between rational and irrational means of augmenting one's appearance and increasing one's feeling of self-worth. Myrrh is one of the rational means. It is made from the resin of several trees and shrubs of the commiphora family (*Commiphora abyssinica* Engler; *C. molmol* Engler; *C. schimperi* Engler), whose range includes the southern portion of Arabia, Ethiopia, and Somalia. Its pleasing spicy odor made myrrh a favorite (and therefore expensive) item for trade. It was used as a powder or dissolved in water or oil to perfume wedding garments (Ps. 45:8 [9]), the bed (Prov. 7:17), or the harem girl before her first visit to the king (Esth. 2:12-13).

Yet myrrh is also an element in the oil used to anoint the most holy vessels and the priests (Exod 30:23). Thus myrrh had its effect because of both its erotic aroma and its sacred associations (a pleasant fragrance signaled the presence of the gods or of the divine).

The amulet character of the small pouch is illustrated not only by its contents but also by its position between the breasts. The only other things reported to be between the breasts in the OT are the amulets and symbols of the goddess, that Hosea rejects as signs of adultery (Hos. 2:2 [4]). An Assyrian oracle concerning Ashurbanipal also mentions an amulet between the breasts. The goddess Mullissu/Ishtar says to the king: "I have placed you like an amulet on my breast."[2]

But the object in v. 13, identified as an amulet by the references to

---

1. F. Lexa, *La magie dans l'Egypte antique: De l'ancien empire jusqu'à l'époque copte,* vol. 2 (Paris: P. Geuthner, 1925) 58.
2. M. Weippert, "Die Bildsprache der neuassyrischen Prophetie," in H. Weippert, K. Seybold, and M. Weippert, *Beiträge zur prophetischen Bildsprache in Israel und Assyrien,* OBO 64 (Fribourg: Universitätsverlag; Göttingen: Vandenhoeck & Ruprecht, 1985) 62; cf. *ANET,* 451.

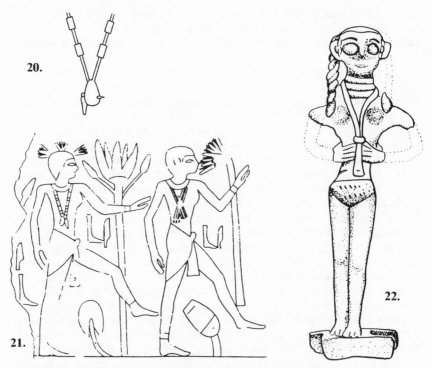

Fig. 20. Cloth bags with various contents served as amulets in ancient Egypt. (From a relief on the tomb of Kagemni in Saqqara; ca. 2250 B.C.)

Fig. 21. The woman dancing (*left*) is wearing a bag amulet. (Painting on tomb 72 in Deir el-Gebrawi, Middle Egypt; ca. 2450 B.C.)

Fig. 22. Figure of a woman with a bag amulet. (Bronze from Cyprus; twelfth century B.C.)

---

the "bag" lying "between the breasts," is not some symbol of the gods or some divine substance like myrrh but the beloved himself. The woman is protected by his sure and intimate solidarity with her. He endows her with vitality and distinction.

In an ancient Egyptian love song, the man also describes his beloved as "my amulet";[3] in another, she is magic for him, allowing him to pass safely to her through a river infested with crocodiles.[4] (See the commentary on 8:6-7 for a view of the beloved as a magical force combating all deadly powers.)

[1:14] The henna bush (*Lawsonia inermis* L.; cf. 4:13), which reaches a height of 10 feet (3 meters), also grows in Palestine, at least in the lower-lying areas. It has thick white flowers that are arranged in erect clusters

3. Papyrus Chester Beatty I, group A, no. 37; Fox, 55.
4. Cairo Love Songs, group A, no. 20D; Fox, 32.

and smell like roses. It is well-known today throughout the Arab world as the source of the red-orange pigment of the same name. There is less data on the use of henna blossoms for their perfume; yet, in analogy to myrrh, this aspect is picked up here. In a treatise on the henna bush a Nubian, S. A. Hissein, writes: "Sometimes women place [henna blossoms] in their hair or in their armpits to drive away the goatlike smell."[5] In all probability, the henna blossom was known in ancient Egyptian as *'anch yimi,* which one might translate as "containing life." The life-giving quality of the plant was related to its pleasant odor. Therefore henna blossoms wrapped in fine linen were placed in graves along with the body.[6] Here the Song ascribes the same kind of amulet character to henna flowers (though for a living person).

Indicating the source of these clusters of henna blossoms—"from the vineyards of En-gedi," the luxuriant oasis in the wilderness near the Dead Sea—emphasizes their special quality. From the end of the seventh century B.C. onward, En-gedi was a carefully tended royal garden producing valuable aromatic substances and high-quality fruits (e.g., grapes and dates).

5. H. Schäfer, *Nubische Texte im Dialekt der Kunûzi,* AKPAW.PH 5 (Berlin: Georg Reimer, 1917); cited by L. Keimer, *Die Gartenpflanzen im alten Ägypten* (Berlin: Ph. von Zabern, 1924) 52D.
6. E. Hornung, *Das Totenbuch der Ägypter,* BAW (Zurich and Munich, 1979) 54 and 420–21.

"Under the linden"

Text

1:15 a Ah, you are beautiful, my love;
ah, you are beautiful.
b your eyes [glances] are doves.
16 a Ah, you are beautiful, my beloved, truly lovely.
b [May] our couch be [fresh greenery];
17 a the beams of our house [(be)] cedar,
b our rafters [wainscoting] [be juniper].

Analysis

The woman has been speaking in 1:13-14, but now in v. 15 the man speaks; the woman answers like an echo in v. 16. Apart from the eyes-as-doves metaphor, this expression of mutual admiration employs quite general terms. But that specificity does not mean the dove metaphor is a later addition copied from 4:1. Like all collections of love songs, the Song uses set pieces. This unit—like other songs of admiration and description (cf. 1:2-4; 1:9-11)—closes with a statement in the first-person plural that spells out the consequences of the conditions that have been described.

Commentary

[1:15a] The "you" in this sentence is emphasized by the "ah" (often translated "behold"): *You* are beautiful, not someone else. In one of the fourteenth-century B.C. letters of Rib-Addi from Byblos, found at Tell el-Amarna in Middle Egypt, a gloss interprets "beautiful" *(yapu)* to mean "desirable" *(chamadu).*[1] But, like the English word "beautiful," Hebrew

---

1. EA 138:126; *The Tell el-Amarna Tablets,* vol. 2, ed. Samuel A. B. Mercer (Toronto: Macmillan, 1939) 463.

יפה has a clear aesthetic sense as well. For the use of "my love," see the commentary on 1:9.

[1:15b] It is no surprise that the eyes receive special attention. Leah's disadvantage over against her more beautiful sister Rachel was the lack of luster in her eyes (Gen. 29:17). David's beauty was due largely to his beautiful eyes (cf. 1 Sam. 17:42 and 16:12). The eyes are still an essential component of a person's radiance or lack thereof. The metaphor "your eyes are doves" has provided fertile ground for commentators trying to determine which of the many possible aspects are being compared here. Many have believed and still believe the eyes of the beloved are being compared to the eyes of a dove. But the dove's eyes are hardly impressive, and other animal comparisons (4:1, 2, 5; 7:3 [4]) always relate to the whole animal, not to individual parts. Using Matt. 10:16 ("be innocent as doves"), earlier exegetes saw innocence and purity as the point of comparison. But the paradoxical instruction to the disciples to be as wise as serpents and as innocent as doves (cf. Hos. 7:11) is surely not the best interpretive context for this metaphor. For a while, some scholars thought that the text referred to the color of the beloved's eyes. But the common rock dove or rock pigeon (*Columba livia* Gmelin), which is what the Hebrew term יונה clearly means (cf. 2:14; Jer. 48:28), is blue-gray, while the eyes of Near Eastern women are dark. The white variation of the rock pigeon, referred to as early as the nineteenth/eighteenth century B.C. (cf. Cant. 5:12), is an even less likely option.

In 1940 Haller claimed that the shape of the human eye resembled a dove, and Gerleman asserts that Egyptian art emphasized this similarity (cf. Krinetzki, Pope). Even though comparisons in form seem appropriate to modern Westerners, they were not appropriate to the Hebrews. When they described parts of the body metaphorically, they normally based the comparison not on external form but on the dynamics of the part in question (see pp. 25–28). Thus the Hebrew עינים ("eyes") comes to mean also "sparkle" or "gleam." The "eye" of the wine (Prov. 23:31, literally in Hebrew) refers to its sparkle, as does the "eye" of copper or bronze (Ezek. 1:7; Dan. 10:6). Thus the commentators who see the point of comparison between eyes and doves in the movement and liveliness of each come much closer to the sense of the Hebrew expression than those who focus on shapes. But even though this interpretation is the "most likely guess" (Pope), it remains only a guess, because no evidence suggests that the ancient world was particularly fascinated by lively motion of the eyes.

Since the beginning of the twentieth century scholars have often pointed out that the dove is a symbol of Ishtar/Astarte—a symbolism commonly explained by the fact that doves nested in the temple of Ishtar. But surely the doves did not distinguish between Ishtar's temple and other temples. The basis for the connection with Ishtar, the prototype and patron of lovers, is more likely the striking love play of doves, especially their billing and cooing. The Roman poet Catullus (84–55 B.C.) writes of one in love:

Fig. 23. A pair of billing and cooing doves, probably presented as votive offerings in a temple of Aphrodite. (Limestone sculpture from Cyprus; fourth/third century B.C.)

Fig. 24. In a world where creation was primarily understood as procreation, sexual provocation was a holy act. This is the sense of this portrayal of a goddess unveiling herself in front of her partner and his son(?). The doves flying from her face signal her love and readiness to conceive. Notice also the dove and the scorpion below the second seated figure. (Ancient Syrian cylinder seal; ca. 1750 B.C.)

Fig. 25. On this seal, whose theme is the same as the one in fig. 24, the dove's direction of flight is even clearer. Along with doves and scorpions (fig. 24), goats and hares belong to the realm of the goddess. (Ancient Syrian cylinder seal; ca. 1750 B.C.)

> Nor did ever dove delight so much in her snowy mate,
> though the dove bites and bills and snatches kisses
> more wantonly than any woman,
> be she amorous beyond others' measure.[2]

2. Catullus 68a.125ff.; tr. F. W. Cornish in *Catullus, Tibullus, and Pervigilium Veneris*,

In the Hellenistic era, billing and cooing doves were presented as votive offerings in the temple of Aphrodite, the goddess of love (fig. 23).

But the iconographic testimony of the ancient Near East is much older than any literary evidence from classical antiquity, and these pictorial images too show how the eye-dove metaphor is to be understood. Two ancient Syrian seals (ca. 1750 B.C.) depict doves flying from the face of a goddess who is opening her clothing in a gesture unmistakably meant to offer herself to her seated partner (figs. 24–25). Even more apparent, on another ancient Syrian seal, is the way the dove flies from the goddess, who has invitingly pushed her skirt to one side, to the weather-god, coming to her across the mountains (fig. 26). A seal from the thirteenth century B.C. shows the dove in the form of a standard between the same couple (fig. 27). The dove was used as a symbol of love across the entire eastern Mediterranean area in the second half of the second millennium B.C. In the first millennium B.C. it also appears in Israel as a terra-cotta figure (fig. 28) and on seals (fig. 29) and other illustrated objects. An Attic dish shows Aphrodite, flanked by a man playing a lyre and a woman playing a double flute, releasing a dove as a messenger of love to fly to Hermes, who is seated opposite her (fig. 30; fig. 39 also depicts a dove between a couple in intimate tête-à-tête). Sometimes the dove flies from the god to the goddess (see the commentary on 5:12), but that scene is rare because the dove is the symbol of the goddess of love (see the commentary on 2:14 and 5:2) and the messenger of her love. In the *Aeneid,* two doves appear to the hero as messengers of the loving care of Venus, his divine mother.[3] The dove at the baptism of Jesus in the Jordan should also be understood as a messenger of love, which the voice from heaven makes clear (Mark 1:10-11 and parallels).

When Cant. 1:15b speaks of "eyes," what it really means is "glances." The same is true in other texts where eyes are said to be enchanting (4:9; 6:5) or, in the view of the prophets and wisdom teachers, seductive (Isa. 3:16; Sir. 26:9). In the present context, given the background of the ancient Near East, one can see the doves only as messengers of love. Thus the sentence would mean: "Your glances are messengers of love!" The man is saying: You are beautiful, and your glances speak to me of love and receptivity.

[1:16a] The woman does not disagree but returns the compliment: *You are beautiful!* Although the OT speaks less often of male beauty than of female beauty, its statements about males are equally unabashed (1 Sam. 16:12; 17:42; 2 Sam. 14:25); it knows that male beauty can work just as seductively on women as female beauty on men (cf. Gen. 39:6-7).

---

ed. G. P. Goold, 2d rev. ed., LCL (Cambridge, Mass.: Harvard Univ. Press, 1988) 147. Cf. also Aristotle *Historia Animalium* 6.2p.560b.26ff.; Pliny the Elder, *Natural History* 10.158; Ovid *Amores,* 2.6.56; *Ars Amandi* 2.465. Cf. B. Steier, "Taube," in PW II, IV A/2, 2479–2500.
3. Virgil, *Aeneid* 6.186ff.

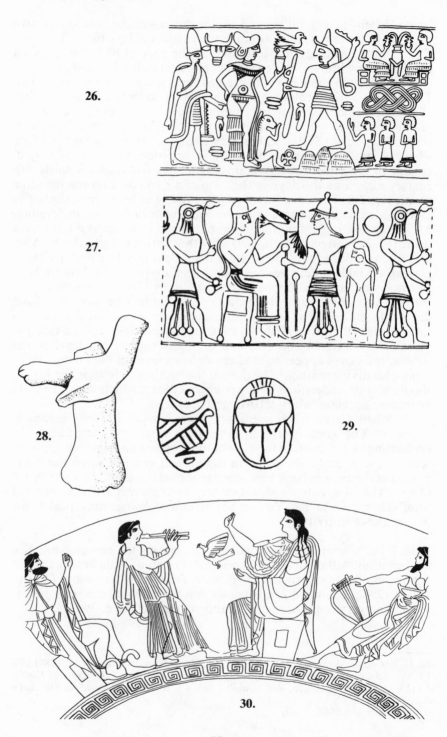

26.

27.

28.

29.

30.

Fig. 26. A goddess who has ostentatiously pushed her dress to one side (cf. fig. 45), offers a welcoming pitcher to her partner, the weather-god approaching across the mountains. The dove flying from her to the weather-god depicts her readiness for love. (Ancient Syrian cylinder seal; ca. 1750 B.C.)

Fig. 27. The seated goddess and the weather-god each hold onto a standard showing a dove flying from her to him. (Mitanni seal from Tell Fakhariyah in northern Syria; thirteenth century B.C.)

Fig. 28. A flying dove on a pillar, found along with a pillar goddess characterized by a young face and very large breasts. (Terra-cotta figure from Lachish; eighth century B.C.) Cf. also fig. 134.

Fig. 29. A dove beneath the symbol of the moon, which, along with the eight-pointed star, represents the Uranian character of the goddess. (Scarab from Lachish; eighth/seventh century B.C.)

Fig. 30. Aphrodite is pictured on the outer rim of an Attic dish decorated with red figures. Flanked by a male playing a lyre (*right*) and a female playing a double flute (*left*), she releases a dove to fly to Hermes who is seated opposite her. (End of the sixth century B.C.)

[1:16b-17] One can properly read the three nominal clauses as wishes rather than statements. In parallelism with the closing clauses of other songs of description and admiration (1:4 and 11), the wish form may be preferable. It is not altogether clear what is meant literally here and what is a figure of speech. Should one envision a chamber with beams crafted of precious cedar as in a royal palace? Or are "couch," "beams," and "wainscoting" figurative terms to describe a love nest in the green forest? Either reading is grammatically possible. The latter seems more probable to me for two reasons. First, the adjective רענה ("green"), used here as a noun, occurs sixteen times with trees (e.g., Deut. 12:2; Ps. 52:8 [10]), twice with parts of trees ("branch" in Job 15:32; "leaves" in Jer. 17:8), and once with oil (translated then as "fresh"; Ps. 92:10 [11]). This usage suggests that רענה is more likely to describe, say, fresh leaves and branches than a freshly made bed (or any other kind of "fresh" bed). Second, when love poets describe actual beds they generally emphasize the luxurious fittings. For example, a Sumerian hymn to the goddess Inanna refers to her sacred marriage to King Iddindagan (ca. 1950 B.C.):

> In order to care for the life of all the lands . . .
> On the New Year, the day of rites,
> A sleeping place was set up for "my queen."
> They [the people] purify it with pots full of rushes, and cedar.
> They set them up for "my queen" as their bed,
> Over it they spread a coverlet,
> A coverlet which rejoices the heart, makes sweet the bed.[4]

---

4. Kramer, *Sacred Marriage,* 65.

A similar hymn to Inanna (but where the corresponding king is not mentioned) includes: "Where a fruitful bed, bedecked with lapis lazuli,/ Gibil [the god of fire] has purified for you in the shrine, the great."[5]

These texts, with all their interest in purification and luxury (coverlets, lapis lazuli), are less reminiscent of Cant. 1:16b-17 than of the bed of the adulteress in Prov. 7:16-17 (who also embellishes what she does with religion; cf. 7:14-15):

> I have decked my couch with coverings,
> > colored spreads of Egyptian linen;
> I have perfumed my bed with myrrh,
> > aloes and cinnamon.

The simple statement of Cant. 1:16b, "may our couch be fresh greenery," is more reminiscent of Cant. 7:12 (13):
"Let us go out early to the vineyards. . . ./ There I will give you my love," or of the ending of the ancient Egyptian love song that claims: "For one who is loved/ how pleasant to go to the fields."[6] Love beneath the trees is the theme not only of Cant. 8:5 but also repeatedly of the ancient Egyptian love songs; one example is the Turin Love Song, where the sycamore, which the young woman has planted with her own hands, says to the young man,

> Come spend the day happily,
> tomorrow and the day after tomorrow, for three days,
> seated in my shade.

Then the tree notes with satisfaction,

> Her friend is on her right.
> She gets him drunk
> while doing what he says.[7]

In another love song, the young woman announces,

> When I retire with you to the trees of the garden house
> I will observe [what you do.]
> My face faces the cottage;
> my arms are filled with Persea (branches).[8]

The context makes clear that the reference is to trees in the temple precincts, which reminds one of the prophetic polemic against sacred fornication:

5. Ibid., 82; see also 76. Cf. *ANET,* 640, 638.
6. Papyrus Harris 500, group B, no. 9; tr. Simpson, 302.
7. Turin Love Song 30; tr. Simpson, 315.
8. Papyrus Harris 500, group A, no. 8; tr. J. B. White, *A Study of the Language of Love in the Song of Songs and Ancient Egyptian Poetry,* SBLDS 38 (Missoula, Mont.: Scholars Press, 1978) 171.

They sacrifice on the tops of the mountains,
>   and make offerings upon the hills,
under oak, poplar, and terebinth,
>   because their shade is good.

Therefore your daughters play the whore,
>   and your daughters-in-law commit adultery. (Hos. 4:13)

The stereotypical reproach of fornication "under every leafy tree" (Deut. 12:2; 1 Kgs. 14:23; 2 Kgs. 16:4; Jer. 2:20; 3:6,13; Isa. 57:5; etc.) provides the majority of the occurrences of רענן ("green," "fresh"), which also appears here in Cant. 1:16b.

As in 1:10-11, the Song and the prophetic critique speak again of the same thing from different perspectives. The prophets combat love-making under every leafy tree because they see it as a continuation of and concession to the cult of Baal. The Song celebrates this love as a way to surround one's own vitality with the life-giving, blooming, all-encompassing vitality of nature, without seeing in it any particular homage to Baal.

[1:17] The poet uses a part to refer to the whole: "beams" means the roof (as in Gen. 19:8), while "wainscoting" means the walls. The OT regards the cedar (*Cedrus libani* Barrel or *Abies cilicica* Kotschy) as the mightiest of trees (1 Kgs. 4:33 [5:13]; 2 Kgs. 14:9); it was planted by Yahweh himself (Ps. 104:16). Because its wood was the most valuable (1 Kgs. 10:27; Isa. 9:10 [9]), it was used throughout the ancient Near East for temples and palaces (1 Kgs. 4:33 [5:13]; 5:10 [24]; 6:9, 18, 20; 7:7, 11; Jer. 22:14).[9] The "juniper" (*Juniperus phoenicea* L. or *Cupressus sempervirens* L.) is frequently mentioned along with the cedar; both are regularly connected with Lebanon (Isa. 14:8; Zech. 11:1-2). Entering the cedar and juniper forests of Lebanon in order to fell these trees is criticized in Isa. 37:24 (= 2 Kgs. 19:23; cf. Isa. 14:8) as an act of imperial arrogance. Behind this criticism stands the old, primarily Mesopotamian, notion that the mountains of cedar were a dwelling place or garden of the gods.[10]

To place the lovers in a "house" of cedars and junipers is to see them more as divine than as royal. To have fresh greenery as a bed is the prerogative of the gods. Zeus comes to lie with Hera on the peaks of Ida (Crete): "There underneath them the divine earth broke into young, fresh grass, and into dewy clover, crocus and hyacinth so thick and soft it held the hard ground deep away from them."[11]

In every age, lovers have usurped this divine prerogative for themselves. Overcome by the power of love, they withdraw from the rational world of social restraints (see the commentary on 7:11-12 [12-13]). Life

---

9. Cf. *ANET,* 25ff., 240, 254, 268, 275, 276, 291, 307, etc.
10. Gilgamesh VI.6ff.; tr. *ANET,* 80; cf. also *ANET,* 104, and F. Stolz, "Die Bäume des Gottesgartens auf dem Libanon," *ZAW* 84 (1972) 141–56.
11. Homer *Il.* 14.347ff.; tr. Richard Lattimore (Chicago: University of Chicago Press, 1951) 303.

can unfold undisturbed in the shadow of the great cedar, the tree of life (Ezek. 31:6). Love takes place under the apple tree (Cant. 8:5). Like many others, Walther von der Vogelweide celebrated such a *retour à la nature* in the meadows and under the shadows of the trees:

> Under the linden
> on the heath,
> there was the bed for the two of us,
> there you can find
> two beautiful broken things:
> flowers and grass.

(Translated here from the contemporary German version of Walther Bulst, *Walther von der Vogelweide, Altdeutsch und übertragen* [Berlin and Leipzig: Tempel, n.d.] 86-87)

"Love's sweet breath,
—a new-born life"*

Text

2:1 a I am [the sea daffodil(?)] of Sharon,
　　b [the lotus] of the valleys.
　2 a As a [lotus flower] among brambles,
　　b so is my love among maidens.
　3 a As an apple tree among the trees of the wood,
　　b so is my beloved among young men.
　　c With great delight I sat in his shadow,
　　d and his fruit was sweet to my taste.*

Analysis

Whereas the previous song (1:15-17) presented the couple's mutual admiration in the second person ("you") and its consequences in the first-person plural ("we"), this song begins with a brief self-description ("I") and then proceeds in vv. 2-3b to mutual admiration in the third person ("she," "he"). Once again, the consequences are in the first person ("I"). Although 1:15-17 is a genuine duet, this song unfolds from the woman's perspective. The brief intrusion of the male voice serves only to confirm her self-assessment and thus to build a bridge to her goal: union with her beloved.

　　Trees obviously play a role in both poems, which is probably why the redactor brought them together. The difference is that while 1:15-17

*This is a line from Goethe, "Suleika," in *The Poems of Goethe,* tr. E. A. Bowring et al. (Boston: Cassino, 1882) 403.

touched on the widespread theme of "love beneath the trees," 2:1-3 employs plants in similes and metaphors.

Commentary

[2:1a] The plant (חבצלת) with which the woman equates herself is not identified. The only other appearance of this flower in the OT is in the context of God's wonderful coming age of salvation (Isa. 35:1). Thus it is probably a noteworthy flower with some splendor, perhaps a kind of lily or iris, rather than a modest little flower like the crocus or meadow saffron. Because it is placed at Sharon, the coastal plain north of Tel-Aviv, the reference could be to the sea daffodil *(Pancratium maritimum* L.). In ancient times, Sharon, now heavily populated, was a region of sand dunes and marshes with few people; it was a habitat for crocodiles even into the nineteenth century.

[2:1b] The second flower mentioned by the young woman, the lotus (שׁושׁנה; the origin of the name Susan) also fits in this milieu. The Hebrew word שׁושׁנה or שׁושׁן is borrowed from Egypt, where it clearly means the water lily or lotus. Nevertheless, most translators have preferred simply "lily," arguing that Israel had no water lilies. But they are wrong; even today one can find there the white water lily (*Nymphaea alba* L.), common also in Europe, and the sweet-smelling African blue water lily (*Nymphaea caerulea* Savigny). When Sharon was full of marshes, there would have been more water lilies than today. But there is an even better argument for translating שׁושׁנה as "water lily" or "lotus." The OT reports that the brim of the molten sea took the shape of the שׁושׁן (1 Kgs 7:26). Vessels in the form of lotus blossoms (like the chalice in fig. 31) are known both in Egypt and in Israel but there are none in the form of lilies. One also reads of capitals in שׁושׁן form (1 Kgs 7:19, 22). All kinds of lotus capitals have been found (fig. 32), but no lily capitals. At least some scholars who equate שׁושׁנה with the lily admit that in these technical expressions relating to construction שׁושׁנה means lotus, but not, they say, in the Song. They follow the translators of the Hebrew Bible into Greek, who rendered שׁושׁנה with κρίνον (lily). But the latter were merely conforming the OT to the Greek world, as Herodotus, the first famous Greek tourist in Egypt, had already done (ca. 450 B.C.): "When the river is in flood and overflows the plains, many lilies, which the Egyptians call lotus, grow in the water."[1]

    I have gone into this matter at some length because the issue is not merely a philological argument; it determines how one envisions the young woman in the Song. Often pietistic and patriarchal, the commentators have desired a chaste and modest maiden. This image works if one compares her to one of the modest spring flowers that grow in thousands on the Plain of Sharon, and to the purity of the lily. But the speaker has more self-confidence than the patriarchal interpreters would like. She

---

1. Herodotus 2.92; tr. A. D. Godley, *Herodotus,* vol. 1, rev. ed., LCL (Cambridge, Mass.: Harvard Univ. Press, 1926, 1966) 377.

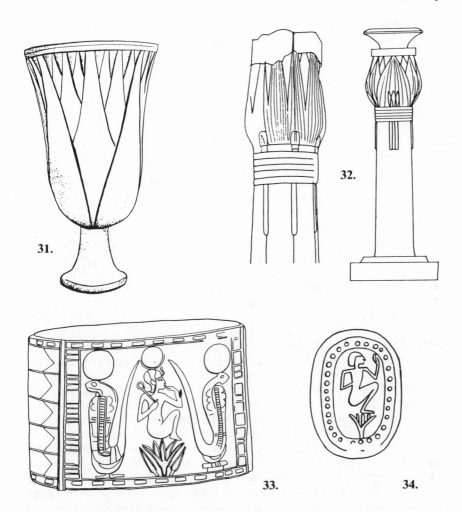

Fig. 31. Egyptian chalice in the form of a lotus blossom (ca. 1500 B.C.)

Fig. 32. Two capitals in the form of lotus blossoms (*left*, from the mortuary structure of Ptahshepses in Abusir, between 2500 and 2350 B.C.; *right*, from the palace of Apries in Memphis, between 590 and 570 B.C.)

Fig. 33. The young sun-god, with the sun disk overhead, sits on the opened primeval lotus, the symbol of the powers that can overcome death and chaos. (He is meant to be within the flower.) The finger in his mouth and the side curl shows him to be a child; the scepter in his right hand show him to be the ruler. He is flanked by two protecting asps. (Bracelet of a son of Pharaoh Sheshonk I, mentioned in 1 Kgs. 14:25; ca. 930 B.C.)

Fig. 34. The young sun-god, seated on the lotus, is also portrayed on a seal that, according to the inscription on the opposite side (not pictured), belonged to a man with the typical Judean name "'Asyo, son of Yokim." *'asyo* means "Yahweh made"; *yoqim*, "Yahweh let arise" (eighth/seventh century B.C.)

Fig. 35. While walking, a man smells a large lotus blossom; its aroma is life renewing (cf. fig. 150). (Scarab from Beth-shan; ca. 1400 B.C.)

Fig. 36. A seated man smells a very large lotus blossom. (Scarab from Beth-shemesh; between 1000 and 800 B.C.)

Fig. 37. A man on a throne smells a lotus blossom. (Wall painting from Kuntillet 'Ajrud; ca. 800 B.C.)

Fig. 38. The head of Tutankhamen emerges from a lotus flower. The head of the dead person was portrayed in the primeval lotus so that, in analogy to the sun (figs. 33 and 34), he might break forth from it filled with renewed vitality. (Wood sculpture overlaid with plaster and painted; tomb of Tutankhamen, ca. 1325 B.C.) This same motif occurs frequently in the death papyri.

---

does not identify herself as one among thousands or as a modest little flower but as a lotus of the plains, embodying its characteristics. In the first millennium B.C. the lotus was one of the favorite symbols in the region stretching from Egypt to Syria. On small objects of Egyptian and Phoenician art, like ivory carvings, metal work (fig. 33), scarabs, and other seal amulets (fig. 34), one finds the sun-god as a child sitting in a lotus blossom. In Egyptian mythology the lotus represents the transition from the dark primeval waters to the ordered world. It is a primary symbol of the Egyptian idea of regeneration. At every opportunity, Egyptian gods and human beings—living and dead—smell lotus flowers in order to capture their regenerative powers, to become as young and fresh as the sun-god at dawn. People in Palestine/Israel were also familiar with this custom, as shown, for example, by scarabs (figs. 35–36), ivories (cf. fig. 64), and wall paintings (fig. 37). In Egypt the head of a person who had died was portrayed in a lotus flower so that the person might go forth from it like the morning sun, new and rejuvenated (fig. 38). Even now, the water lily, opening out of the water in all its radiance, serves to symbolize the freshness provided by soaps, bath accessories, and cosmetics of all kinds. When a woman in an ancient Egyptian love song calls her beloved "my lotus,"[2] or when the woman here calls herself a lotus flower, it means they are able and willing to bestow renewed power—"Love's sweet breath—a new-born life."

[2:2] The man supports the proud claim the singer has made about herself; he contrasts the life and refreshment he receives from his partner with the troubles and deadly boredom associated with other women. The Hebrew word for the other women is "daughters" (בָּנוֹת), but apparently, as in Gen. 30:13, this means the women of a particular group, such as a city ("the daughters of Jerusalem") or a clan ("the daughters of Jacob") (cf. Cant. 1:5). The comparison with brambles is not meant as a photographic representation of nature, because it would be hard to picture actual water lilies among bramble bushes. Thorns are a symbol of misery (2 Kgs 14:9) and curse (Hos. 9:6), of a bleak and deadly world (Isa. 34:11-

---

2. Cairo Love Songs, group A, no. 20C; tr. Fox, 32.

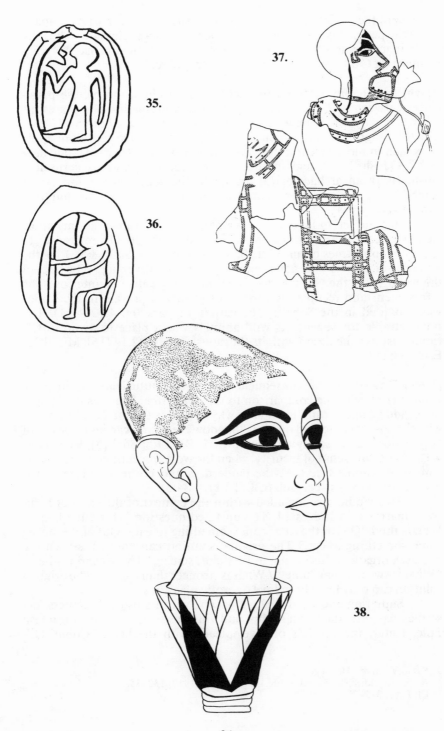

35.

36.

37.

38.

81

15), where the radiance of the mysterious water lily clearly sets it apart. From the perspective of Jerusalem—where the songs originate—the relatively inaccessible Plain of Sharon imparts an exotic air. See the commentary on Cant. 1:9 regarding the title "my love."

[2:3ab] In a happy relationship feelings are mutual; the precise parallelism between v. 2 and v. 3ab expresses this mutuality. She shares his feelings exactly. In Hebrew, "apple" and "apple tree" are both תפוח ("that which is fragrant"). In ancient times Israel apparently had more apple trees than in more recent times. Two villages were called תפוח—one near Hebron (Josh. 15:34) and another 32 miles (52 km.) north of Jerusalem (Josh. 16:8); an archaeological dig far to the south (at the fortress of Kadesh in the northeastern Sinai) uncovered more than two hundred carbonized apples.

In a Sumerian love song, a woman praises her lover as "my apple tree that bears fruit up to its crown."[3] Four of the six OT references to apples or apple trees occur in the Song (cf. also 2:5; 7:8 [9]; 8:5). Like the lotus flower, apples were apparently regarded as enlivening. "The trees of the wood," like the "brambles," function as a negative counterfoil. The refreshment and recuperation moderns gain from a walk in the woods was provided in the Song by the garden or park (cf. 4:12—5:1). The impenetrable forest with its wild animals was a place to avoid in OT times, just like the desert with its thornbushes (Hos. 2:14 [16]; Mic. 3:12; Ezek. 34:25).

[2:3cd] Describing the consequences of their mutual admiration, the woman continues the comparison to the apple tree. She uses the images of "shadow" and "fruit" to explain why she finds the man desirable and why she has firmly settled on him. "Shadow" regularly carries the sense of "protection" and "safety" in Hebrew (cf. Ps. 17:8; 36:7 [8]; 91:1; Hos. 4:13). With this sense of security, when the woman ventures a taste of the fruit of the apple tree (i.e., the tenderness and erotic attention of the lover), she finds it sweet (Job 6:30; 12:11 = 34:3).

Two riddles are included within the context of the story of Samson's marriage in Judges 14. The unstated question behind the first is: Who is this? "Out of the eater came something to eat. / Out of the strong came something sweet." The original solution can only have been the male sex organ, or, according to Eissfeldt, semen.[4] The second riddle is: "What is sweeter than honey?/ What is stronger than a lion?" The original solution can only have been love or erotic pleasures.

Sumerian and Ugaritic love poetry, with its usual directness, describes explicitly the woman's lips and vulva as sweet.[5] In the Gilgamesh Epic, Ishtar, the goddess of love, pleads with the hero: "Come, Gil-

3. Kramer, *Sacred Marriage*, 96.
4. A. O. Eissfeldt, "Die Rätsel in Jdc 14," *ZAW* 30 (1910) 132–35.
5. Cf. Pope, 372–73.

gamesh, be thou (my) lover!/ Do but grant me of thy fruit [i.e., virility]."[6] But, like many others, the fruit metaphor is not gender specific. In 4:13 and 16 it evokes the charms of the woman. Sappho (ca. 600 B.C.) uses the image of the apple to portray her sweet and proud (female) lover: "Like a sweet apple reddening on the high tip of the topmost branch and forgotten by the pickers—no, beyond their reach."[7] For the apple as an aphrodisiac, see the commentary on 2:5b; on the pleasures of love as food, see 4:16cd.

6. Gilgamesh VI.8; tr. *ANET,* 83; cf. Pope, 591.
7. Fragment 116D; tr. Willis Barnstone, *Sappho* (Garden City, N.Y.: Anchor, 1965) 43.

Sick with Love

Text

2:4 a He brought me to the [wine hall],
     b and his [banner over] me was ["Love."]
   5 a Sustain me with [raisin cakes],
     b refresh me with apples;
     c for I am [sick] with love.

Analysis

In 2:1-3 the woman was the initiator, one who had achieved her intended goal; but in 2:4-5 she is the object, pleading for help in her need. Now the elegant, if somewhat forced, plant metaphors give way to the roughness and vehemence of wine, military life, and consuming illness. No doubt the catchword "apple" was the occasion for the redactor's placement of 2:4-5 after 2:1-3.

Commentary

[2:4a] To bring someone to a particular place frequently means putting him or her in a new situation, giving the person a new experience (Ezek. 40:2; Ps. 78:71). The expression often has a violent connotation, as in hauling away prisoners (Ezek. 12:13; 17:4, 12, 13, 20; 20:35) or booty (2 Chron. 36:17-18; see the commentary on Cant. 1:4ab). An Egyptian love song, with the same structural elements as the poem here, reports:

> My brother roils my heart with his voice,
>   making me take ill. . . .
> Come to me that I may see your beauty![1]

---

1. Papyrus Chester Beatty I, group A, no. 32; tr. Fox, 52–53.

What the Egyptian poem calls "roiling the heart" is paraphrased in the Song by the forced visit to the wine hall. The "wine hall" might be a room in the palace (Esth 7:8; cf. Dan. 5:10) or a garden arbor. The term can probably also refer to a private home where for a time (e.g., during the harvest) wine is publicly served. This service would be made known on a sign, called a *ghaya* ("banner," "standard") in ancient Arabic poetry. Finally, in ancient Egypt[2] and in Canaan public houses made available both wine and prostitutes (cf. Josh. 2:1). It is not crucial to know exactly what "wine hall" means in v. 2:4a; what is important is its erotic connotation. At normal dinner parties, men and women drank separately (cf. fig. 6). In the ancient Near East, if they were seen drinking together, erotic associations would be unavoidable. Significantly, an ancient Syrian cylinder seal depicts a dove (cf. figs. 24–26, 30) flying from a man toward the woman with whom he is drinking (fig. 39; cf. also fig. 64). The famous scene of Ashurbanipal's arbor banquet (fig. 40) includes features that point discreetly but unmistakably in the same direction, e.g., the decorations on the bedstead, including the erotic motif of the "woman at the window," and the queen's heavy ceremonial chain, now removed and hanging on the head of the bed (cf. also fig. 128).

"Wine" probably functions here as a metaphor for the joys of love, as it does in 5:1; 7:9 [10]; and 8:2. This interpretation is confirmed by the following half verse.

[2:4b] The Hebrew word דֶּגֶל, the "banner" under which a military unit gathers (cf. Num. 1:52; 2:2), can also refer to the unit itself (like the German word *Fähnlein;* cf. Num. 2:3, 10, etc.). The symbols on such a banner portray the unit's mission or its patron deity. For example, the standard of an Egyptian unit pictures the pharaoh smashing the enemy (fig. 41), while the standard of a group of Egyptian wrestlers, pictured in a tomb, shows two wrestlers in action (fig. 42). The standards on the relief of the Assyrian King Ashurnasirpal II depict the weather-god in combat on a bull; the soldiers' invasion of the enemy land comes under the protection and the mandate of the god (fig. 17). But the banner erected over the female recruit in the wine hall carries the symbol "Love." "Love" is her mission and her patron goddess. A concrete image for this symbol could well be the dove (cf. fig. 39).

[2:5ab] The woman takes her task so seriously that she asks for nourishment—cakes made from pressed dried grapes and apples—from an unnamed source (no doubt the "daughters of Jerusalem," the perpetual extras in this drama; cf. 1:5). Raisin cakes were used in the cult of Canaanite goddesses (Hos. 3:1; cf. Jer. 7:18; 44:19). Forms may have been used to impress the image of the goddess on them; such forms have been found in the Mari palace kitchen in Syria (fig. 43).

---

2. Cf. the *iwyt* in Papyrus Anastasi IV.12.3; R. A. Caminos, *Late-Egyptian Miscellanies* (London: Oxford Univ. Press, 1954) 182 and 187.

Fig. 39. A man and woman toast one another in an intimate tête-à-tête. Meanwhile, a bejeweled(?) dove flies between them as a messenger of love. On the erotic connotations of this scene, cf. fig. 128. In the accompanying scenes, one sees a lion attacking a leaping gazelle (perhaps a symbol of death) and two cherubs, face-to-face, symbolizing protection and care. (Ancient Syrian cylinder seal; ca. 1750 B.C.)

Fig. 40. Following his victory over the Elamites, Ashurbanipal celebrates in an arbor with this wife. Normally men and women celebrated separately (cf. fig. 6 and Esth. 1:10-12). Seated upright and wearing a crenellated crown (cf. fig. 83), the queen may symbolize an undefeated Assyria with whom the victorious king reunites. The bed is decorated with erotic motifs, e.g., women at the window under the seat of the queen, and lions as the symbol of Ishtar(?); cf. figs. 46, 59, 94–99. (Relief from the palace of Ashurbanipal in Nineveh; ca. 640 B.C.)

Fig. 41. A group of Egyptian soldiers is presented with their standard; it depicts the unit's task, the submission of pharaoh's enemies. (Relief in the tomb of Mahu in Tell el-Amarna; ca. 1340 B.C.)

Fig. 42. A group of wrestlers and cudgel fighters carry their standard; it shows two wrestlers in action. (Painting in the tomb of Tjaneni, West Thebes, no. 74; ca. 1390 B.C.)

I have already mentioned the apple as an erotic symbol in 2:3. According to an Assyrian incantation, it was also an aphrodisiac:

> [Incan]tation. The beautiful woman has brought forth love.
> Inanna [the goddess of love], who loves apples and
> pomegranates [cf. fig. 125],
> Has brought forth potency. . . .
> Its [i.e., the incantation's] ritual: either ⟨to⟩ an apple or a pomegranate
> You recite the incantation three times.
> You give (the fruit) to the woman (and) you have her suck the juices.
> That woman will come to you; you can make love to her.[3]

Like many aphrodisiacs, raisin cakes and apples are also symbols of erotic pleasure. One who is consumed in the service of love can be cured only by love. This point is even more clear in the following ancient Egyptian love song than in the one just quoted:

> Seven whole days I have not seen (my) sister.
> > Illness has invaded me.
> Should the master physicians come to me,
> > their medicines could not ease my heart.
> More potent than any medicine is my ⟨sister⟩ for me.
> (I) see her—then (I) become healthy.[4]

[2:5c] The Hebrew word for "sick" literally means "weak." Now that the singer is in the service of love, her strength is consumed—until it is restored by new lovemaking.

---

3. Quoted by Pope, 381.
4. Papyrus Chester Beatty I, group A, no. 37; tr. Fox, 55.

Do Not Stir up Love! I

Text

2:6 a [His left hand (lies) under my head,
    b and his right hand embraces me.]
   7 a I adjure you, O daughters of Jerusalem,
    b by the gazelles or the wild does:
    c do not stir up or awaken love
    d until it is ready!

Analysis

The woman speaks of her beloved in the third person and addresses the daughters of Jerusalem who appear in the scene as extras (cf. 1:5). Thus this song has the same constellation of persons and action as the preceding song. For this reason, many exegetes regard 2:4-5 and 2:6-7 as a unit, but the contents differ too much for this to be so. In 2:4-5 the lovesick woman is consumed with longing, while here in 2:6-7 she adjures those around her not to disturb the fulfillment of love. Another fact pointing to 2:6-7 as an independent unit is the recurrence of the same song (with only minor variations) in 8:3-4—just as some psalms occur as doublets in the Psalter (Psalm 14 = 53; Psalm 70 = 40:13-17 [14-18]). The exhortation of 2:7 occurs a third time in 3:5. There too it is connected to a statement about fulfilled love, though quite a different one.

Commentary

[2:6] This verse describes a classic position in which lovers are portrayed, as on ancient Babylonian terra-cottas (fig. 44).

[2:7a] The solemn commitment asked of the daughters of Jerusalem draws their attention to the inviolability and sanctity of this relationship, one that should be left to develop according to its own rules. Here the two

89

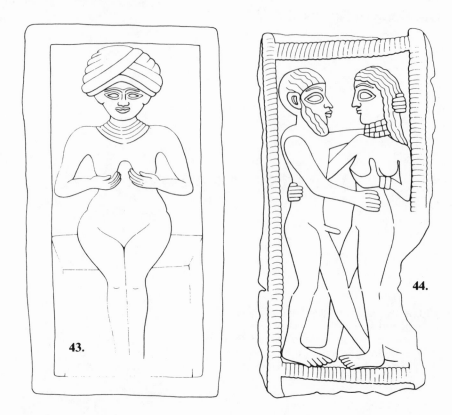

43.

44.

Fig. 43. Baking form from the palace kitchen in Mari, showing a naked goddess holding her breasts. (Clay; ca. 1750 B.C.)

Fig. 44. A man and woman on a bed, both naked except for the woman's three-tiered necklace and two bracelets. His left hand is under her head, while his right hand lies on her abdomen; she holds his waist with her right hand, while presenting her right breast with her left hand. (Old Babylonian terra-cotta; ca. 1750 B.C.)

Fig. 45. A goddess appears to offer a fruit to a royal figure with broad-brimmed cap and club; at the same time, she is pushing aside her robe with her left hand (cf. fig. 26). A variety of nursing and copulating animals romp behind the goddess (*lower register*), including a pair of deer and a female goat with her offspring. (Ancient Syrian cylinder seal; ca. 1750 B.C.)

Fig. 46. Goddess with garment opened in the front; behind her a goat's head and a bird of prey(?) or dove, along with a hare (cf. fig. 25), a running gazelle, and a nursing goat. (Fragment of an ancient Syrian cylinder seal; ca. 1750 B.C.)

Fig. 47. Frontal view of a naked goddess, with a hairstyle like Hathor, bejeweled neck and arms, and belt; she stands over a lion (cf. figs. 59, 94–99). Two snakes cross behind her waist (cf. fig. 96). In each hand she holds a gazelle. The small circles surrounding her may symbolize stars. (Gold pendant from Minet el-Beida, the harbor of Ugarit; ca. 1350 B.C.)

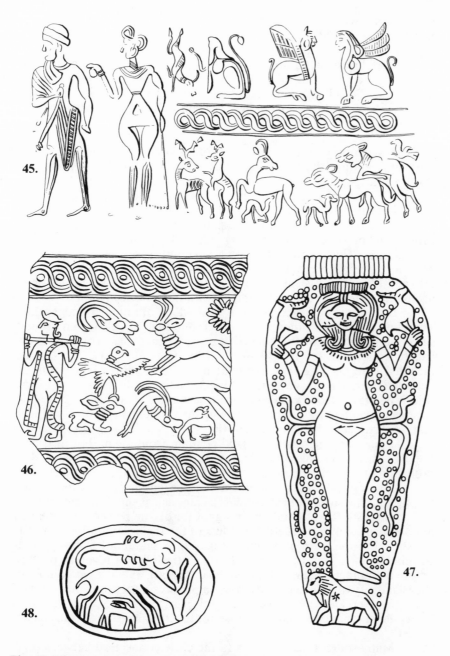

Fig. 48. The scorpion above a nursing gazelle on an Egyptian scarab shows that the Syrian goddess and the animals associated with her also found a place in Egypt in the New Kingdom (1540–1075 B.C.). (Cf. fig. 96; regarding the scorpion, cf. fig. 24.)

lovers do not withdraw under the trees as in 1:15-17; rather, the solemn oath assumes a public occasion, although at the same time it keeps the witnesses to this love at a discreet distance.

To obligate oneself or another through a solemn oath is a frequent OT occurrence; the God of Israel is regularly called on as guarantor in such a case. To call on another deity in this way would be idolatry (Jer. 5:7; 12:16). What does it mean here in Cant. 2:7 or in 3:5 when gazelles and wild does take the place otherwise reserved for God?

[2:7bcd] According to an opinion common since the beginning of the twentieth century, the צבאות ("gazelles") stand for *(Yahweh)* צבאות, the "Lord of hosts," and the אילות השדה ("wild does") for אלשדי, "God Almighty." According to this view, the poet hesitated to use the ancient and honorable titles for the God of Israel in this erotic context; instead, the names are bowdlerized in much the same way Americans replace "God" with "gosh" in some curses (or the French replace *"Dieu"* with *"bleu"* and the Germans *"Gott"* with *"Potz"*). But two points speak against this interpretation: (1) such precautionary measures are otherwise unknown in the OT, and (2) when this substitution happens in modern languages or in postbiblical Hebrew, the replacement word makes no sense.

But in this context "gazelles" and "does" do indeed make sense. Therefore, I prefer a different proposal, one that has also been around since the beginning of the twentieth century, that these shy and easily frightened animals (cf. Isa. 13:14; Ps. 29:9 [NRSV margin]; Job 39:1) are included here because they are related to the goddess of love. On an ancient Syrian seal (fig. 45), the goddess, who has pushed her dress to one side, is portrayed along with copulating deer and a wild goat nursing a kid (among other creatures). Accompanying the goddess on another cylinder seal, unfortunately badly damaged (fig. 46), are a leaping gazelle and a suckling goat (among others). A gold pendant from the harbor in Ugarit (fig. 47) shows the naked goddess with a gazelle(?) in each hand. The probability that similar connections were made in Egypt is demonstrated by a scarab (fig. 48) that combines a nursing gazelle and a scorpion (which belonged to the sphere of the goddess as far back as the third millennium B.C.; cf. fig. 24). It was common in Egypt for divine powers to appear in animal form. For example, the goddess of the region around Aswan was worshiped in the form of a gazelle (fig. 49). A scaraboid from approximately 600 B.C., found in Israel, shows a priest(?) in a reverent posture before the prancing figure of a male goat (fig. 50), and a silver coin from the island city of Arwad (Ruad) in Syria pictures a deer in front of a date palm (fig. 51). Deer and date palms (cf. figs. 59, 93, 95, 135–45) were sacred to Ishtar and similar goddesses (or to Artemis in the Syrian coastal cities).

Many sources bear witness to the close connection between goddesses of love and gazelles, hinds, and similar wild animals (cf. also figs. 8–11). Their habitat, the wilderness or open country, says something about love's passion, which is out of place in the ordered day-to-day world (cf. 7:11 [12]). To swear by the creatures of the wild is similar to

49.

50.   **51.**

Fig. 49. The goddess of the First Cataract, Anukis, appears in the form of a gazelle from the mountains of Thebes. A worshiper has placed a virtual mountain of sacrificial offerings before her. (Sketch from a limestone shard from Deir el-Medina; thirteenth/twelfth century B.C.)

Fig. 50. A priest(?) wrapped in an Assyrian garment stands in a reverent posture before a prancing male goat (regarding the goat as a representative of the goddess, cf. figs. 45 and 124); behind the man is a stylized tree. This scaraboid, found in Israel, is probably a local imitation of a Mesopotamian original (eighth–sixth centuries B.C.)

Fig. 51. A deer in front of a date palm; a bee, on the opposite side, is not pictured. (Silver coin from the city of Aradus [modern Arwad]; ca. 150 B.C.)

swearing by heaven as the throne of God, or by the earth as his footstool, or by Jerusalem as the city of the great King (Matt. 5:34-35). One does not swear by the deity itself but by its attributes—in this case, by the shy, agile creatures of the wild, who are potent with love. Substituting these representatives for the deity herself diminishes a polytheistic interpretation of the Song while maintaining for the oath a sacred aura and imparting a stronger emphasis than merely adjuring the daughters of Jerusalem by "love" itself (1 Sam. 20:17) not to disturb or stir up love (see the commentary on 8:3-4).

"Nothing restrains love"*

Text

2:8 a The voice of my beloved!
   b Look, he comes,
   c leaping upon the mountains,
   d bounding over the hills.
 9 a My beloved is like a gazelle
   b or a young stag.
   c Look, there he stands
   d behind our wall,
   e gazing in at the windows,
   f looking through the lattice.

Analysis

In this poem the woman again speaks of the man in the third person. Unlike what goes before, however, no other characters are included here, at least not explicitly. The woman is speaking to herself. The situation differs completely from 2:6-7. Rather than already resting at her side, the beloved is approaching. The inclusion of this brief song here is based on the catchwords "gazelle" and "stag," the feminine forms of which appear in 2:7b.

Commentary

[2:8ab] Lovers, whose thoughts and feelings incessantly revolve around each other, are inclined to hear or see the coming of the beloved in every noise or in every person appearing on the horizon. This continuing but often disappointed expectation makes the real event always a happy surprise. Regarding the title "beloved," see the commentary on 1:13.

*This is the first line of "Die Liebe," a poem by Matthias Claudius.

[2:8cd] The desire to be with his beloved enables the man to leap over the mountains and hills that separate them (cf. Ps. 125:2; 121:1). Love brings superhuman power. In Ps. 18:29 (30) God himself gives the king the ability to jump over walls.

[2:9ab] In the same psalm, the king praises God as the one who makes his feet like hinds' feet (Ps. 18:33 [34]). The speed and leaping ability of gazelles and hinds is proverbial in the OT and in the entire ancient Near East (cf. Cant. 2:17; 8:14; 2 Sam. 2:18; 1 Chron. 12:8 [9]; Sir. 27:20; Isa. 35:6; Hab. 3:19). An ancient Egyptian love song works particularly well as a parallel here:

> If only you would come to (your) sister swiftly,
>   like a gazelle bounding over the desert,
> whose legs are shaky, whose body is weary,
>   for fear has entered his body.
> A hunter, dog with him, pursues him,
>   but they can't even see his dust.
> He regards a resting place as a trap(?)
>   and takes to the river as a road(?).
> (Then) ere (you) kiss your hand four times,
>   you will arrive at her "cave."[1]

In this song the natural speed of the gazelle is dramatically intensified through the introduction of the theme of the hunt (an intensification lacking in the Song). Leaping and jumping express agile grace and a heightened feeling of life more than they do unbridled passion. The leaping fallow buck on a Middle Assyrian cylinder seal seems to characterize the same kind of happy and excited feeling of life (fig. 52). The young fallow buck on an ivory toy chest from Kamid el-Loz in Lebanon is turning its head to look for a following fox or jackal, but its wide-paced gallop gives the predator no opportunity to attack (fig. 53). Their back-to-back placement brings a playful element to the pair of leaping gazelles pictured on a scarab from Ashdod and on a Hebrew seal (figs. 54 and 55).

[2:9cd] With this kind of agility, it is no wonder that the beloved shows up behind the wall just as suddenly and unexpectedly as he did on the hills (notice the repetition of "Look!" in vv. 8b and 9c). "Behind the wall" is his position in relation to the woman speaking, but the term is also a play on coming after her from behind (Gen. 37:17). The precise designation *"our* wall" is unique. Shifting protectively from the singular to the first-person plural in a decisive moment is reminiscent of Cant. 1:4, where the woman takes refuge among her companions. Here the "our" probably means to include her mother. In 3:4 and 8:2 the mother's house or chamber is the place the woman chooses to give herself to her beloved.

1. Papyrus Chester Beatty I, group B, no. 40; tr. Fox, 66–67.

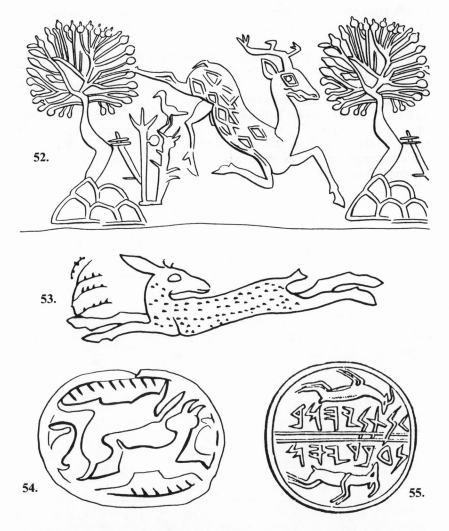

Fig. 52. A Mesopotamian fallow buck jumps over a mountain topped with a tree and a bush holding a bird. (Middle Assyrian cylinder seal; thirteenth century B.C.)

Fig. 53. A young stag in a flying gallop runs from a jackal or fox (not visible here). (Engraving on ivory from Kamid el-Loz in the Bekaa region of Lebanon; fourteenth/thirteenth century B.C.)

Fig. 54. Two young ibexes or gazelles, back-to-back; the upper and lower margins are developed into branches; an asp appears on each of the narrow edges. (The scarab was found in Ashdod at a seventh-century level, but, based on its style, it belongs in the thirteenth/twelfth century B.C.)

Fig. 55. Two back-to-back gazelles that, in contrast to those in fig. 54, are both jumping in the same direction. The seal's owner has the typical Judean name "Natanyahu, son of Abadyahu" (eighth/seventh century B.C.)

[2:9ef] The reference to "standing" in v. 9c contrasts sharply to the earlier "leaping" and "bounding." For a moment all movement ceases, but then the energy of leaping and jumping is transformed into that of gazing and looking. In both cases, the Hebrew participles denote a total participation in the activity on the part of the beloved. During the leaping and jumping, the woman is the observer, but now that the beloved stands behind her wall, she is the one observed. The intensity of his gaze is emphasized by using plural forms for both the windows and the lattices (which cover the larger openings). The more windows, the more searching eyes looking through them. The brief clauses, constructed in strict parallelism, betray the excitement of the woman who has been sought so fervently and watched so intently.

The Time Has Come

Text

2:10 a My beloved speaks and says to me:
   b "Arise, my love,
   c my fair one, and [go];
 11 a for now the winter is past,
   b the rain is over and gone.
 12 a The flowers appear [in the land];
   b the time of singing has come,
   c and the [cooing] of the turtledove
   d is heard in our land.
 13 a The fig tree puts forth its figs,
   b and the vines are in blossom; they give forth fragrance.
   c Arise, my love,
   d my fair one, and [go]."

Analysis

Many interpreters regard 2:8-13 as one poem (some include also v. 14). They argue that the beloved arrives and invites his lover to go with him to the vineyards. But the invitation to the woman in vv. 10b-13 has no direct connection to the situation of vv. 8-9. For example, the woman receives no invitation to come out of the house to meet her lover, even though, according to v. 9c-f, that is where she was when he was looking for her. Therefore the clause in v. 10a, which now combines the two parts (vv. 8-9 and 10b-13 [14]), appears to have been added by a redactor in order to connect the two songs and neatly turn them into a single unit (cf. Krinetzki). The combination would have been even more convincing had he inserted v. 14 after v. 9.

I treat the three songs independently here because they were probably originally independent. A redactor has contrived to combine them, which is one of the things that has led many exegetes over the centuries to mistakenly interpret the Song as a unified drama; this interpretation has required the fanciful invention of a complicated love story, often elaborate and totally improbable (cf. pp. 13-15).

Structure

The structure of the poem in 2:10b-13 is marked by the use of identical invitations at beginning and end. In between, introduced by "for," is the basis for the invitation. This poem has been praised as "the most beautiful nature song in the OT" (Rudolph). "The tone of this song of spring seems remarkably modern. Here the natural phenomena are not described in metaphors, but are instead part of a lyrical and sensitive observation of nature for its own sake; this is found nowhere else in the OT nor in the Egyptian love poetry" (Gerleman).

But is this view correct? Does this poem merely describe the awakening of nature for its own sake, or does the awakening of nature imply the blossoming of the young woman to sexual maturity, thus justifying the invitation to "arise" and "go"? The latter interpretation would parallel Mörike's poem "Liebesvorzeichen" (Signs of love), where the swelling pomegranate buds unexpectedly turn out to be lips, which overnight are awakened to sexual maturity. A clear answer to this question is made difficult by the occurrence in the brief poem of several rare words, no longer unequivocally translatable.

Commentary

[2:10bc] See the commentary on 1:9 for a discussion of the address "my love." Most commentators translate the two imperatives קוּמִי and לְכִי with "arise" and "come." But these two imperatives often occur in combination, where they always have the sense of "arise" and "go" (cf., e.g., 2 Sam. 13:15; 1 Kgs 14:12; 2 Kgs 8:1; Mic. 2:10). The translation "come" does not arise from the Hebrew words themselves but only from the context—the secondary connection of the two songs in 2:8-9 and 2:10b-13. After each imperative the Hebrew inserts the so-called *dativus commodi* ("for yourself," "for your sake"). That construction and the frequent use of *l* and *i* lend a brusque urgency to the command to rise and go.

This understanding of vv. 10bc and 13cd immediately suggests the question of where the woman should go. One must seek the answer in vv. 11-13b, which provide the basis for the imperatives.

[2:11] First, this verse states merely that it is a favorable time to go. The winter is past, along with the cold and flooding rains that often accompany it in Palestine/Israel. Both London and Jerusalem average 21.45 inches (550 mm.) of rain annually, but in London it rains three hundred days every year, while in Jerusalem the same amount is concentrated in fifty days. These days of heavy precipitation are over by the end of April.

[2:12] The statements of this verse, like those of v. 11, emphasize primarily the propitiousness of the hour. The Hebrew word for "flowers" in v. 12a (נצה) does not refer merely to the splendor of the flowery meadows but to the blossoming of bushes and trees, especially the grapevines (Gen. 40:10; Sir. 50:8). Verse 12b explicitly emphasizes the temporal aspect: "The favorable time for the זמיר has arrived." זמיר can refer to the pruning of vines or the wine harvest, but it can also mean accompanied singing. The vines are pruned or cut between January and March, before the new sap rises and before the time of the other signs enumerated in this verse. The grapes are harvested in August/September, much too late for the other phenomena mentioned here. Thus, in this verse זמיר has to mean singing (Isa. 24:16; 25:5; Job 35:10 RSV). The definite article could indicate that the author has a particular kind of singing in mind. The turtledove mentioned in v. 12c is a migratory bird (cf. Jer. 8:7), as it is in Europe; it shows up in Israel about the middle of April (at the end of the rainy season). Its amorous cooing seems to provide the beat for the song of v. 12b. Verse 12 seeks to motivate the call to go (in vv. 10bc and 13cd) primarily by calling attention to the favorable time. But, the repetition of references to the land ("in the land" [v. 12a], "in our land" [v. 12d]) also introduces a spatial element. "Land" here obviously means the open country in contrast to the houses of the walled city (cf. Lev. 25:23-31).

[2:13ab] The fig tree, whose early fruit ripens on the new branches as early as May, and the grape vines, which blossom in April/May, point again to the favorable time; in addition they call to mind a location (the vineyard) that plays a major role in the love poetry of the Song (1:6; 2:15; 8:11-12; cf. 6:11; 7:8, 12 [9, 13]). Vineyards almost always include also a few individual fig trees.

The blooming vineyard may well indicate the place where the young woman is supposed to go, because its mention closes the section of the man's speech that seeks to motivate her movement. It is followed by the renewal of the invitation. According to traditional Jewish literature of the first centuries A.D., young Jerusalem women journeyed into the vineyards on the 15th of Ab and on Yom Kippur. According to the Mishnah: "There were no days better for Israelites than the fifteenth of Ab and the Day of Atonement. For on those days Jerusalemite girls go out in borrowed white dresses. . . . And the Jerusalemite girls go out and dance in the vineyards." And the Gemara comments: "Whoever [among the men] was unmarried repaired thither."[1]

These trips to the vineyards afforded young people the opportunity to meet. The narrative in Judg. 21:15-23 shows that this meeting was an ancient custom. It speaks of a festival during which the daughters of Shiloh went out into the vineyards to sing and dance. The Benjami-

---

1. Mishnah, *Ta'an.* 4:8; tr. J. Neusner, *The Mishnah: A New Translation* (New Haven and London: Yale Univ. Press, 1988) 315. Babylonian Talmud, *Ta'an.* 31a; tr. J. Rabbinowitz (London: Soncino, 1938) 164.

nites, who had no wives, took this opportunity to kidnap them. The text says nothing of the time of year for this festival. The 15th of Ab normally falls in August, the Day of Atonement in October. Cant. 2:10-13, along with 7:11-12 (12-13), seems to indicate that at the time these songs were written there was another such festival at the end of April or in May, occasioned by the budding or blooming of the vineyards. Perhaps the joyful holiday Lag ba-Omer, celebrated in May, derives from this festival, because the historical bases for the present holiday all seem to be clearly secondary (e.g., the day is said to mark the end of a great plague to which large numbers of the students of Rabbi Aqiba succumbed; the warlike games of the boys are said to be reminiscent of the excitement during Bar Kokhba's rebellion against Rome; the day is said to mark the death of Rabbi Simeon ben Yohai, the alleged author of the *Zohar,* the most important of the Kabalistic writings; etc.).

Purpose and Thrust

In 2:10-13 the man urges the woman to go out and participate in this festival; it is time for them to hear the amorous cooing of the turtledoves and to enjoy nature's budding and blooming—nowhere does this song distinguish clearly between what is a description of natural reality and what is metaphor. In any case, the Song quite clearly often uses vines and vineyards to describe feminine charms (cf. especially 1:6, but also 2:15; 8:11-12; 6:11; 7:7, 12 [8, 13]). In 1:12, "giving forth fragrance" probably signals the intensity of erotic presence (cf. 7:13 [14]).

The Dove in the
Clefts of the Rock

Text

2:14 a O my dove, in the clefts of the rock,
  b in the covert of the cliff,
  c let me see your face,
  d let me hear your voice;
  e for your voice is [infatuating],
  f and your face is [ravishing].

Analysis

This brief song, like the previous one, seeks to bring about a movement on the part of the woman that will make her accessible to the lover. But whereas the former song wanted her to visit the vineyard where the speaker hoped to meet her(?), this one is a straightforward request to show herself to him. The pronouns clearly emphasize the wish: a relationship between the one speaking and the one addressed; the basis, introduced with "for," sounds like a more objective remark. But every man in love thinks that whatever infatuates and enchants him personally has the same effect on everyone else.

Commentary

[2:14ab] As we saw in 1:15 (cf. figs. 23–30, 39), the dove is an animal belonging to the realm of the goddess of love; it can serve as a messenger of love or as a representative of the goddess. That connection is particularly clear when doves are used to designate sanctuaries as temples of the love-goddess. A coin from the time of Roman emperor Caracalla depicts the famous temple of Aphrodite in Paphos (Cypress); it is identified by, among other things, three doves (fig. 56). A dove is perched

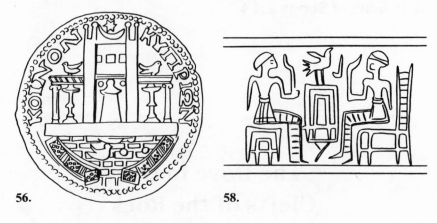

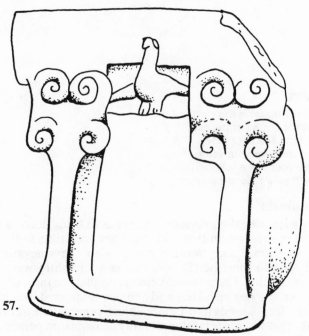

Fig. 56. Three doves identify the "common place [sanctuary] of the Cypriots" (coin inscription) as the temple of Aphrodite of Paphos. (Coin from the time of Caracalla; ca. 200 A.D.)

Fig. 57. Clay model of a temple, the entrance flanked by two palmette pillars, which is identified as a temple of a Syrian goddess by the dove over the entrance. (From Palestine/Israel; ninth/eighth century B.C.)

Fig. 58. Two people, seated in reverent posture, flank a temple whose most prominent symbol is a dove. (Cylinder seal from Salamis, Cyprus; thirteenth-eleventh century B.C.)

59.

105

above the entrance on a model of a temple found in Palestine/Israel (fig. 57).

Two worshipers flank a dove-crowned temple on a cylinder seal from Salamis on Cyprus (fig. 58). The oversized dove on a palm tree in the courtyard of the Ishtar temple in Mari (fig. 59) demonstrates that the dove could be used to symbolize the presence of the goddess already in the second millennium B.C.

The address "my dove" (cf. also 5:2 and 6:9) does not imply a claim of ownership (contra Krinetzki); it confesses that in the beloved the speaker encounters love—if not the love-goddess—in person. The location of the encounter with the dove (or beloved) betrays a dissociation from the tradition of the love-goddess. It does not take place in a temple but in the natural habitat of the rock dove (*Columba livia* Gmelin)—the clefts and cracks of the rocks. These features characterize the relative inaccessibility of Edom (Obad. 1:3) and provide nesting places for the raptorial birds (Jer. 49:16). "The covert of the cliff," paralleling "the clefts of the rock," refers to this wild and inaccessible region. The Hebrew מדרגה, translated here as "cliff," actually refers to stair-step ledges in the rock (cf. Ezek. 38:20). To a viewer standing in a ravine or at the base of a mountain the wild dove would be visible only for a moment when it came to the edge of such a ledge, usually to disappear again quickly. Thus, as in 4:8, the woman is portrayed as unreachable; as in 2:2-3, her splendor is emphasized by the contrast to this wild and desolate landscape.

[2:14c-f] The speaker's request to be permitted to see the face of his beloved, especially in the Hebrew wording, is reminiscent of Moses' request that the Lord permit him to see his glory (Exod. 33:18). The Hebrew מראה, like the English "appearance," can refer either to external appearance or shape (Gen. 12:11; 29:17; 39:6) or to supernatural appearance or vision (Exod. 3:3; 24:17).

Fig. 59. In the middle of the famous symmetrical wall painting from Mari (a portion of the left half is not included here because it is severely damaged) stands the warlike Ishtar in the cella of a temple, with her right foot on a lion. Behind her stand a protecting goddess and a warlike god, before her the king of Mari, who is touching her ring and her staff. Another protecting goddess stands behind the king. In the anteroom to the cella are two goddesses holding spherical vessels; a stylized tree and four rivers (with fish) emerge from each of these vessels (cf. figs. 80 and 104–7). The temple is flanked by two stylized trees; in addition, six composite beings serve as guardians, two palms—each being climbed by two men to pick the dates—and two gigantic doves on the palms. Although the water deities, trees, and composite beings could characterize any temple, the lions (figs. 47, 94–99), palms (figs. 93, 95, 135–46), and doves are typical of the sphere of the love-goddess.

Purpose and Thrust

Although the request mentions the visual appearance first and then the voice, this order is reversed in the basis, yielding an *abb'a'* structure or chiasm. The structure emphasizes the strict correspondence of the comparison—the voice is just as infatuating (or "sweet"; cf. Prov. 20:17) as the face is ravishing. The numinous quality common to both the request and the basis justifies these strong words. The usual translations ("pleasant," "lovely," etc.) are too pallid, failing to do justice to the intensity that enlivens this little song.

The Free-Running Admirers

Text

2:15 a Catch us the foxes,
    b the little foxes,
    c that ruin the vineyards—
    d for our vineyards are in blossom.

Analysis

The collector/redactor has probably placed the song in its present location (i.e., after the song of the dove, as close as possible to 2:10-13)
solely because of the catchword "vines [or vineyards] in blossom" in vv.
13b and 15d. Now, in contrast to 2:14, we do not hear an individual addressing his one-and-only love but a group addressing a group. The group
(in the first-person plural) is made up of women or girls (see p. 110).
Because their vineyards are in bloom, the foxes must be caught. It is not
clear who is meant by the masculine plural imperative. It would be best to
think of an indeterminate addressee—something like, "Won't someone
catch us the foxes?" (cf. Krinetzki).

Commentary

[2:15] The content of the song is determined by the double use of "vineyards" and the similar repetition of "foxes." The latter must be caught
because they are destroying the former. The Hebrew שׁוּעָל can mean the
golden jackal (*Canis aureus* L.; cf. Ps. 63:10 [11]; Ezek. 13:4), which, in
the open, is hardly distinguishable from a fox (*Vulpes vulpes* L.) to an un-
trained observer; but the fox is the more likely ravisher of vineyards. Its
burrowing endangers both the vines and the walls (cf. Neh. 4:3 [3:35]);
moreover it is a great fancier of ripe grapes. Thus, in about 275 B.C.,
Theocritus has Comatas the goatherd say: "I hate the brush-tail foxes,

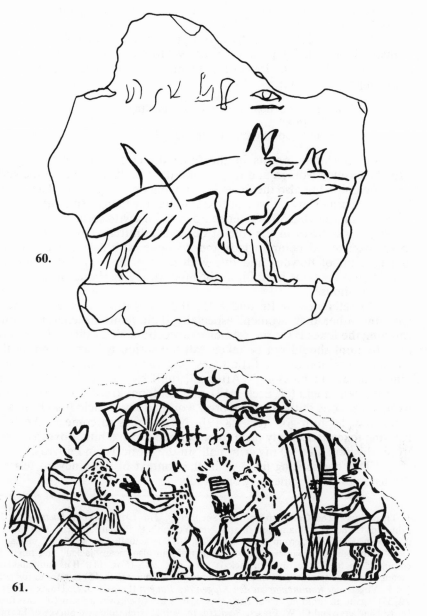

Fig. 60. Two foxes or jackals copulating. (Sketch on a limestone shard from Deir el-Medina; thirteenth/twelfth century B.C.)

Fig. 61. Three foxes admire an elegant lady mouse. The first is carrying a fan or parasol in the form of a gigantic flower, the second an artistic bouquet of flowers, and the third a harp. (Ostracon from Deir el-Medina[?]; thirteenth/twelfth century B.C.)

that soon as day declines/ Come creeping to their vintaging mid goodman Micon's vines."[1]

But Cant. 2:15 is hardly about production problems in the wine industry. In ancient Egyptian love poetry, "fox" or especially "young fox" is a metaphor for a great lover or womanizer. In one such Egyptian song, the young woman says:

> My heart is not yet done with your lovemaking,
>   my (little) [fox]!
>   Your liquor is (your) lovemaking.[2]

A hymn to Hathor points in the same direction when not only the wreathed young women and the drunkards raise their heads to the goddess of passion but also the foxes.[3] A drawing on an Egyptian shard from Deir el-Medina shows a pair of foxes, noted for their sexual prowess, in the act of mating (fig. 60). Other shard drawings with scenes from animal fables portray foxes in the role of dubious admirers. On one ostracon, three foxes stand before a lady mouse—one with a fan, one with an arrangement of flowers, and one with a harp (fig. 61). No doubt the drawing has the same meaning as the modern saying about the fox guarding the henhouse.

In reference to 1:6 and 8:12, the vineyards can scarcely mean anything other than women, especially their feminine charms. Thus, catching the foxes is for the women's protection. Yet, as Rudolph points out, the hunt should not be taken "all too seriously," as is seen by the "tender repetition of 'the little foxes' and the provocative closing: 'our vineyards are in blossom.'" After all, the foxes are only to be taken, snared (אחז), caught (cf. Eccl. 9:12), and held, not killed. In Cant. 3:4 the woman uses one of the same Hebrew words to say, "I held (אחז) him, and would not let him go!" (cf. 7:8 [9]). No harm is to come to the free-running foxes. They only need to be calmed down a bit. "Foxes" is used ironically here, like "O my criminal!" in the erotic Turin Papyrus.[4]

This comic song fits well in the context of the vineyard festival discussed in the commentary on 2:13ab.

---

1. Theocritus, "The Goatherd and the Shepherd," *The Greek Bucolic Poets;* tr. J. M. Edmonds (London: William Heinemann; New York: G. P. Putnam's Sons, 1912) 77.
2. Papyrus Harris 500, group A, no. 4; tr. Fox, 10. Fox actually has "wolf cub" instead of "fox," although he recognizes that the term *wnš* can also mean "jackal" and might be compared to the "little foxes or jackals" in Cant. 2:15 (Fox, 11). *Wnš* unmistakably means "fox": the term is used in the "Laments of the Peasant" (r. 15) to refer to fox pelts (cf. F. Vogelsang, *Kommentar zu den Klagen des Bauern* [Leipzig: J. C. Hinrichs, 1913] 29–31); again, in tomb no. 15 at Beni Hasan, it is inscribed over a picture of two foxes (P. E. Newberry and G. W. Fraser, *Beni Hasan,* vol. 2, Archaeological Survey of Egypt 2 [London: K. Paul, Trench, Trubner & Co., 1893] pl. 4).
3. E. Drioton, *Rapport sur les fouilles de Médamoud (1926): Les inscriptions* (Cairo: Institut français d'archaeologie orientale, 1927) 27–28; cf. S. Schott, *Altägyptische Liebeslieder: Mit Märchen und Liebesgeschichten,* BAW, 2d ed. (Zurich: Artemis, 1950) 80.
4. J. A. Omlin, *Der Papyrus 55001 und seine satirisch-erotischen Zeichnungen und Inschriften,* Catalogo del Museo Egizio di Torino 1/3 (Turin: Edizione d'arte fratelli Pozzo, 1973) 68 no. 12.

"You are mine, I am yours"*

Text

2:16 a My beloved is mine and I am his;
     b he [grazes] among the [lotus flowers].
  17 a [When] the day [(wind) begins to blow]
     b and the shadows flee,
     c turn, my beloved,
     d be like a gazelle
     e or a young stag
     f on the [*beter*] mountains.

Analysis

The delineation of the songs at the end of chap. 2 is controversial. For example, Gerleman regards 2:15-17 as a single song, whereas Krinetzki thinks each verse (15, 16, and 17) is an independent poem. Form (plural) and content (fox and vineyard theme) make a clear separation between 2:15 and what follows. Perhaps the redactor wanted to contrast the free-roaming foxes with the faithful gazelle (the lover).

      It is difficult to decide what to do with 2:16-17 because the verses obviously contain many favorite and frequently used expressions, often found with somewhat different meanings. Verse 16 is repeated almost verbatim in 6:3, where it is triggered by the picture of the man "in the garden," picking lotus flowers (6:2). Verse 2:17ab is repeated exactly in 4:6ab, where it is connected to a detailed description of the woman (4:1-5) and builds a transition to the man's intention to "hasten to the mountain of myrrh" (4:6c) when "the wind begins to blow" (4:6a). These parallels suggest that one can easily read 2:16-17 as a unit, where 2:16 is

---

*This is the first line of a well-known medieval *Minnelied* (love song), "Dû bist mîn, ich bin dîn."

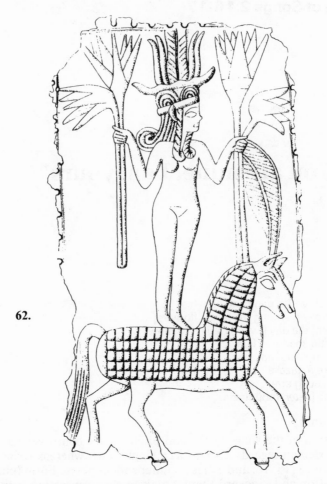

62.

Fig. 62. A naked goddess standing on a warhorse (instead of the customary lion; cf. figs. 47, 96). She holds two gigantic lotus blossoms in each hand. While the lion or warhorse embody her aggressive side, the lotus flowers express her fascinating and life-renewing powers. (Gold foil from Lachish; thirteenth/twelfth century B.C.)

Fig. 63. Ankhesenamen holds a bouquet of lotus flowers and love apples under the nose of her husband Tutankhamen (cf. figs. 149–52), thereby arousing the king's love (cf. the flowers under the nose of Min in fig. 96). The queen's readiness to receive her husband's love is shown by her bared lower abdomen, which her garment emphasizes. (Painted ivory tile on the cover of a small chest from the tomb of Tutankhamen; ca. 1325 B.C.)

Fig. 64. A Canaanite king, returned from a victory, seated on his cherub throne. The princess (cf. figs. 39 and 40) offers him a lotus blossom and a towel. The musician at the right plays the lyre, while, at the left, two servants draw wine from a large mixing vessel. (Ivory engraving from Megiddo; ca. 1300 B.C.)

63.

64.

the actualization of a happy situation and 2:17 expresses the wish to experience this happiness again and again (the move from indicative to imperative implies a connection). In content, the "grazing" of 2:16 and the gazelle comparison of 2:17d unite the two parts. Verse 17c-f occurs again in 8:14, although with a significant variation ("make haste," i.e., flee, instead of "turn," i.e., return). The connections in 8:14 are too opaque to be of any help in a decision here.

Commentary

[2:16a] The classic solidarity formula with its emphasis on mutuality does not imply an owner's pride in the other, but, like the relational formula of Gen. 2:23 ("This at last is bone of my bones and flesh of my flesh"), it expresses the feeling of deepest and most intimate connectedness. The misery of loneliness ("It is not good that the man should be alone"—Gen. 2:18) is overcome by the realization that she is there for him and he is there for her. The human finds fullness, security, peace, and freedom in this happy duality. The Jewish tradition comments: "Any man who has no wife is no proper man; for it is said, *Male and female created He them and called their name Adam.*"[1]

This happy situation of full humanity is based on the mutuality of love; when a relationship becomes one-sided it can easily degenerate into one of dominance and ownership (see the commentary on 7:10 [11]).

[2:16b] The woman uses the image of her beloved as a gazelle grazing among lotus flowers to characterize the content of their solidarity. Her beloved finds in her love refreshment and renewal of life, which is what binds him to her (2:1-2). The "grazing" looks forward to the explicit mention of the gazelle or stag in v. 17. The lotus flowers stand for the woman's charms. Like the flowers, the woman brings forth renewed vivacity and vitality (cf. 2:1-2 and figs. 33–38). In an ancient Egyptian story, the sun-god Re, the creator and progenitor, has become old and tired and is ready to relinquish his creative work: "Then Hat-Hor, the Lady of the Southern Sycamore, came, and she stood before her father, the All-Lord, and she uncovered her private parts before his face. Then the great god laughed at her."[2] Whereupon he resumed his providential rule (cf. figs. 24–26).

The Canaanite love-goddess Qodshu signals the life-renewing power of her charms by holding gigantic lotus flowers in her hands (see, e.g., the gold foil from Lachish in fig. 62). In a famous painted ivory carving from the tomb of Tutankhamen, the pharaoh's young wife Ankhesenamen holds a bouquet of lotus blossoms to his nose (fig. 63). She is wearing a dress that calls attention to the abdominal region. With the lotus flowers, she is apparently offering him her own regenerative powers. For more on the image of the gazelle grazing among the lotus blossoms—

---

1. Babylonian Talmud, *Yebam.* 62b; tr. I. W. Slotki, 2 vols. (London: Soncino, 1936) 1:419.
2. The Contest of Horus and Seth for the Rule 4:1ff., *ANET,* 15; cf. Prov, 8:21–22.

a picture pregnant with meaning, even though artificially contrived—see the commentary on 4:5 and figures 66 and 85–90. The motif of the beloved woman offering her love to her partner in the form of a lotus (or a drink; cf. 7:2 [3] and fig. 128) shows up again in the well-known ivory carvings from Megiddo (fig. 64). Like the arbor feast of figure 40, this scene is connected to a victory. While the lotus flower is simply being presented in figure 64, in figure 40 it is already in the hand of King Ashurbanipal.

The life-giving and life-enhancing power of the lotus is also demonstrated by the fact that both in the Levant and in Egypt the ancient symbol of the "tree of life" is often strengthened and clarified by the addition of the Egyptian lotus symbol—for example in a shard drawing from Kuntillet 'Ajrud in northern Sinai (fig. 65) or in the painting of a lotus/ tree of life flanked by two nursing gazelles on a small Egyptian chest (fig. 66).

[2:17ab] The indicative statement about happy mutuality is followed by a wish to enjoy this mood forever. One could read the wording of v. 17 to mean that the woman requests her lover to go when the day begins and the shadows disappear. But the context and careful attention to the traditional meaning of the images employed here suggest a different interpretation. The Hebrew is literally "the blowing of the day," which alludes to the daily wind (Gen. 3:8) that begins to blow from the sea in the course of the afternoon. The "fleeing" of the shadows means they are getting longer (cf. Jer. 6:4). For the people of the Bible, who regularly rose early, the day already began to grow old and turn toward evening at a time most moderns would call midafternoon (Judg. 19:9).

[2:17c-f] At this time the man is supposed to go on his way. The two imperatives, "turn" and "be like" (both together in v. 17c in Hebrew), may be an example of hendiadys, that is, a single expression formed from two seemingly unrelated contiguous words. If so, the meaning could be something like: "Be like a gazelle again and again" (cf. Eccl. 1:6). On the comparison with the gazelle or the young stag, see the commentary on 2:9a.

The term *"beter* mountains" has no clear explanation. The simplest explanation would be to follow the example of many classical translators (Aquila, Symmachus, Jerome), who saw נתר as a place-name (cf. Josh. 15:59 and 1 Chron. 6:44 in Codex Alexandrinus), referring it to Battir or Khirbet el-Jehud, 6 miles (10 km.) southwest of Jerusalem. Battir lies on the south side of the Rephaim Valley at the beginning of a chain of low-arched mountains; thinly populated in ancient times, the chain stretches toward the south and could easily be seen as the habitat of a significant population of deer or, to a lesser degree, gazelles. For a similar use of place-names in the Song, cf., e.g., En-gedi in 1:14 or Sharon in 2:1.

From the context, the most probable translation—although problematic in a philological sense—is to interpret נתר as an Indian spice,

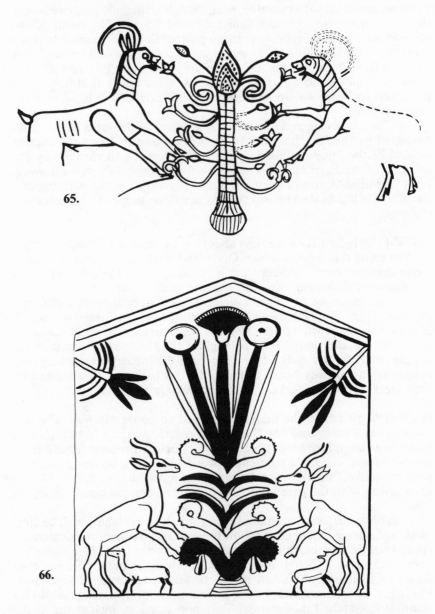

Fig. 65. Two goats prop their front feet on the "tree of life"; its branches extend into lotus blossoms. (Painting on a storage jar from Kuntillet 'Ajrud; ca. 800 B.C.)
Fig. 66. Two nursing gazelles prop their front feet on a "tree of life" formed by the combination of all sorts of floral elements, the most important of which is a large lotus flower. (Painting on a small Egyptian chest; fourteenth/thirteenth century B.C.)

116

Fig. 67. A goddess representing the earth bringing forth vegetation; to her left a variety of animals, to her right another goddess (or the same one, now fully in human form; cf. fig. 143). (Cylinder seal from Shadad near Kerman in Iran; mid-third millennium B.C.)

known in Greek as μαλάβαθρον (*Cinnamon tamala* Nees). In the first century B.C., Pliny reported that the plant was also cultivated in Syria and Egypt; among other things, he compared it to nard.[3] This notion seems to have been available already to Theodotion and the ancient Syriac translators, when they rendered "*beter* mountains" as "fragrant mountains."

In 4:6 the man says, "When the day wind begins to blow and the shadows flee, I will hasten to the mountain of myrrh and the hill of frankincense"; again, in 8:14, the woman calls on her lover to be like a gazelle or a young stag "upon the mountains of balsam." These aromatic mountains and hills refer to the pleasures that the woman has to offer. The stag standing on the (Mala)Batron mountains (2:17ef) is parallel to the gazelle grazing among the lotus flowers (2:16b). The rather peculiar hill or mountain metaphor may relate to the ancient Near Eastern tradition that saw the woman as a model (metaphor) for the earth. The impression of the cylinder seal in figure 67 shows the earth goddess bringing forth all kinds of plants. The same tradition stands behind the word of the goddess Inanna to King Shulgi (ca. 2000 B.C.): "To prance on my holy bosom like a 'lapis lazuli' calf, you are fit."[4]

Cant. 2:17 may also be influenced by the ancient Egyptian motif of identifying the beloved with the wonderland of Punt (eastern Sudan, northern Eritrea). The legendary expedition of Queen Hatshepsut was said to have brought large quantities of incense and other aromatic substances from Punt. According to an Old Egyptian love song:

3. Pliny *Natural History* 12.129.
4. Kramer, *Sacred Marriage,* 64.

> I embrace her,
> and her arms open wide,
> I am like a man in Punt.[5]

For more information, see the commentary on 4:6.

5. Cairo Love Songs, group A, no. 20F; tr. Simpson, 310.

Yearnings in the Night

Text

3:1 a Upon my bed at night I sought him
    b whom [I fervently love];
    c I sought him, but found him not.
    d [*Hebrew lacks this line.*]
  2 a "I will rise now and go about the city,
    b in the streets and in the squares;
    c I will seek him whom [I fervently love]."
    d I sought him, but found him not.
  3 a The sentinels found me,
        as they went about in the city.
    b "Have you seen him whom [I fervently love]?"
  4 a Scarcely had I passed them,
    b when I found him whom [I fervently love].
    c I held him, and would not let him go
    d until I brought him into my mother's house,
    e and into the chamber of her that conceived me.
  5 a I adjure you, O daughters of Jerusalem,
    b by the gazelles or the wild does:
    c do not stir up or awaken love until it is ready!

Analysis

In 3:1-5 the woman speaks of herself in the first person and of her beloved in the third person. This form of address distinguishes the poem from 2:16-17b, where she addresses the beloved directly. He is not a partner in conversation here but only the object of her fervent emotional stirrings, which express themselves sometimes in abrupt declarations (v. 1) and sometimes in firm resolutions (v. 2a-c). The poem was probably inserted here because of the catchword "night" since 2:17ab spoke of the evening.

Interpreters have long debated whether these activities, described also in 5:2-8, are a dream or a conscious experience. Some have argued

119

that a woman wandering the city at night or bringing her lover into her mother's house would be unthinkable under the strict moral code of the real world. According to Sir. 42:11, the unmarried daughter should not only be kept off the street but if possible away from the windows (cf. also 2 Macc. 3:19). In light of these considerations, some have claimed that Cant. 3:1-5 (and 5:2-8) can only reflect a dream. By contrast, others have correctly observed that the moral code became so strict only in inter-testamental Judaism, that women in antiquity had much more freedom. They have referred, for example, to the possibility of encountering men on the daily journey to the well (cf. Gen. 24:14ff.; 29:10ff.; Exod. 2:16; 1 Sam. 9:11). Other indications of a woman's relative freedom in ancient times include the discussion of rape in Deut. 22:25ff., which recognizes that in cases of extramarital intercourse one must distinguish between voluntary and forced behavior; and especially Ruth's nocturnal journey to the threshing floor to court Boaz (Ruth 3).

The whole discussion has often overlooked the fact that poetry does not merely reflect reality—whether the reality of dreams or of conscious experience—but uses artistic means to create a reality of its own.

A third song, thematically similar to 3:1-5 and 5:2-8, is formulated as a wish, making clear that it is about desire created in the poem itself:

> O that you were like a brother to me,
> who nursed at my mother's breast!
> If I met you outside,
> I would kiss you,
> and no one would despise me.
> I would lead you
> and bring you into the house of my mother. (8:1-2)

The wish form and the unreality of 8:1-2 suggest that the scenes sketched by the poem in 3:1-5 were unacceptable in the framework of the given social structures. The woman speaking in 8:1-2 wants to have the same kind of close and uncomplicated relationship with her lover that she might have with her biological brother—seeking him in public, greeting him with a kiss, bringing him to her mother's house—all without social reproof. But in reality this relationship was hardly possible. Significantly, in a modern Arab love song from Palestine, it is the man who seeks his beloved at night.[1] The picture of a woman seeking her lover after dark is no longer possible even in poetry.

"Wily of heart" (NRSV) is how the OT wisdom literature describes the married woman whose feet will not stay at home, who pursues the adventurous young man in the streets and public squares, seizing and kissing him and bringing him home; she disdains all sacred laws and brings misfortune and death (Prov. 7:11ff.). Yet who has never envied those who fear neither death nor the devil (Ps. 73:3)! Nevertheless, in everyday life both unmarried and married women would have instinc-

---

1. Dalman, *Diwan*, 76, no. 36.

tively protected themselves (and been protected) against the danger of doing anything to force a comparison with such a negative figure.

In the story of Ruth, it is the experienced and hard-pressed Naomi who comes up with the idea of encouraging Ruth to address her need in a decisive act; she is to seek to win Boaz, who was already well disposed and obligated to her, by a bold nocturnal visit to the threshing floor where he was guarding the harvest. But the poem in Cant. 3:1-5 does not include the kind of special circumstances that determine the actions of Naomi and Ruth. It is totally unrealistic. No reasons are given to explain why the woman should be on the streets at night, and the way she describes to the sentinels the one she is seeking ("him whom I fervently love") does not give them any helpful information. Yet it is precisely this relative clause, repeated four times (vv. 1b, 2c, 3b, 4b), that provides the key to understanding the conditions and wishes described in 3:1-5. The clause is usually translated with the rather platonic-sounding formula "him whom my soul loves"; it already appeared in 1:7a, also in the context of seeking. The Hebrew word translated "soul" is נפשׁ, which means "gullet" or "throat," plus the "heavy breathing" related to these and the "longing" and "desire" such breathing implies. Finally, the term נפשׁ can mean the whole person, seen from the perspective of human need and desire, longing and passion. Thus the refrain "him whom my נפשׁ loves" does not at all mean that the woman loves her beloved only spiritually or deeply, but that her whole desire, all her yearnings, her thoughts, her feelings, and her physical needs are directed toward him. It is this kind of longing and passion that the poem wants to portray.

Commentary

[3:1ab] Seeking (and finding) are the activities of life that appropriately correspond to such passion. Both "seeking" and "finding" occur four times in this brief poem. They are the key words that provide the structure for the entire unit, as any reader can easily ascertain.

The passionate search for the absent lover is an element of the mythology of several ancient Near Eastern goddesses. Thus this poem provides a particularly clear indication that a goddess was the original protagonist of the Song. The Baal texts from Ugarit describe the Canaanite goddess Anat after Baal's disappearance:

> Like the heart of a [heifer] (yearning) for her calf,
> like the heart of a ewe (yearning) for her lamb,
> so the heart of Anat (yearned) after Baal.[2]

After the disappearance of Osiris, Isis is said to have sought him not only throughout Egypt but even to Byblos:

> Mighty Isis who protected her brother,
> Who sought him without wearying,

---

2. Baal and Mot 6.ii.7–9, 28–30; tr. Gibson, 76–77.

Who roamed the land lamenting,
Not resting till she found him.[3]

But the theme of the woman seeking her lover is not limited to mythology. This relational fantasy also turns up, for example, in an Akkadian incantation. The woman, now touched by love's magic, encircles the man she had previously rejected "like the she-goat her kid, the mother sheep her lamb, the ass her foal."[4]

The Hebrew verb used in 3:1 covers more than merely "to look for." It can also mean "to desire," "to yearn for" (cf., e.g., Ps. 27:4; Jer. 2:33; 5:1). Only this meaning makes sense with "upon my bed at night."

"Bed" and "night" are associated primarily with inactivity, rest, and sleep. The two words marking the place and time of the lover's yearning and seeking are emphasized here at the beginning of the poem to say that love's desire, like other passions (Ps. 36:4 [5]; Mic. 2:1), cannot find rest even at night—when otherwise only the wild animals are up and about (Ps. 104:20-21). A sketch on an Egyptian shard from Deir el-Medina illustrates this theme nicely with a young woman in bed, kept awake by her longings (fig. 68); cf. also the commentary on 5:2a and figures 113–15. It is only in the picture on the erotic and satirical Turin Papyrus that the woman finds her lover under the bed (fig. 69). Resolution does not come so easily in Cant. 3:1-5.

[3:2] Unlike the more timid girl in 1:7-8, the woman here resolves to get up and wander the city, seeking her lover—not unlike the adulteress, driven by her passion, in Prov. 7:11. Another poem characterized by great passion, Cant. 2:4-5, uses a military metaphor to describe the woman; she acts "under orders," under the banner of "love." That image seems to apply here as well. Like the sentinels seeking potential criminals and disturbers of the peace (cf. v. 3a; 5:7; Isa. 21:11; 62:6; Ps. 127:1; Neh. 4:9 [3]), the woman patrols the darkened city "under orders of Venus." But for the moment her search is without success.

[3:3] Instead, the implied justification for her shocking behavior (being "under orders") is called into question. The sentinels appear. According to the Middle Assyrian law code (eleventh century B.C.), even in daytime women were permitted on the streets only under particular conditions (e.g., wives and daughters of free men must be veiled; slaves and prostitutes must be unveiled).[5] Women on the streets at night were immediately suspect (cf. Prov. 7:11) and could not expect respectful treatment by the sentinels (cf. Cant. 5:7). Nevertheless, the young woman in this

3. The Great Hymn to Osiris on the stela of Amenmose; cf. M. Lichtheim, *Ancient Egyptian Literature: A Book of Readings,* vol. 2, *The New Kingdom* (Berkeley: University of California Press, 1976) 83.
4. J. and A. Westenholz, "Help for Rejected Suitors: The Old Akkadian Love Incantation MAD V 8," *Or* 46 (1977) 202–3, lines 21–24.
5. R. Borger et al., *Rechts- und Wirtschaftsurkunden,* Texte aus der Umwelt des Alten Testaments 1/1 (Gütersloh: Gerd Mohn, 1982) 87-88 §40.

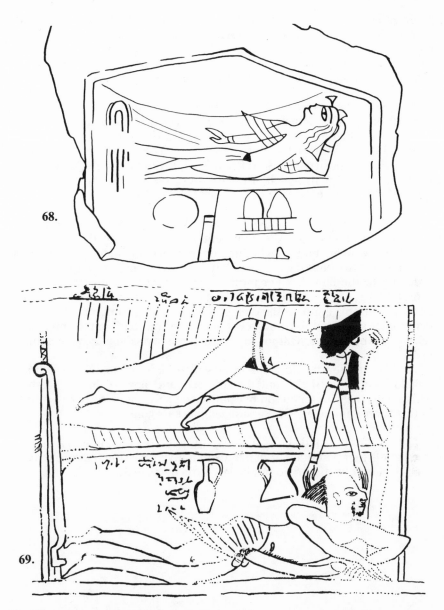

Fig. 68. A young woman lies in bed, clad only in a transparent veil. She supports her head by her left hand, giving the appearance of dreaming. Beneath the bed are ointments and toilet articles. (Sketch on a limestone shard from Deir el-Medina; twelfth century B.C.)

Fig. 69. The woman on the bed desires the man under the bed. (He may be drunk; notice the two pitchers.) As always on this papyrus, the man's phallus is pictured overly large. (Satirical and erotic Turin Papyrus; twelfth century B.C.)

123

poem greets them with an impudent question about her lover, just as one patrol might ask another if they have seen anything suspicious. To be in the service of Venus makes one bold, for "she never dwells in cowardly hearts" (according to "Estuans intrinsecus," a poem of the medieval *Carmina Burana* [songs of the Benediktbeuern monastery]).

[3:4a-c] After she has overcome this obstacle, the third attempt (cf. vv. 1c and 2d) brings surprisingly quick success. The woman's patrol leads to the arrest of the one she has been seeking (on the term אחז, "arrest," cf. Judg. 16:21; 2 Sam. 4:10; Ps. 56:title [1]). The word can also mean "holding" in a positive sense (cf. Ps. 73:23). Equally ambiguous is the following term (רפה), which, with the negative, can mean either "not forsake" (Deut. 31:6, 8) or "not let alone" (Job 7:19).

[3:4de] Once found, the beloved is not taken to jail after all but to the house of the mother (cf. the commentary on 3:11)—to the very place where the woman had sought him on her bed at night. The parallel expression, "the chamber of her that conceived me," is meant to call attention to the fact that her mother, her model and her confidant (cf. 3:11; 6:9; 8:1, 5; cf. also Naomi in the story of Ruth), has also known the passion that now controls the daughter. The young woman now assumes her mother's role. To some degree at least, the "mother" in the Song plays the role of the goddess Hathor in the Egyptian love song: the protector of love.

 The tension between the interests and laws of society, which are upheld by the sentinels, and the interests and laws of love's passion, which send the woman out on her patrol, are solved playfully and calmly in this poem (unlike 5:2-8). Passion achieves its goal.

[3:5] This point is made clear by the oath that closes the poem. As in 2:7 (see details there) and 8:4, it demands that love's passion, having arrived at its goal, not be disturbed but be left to its own rules.

Tremendum et fascinosum* I

Text

3:6 a [Who is this] coming up from the wilderness
   b like [(palm) columns] of smoke,
   c perfumed with myrrh and frankincense,
   d with all the fragrant powders of the merchant?
  7 a Look, it is the litter of Solomon!
   b Around it are sixty mighty men
   c of the mighty men of Israel,
  8 a all equipped with swords,
   b and expert in war,
   c each with his sword at his thigh
   d because of alarms by night.

Analysis

There is no doubt that a new poem begins with v. 6. Unlike the previous section, here the woman no longer speaks or exhorts those around her; instead, observers use questions (v. 6a) and exclamations (v. 7a) to announce a dramatic event: the approach of a litter. The insertion of the poem at this point in the collection may be due to the catchword "night" (3:1a and 3:8d) or perhaps the contrast between "city" (3:1-5) and "wilderness" (3:6-8).

Commentary

[3:6a] The question "Who is this [fem.]?" makes one expect a woman's name or title as answer. In rare instances, the Hebrew expression can be used to inquire about an object (neuter); but to make such an inquiry precisely would require the use of מָה ("what?") instead of מִי ("who?").

---

*"Fear and fascination"

125

"Who is this?" must certainly be used deliberately to suggest the arrival of a woman.

On the surface, the wilderness or desert from which "she" comes would be the Judean wilderness east of Jerusalem—because the questioners must be the usual extras in the Song, the "daughters of Jerusalem." Moreover, it is customary to speak (as here) of "going up" or "coming up" to Jerusalem, which sits on a hill (Ps. 122:4). But beneath the surface, "wilderness" connotes a distant, dangerous, inaccessible area (cf. also Cant. 8:5), analogous to the mountains in 4:8 (see the commentary there). To call the great love-goddesses Ishtar and Astarte *belit zeri* ("lady of the wilderness") and *'ashtarat shad* ("Astarte of the wilderness [or desert]")[1] is to characterize them as wild beings, surrounded by desert animals (cf. figs. 45–47) and belonging to a realm inaccessible to human beings. But now a mysterious "she" is coming up out of this realm into the immediate vicinity of the speakers.

[3:6bc] At first, one senses only the atmosphere surrounding the event, not yet the person. The word used here for "columns" may be related to תמר, "palms," or תמרה, "palm ornamentation" (1 Kgs. 6:29, 32, 35) because the typical form of columns or pillars in monarchical Israel employed a stylized palm crown as its capital (fig. 70).

Palm columns suggest royal splendor, as does the information that all this smoke is not coming from some catastrophic fire but from expensive perfume and incense. Being "perfumed" in this way is the origin of the name of a fictitious concubine of Abraham (Keturah, Gen. 25:1-4), introduced to connect Abraham to several tribes of Arabia, the land of precious aromatic substances. But the mention of one "perfumed with myrrh and frankincense" also calls to mind the queen of Sheba. "Never again did spices come in such quantity as that which the queen of Sheba gave to King Solomon" (1 Kgs 10:10).

In the commentary on 1:13, I have already discussed the cosmetic use of resin from myrrh bushes and myrrh trees in romantic affairs. For Christians, frankincense is closely connected to worship. The same is true in the OT, where, unlike myrrh, it is mentioned only in a cultic context (except here in the Song) and only in relatively late texts. The oldest passage is Jer. 6:20 (seventh century B.C.). Like myrrh, frankincense is also an exudate or resin of trees and bushes (of the genus Boswellia, which has 24 varieties). Genuine frankincense is *Boswellia sacra* Flueckiger, a medium-sized shrub with pinnate leaves and small green or white blossoms. But *Boswellia Carteri* Birdwood and *Boswellia Frereana* Birdwood are also known. The natural secretion of resin can be hastened by making small cuts in the plant. The Hebrew name לבונה, "something white," comes from the whitish (or yellowish or reddish) globules of resin, which have a very bitter taste. When burned, they produce a heavy, almost narcotic, sweet aroma. Frankincense was imported from southern Arabia (Sheba; cf. Jer. 6:20; Isa. 60:6) and perhaps also from East Africa.

1. See *UT,* 235, 1106.52, 55.

70.

71.

Fig. 70. Reconstructed Samarian pillars with palmette capitals (ninth century B.C.)

Fig. 71. A lion-headed guardian angel, in the form of a short sword, at the entrance to the holy of holies in a temple. (Limestone sculpture from Tell al-Rimah; beginning of the eighth century B.C.)

127

[3:6d] The report that the one coming is perfumed "with all the fragrant powders [or 'dust'] of the merchant" both recapitulates what has already been said and adds to it. The dust stirred up by horses and people (Ezek. 26:10; Isa. 5:24; Nah. 1:3) is part of every procession through the desert. But here "the dust of the merchant" refers to the powdered and burned spices. Ten of the seventeen OT references to merchants occur in Ezekiel 27, which speaks of Tyre as the great center of commerce. In that chapter, the traders from Sheba are specialists in spices (v. 22). They have brought their precious wares over endless caravan routes through the desert to the shores of the Mediterranean Sea. Now, amid the exotic aura of these caravans and their treasures arrives the one about whom the onlookers had asked: "Who is this?"

[3:7a] This line brings the answer. But instead of the woman one expects, it is the litter (or, better, the portable bed) of Solomon. One can ask about this sentence: Is it a clumsy insertion, answering a question meant to have no explicit answer, a question meant to keep the imagination in tension until the end (cf. 6:10; 8:5; Isa. 60:8)? Or is it a brilliant response, lifting the veil of incense only enough to sharpen the question without solving it: Who is this woman arriving on Solomon's litter? Although the litter belongs to Solomon, the introductory question ("Who is she?") does not permit one to picture Solomon riding on it. Great lords like Solomon did not pick up their wives and concubines themselves but sent an escort party to fetch the bride and bring her to them (cf. Genesis 24). Witnesses to that practice extend from the Hellenistic period (1 Macc. 9:37) back into the Bronze Age. For example, Ramses II (thirteenth century B.C.) sent "the army and the princes" to accompany a daughter of the Hittite king to Egypt and to him for their wedding ceremony.[2]

[3:7bc] These lines describe this kind of honor guard, which then blocks the view of the litter before one can see who it is that is being brought to Solomon. Since the time of the Davidic dynasty the "mighty men" were an elite troop with thirty members (cf. 2 Sam. 23:18-19, 23). Similarly, the Philistines sent thirty young men to Samson's wedding (Judg. 14:11). Thus the double size of this honor guard (sixty members) means to imply a superlative force. The addition "of the mighty men of Israel" has the same function. These men are the best of the best; it may be that five men were included from each of the twelve tribes. The combination of the exotic (perfumes from Sheba) and the nationalistic (mighty men of Israel) was also present in the text describing the marriage of Ramses II just cited: "They [the Egyptian army] were mingled with foot and horse of Kheta [the Hittites]" (cf. also Ps. 45:10, 12 [11, 13]).

[3:8] Their skill with the sword shows the warlike aspect of the mighty men. The "sword" often stands for war in the OT (compare "sword, famine, and pestilence" in Jer. 14:12 with "war, famine, and pestilence"

2. *ARE*, 3:185–86.

in Jer. 28:8). It is often described as an independent agent. A flaming sword guards the tree of life (Gen. 3:24). Two swords guarded the entrance to the holy of holies in the Hadad temple at Tell al-Rimah in northwestern Iraq (fig. 71). The reference to "alarms by night" emphasizes that the swords are meant to ward off danger—apparently not an attack by highwaymen or soldiers but, as in Ps. 91:5 (cf. also Gen. 32:23ff.), one by demonic powers. The ancients assumed that a particularly beautiful woman could provoke such an attack. For example, the apocryphal story of Tobit tells of an infatuated demon who kills anyone who comes near the beautiful bride (Tob. 3:17; 6:14ff.). In the fairy tale that lies behind this story the demon must be killed by the sword before the bridegroom can go in to her.[3]

Purpose and Thrust

Like the little song in Cant. 6:10, which also begins with "Who is this?" 3:6-8 serves to characterize the bride. In this case, the enchanting allure *(fascinosum)* and awesome magnificence *(tremendum),* radiated by every extraordinary beauty, is not presented by describing the woman herself but by picturing her surroundings—just as clouds and lightning announce the coming of an invisible holiness.

3. Cf. P. Deselaers, *Das Buch Tobit: Studien zu seiner Entstehung, Komposition und Theologie,* OBO 43 (Fribourg: Universitätsverlag; Göttingen: Vandenhoeck & Ruprecht, 1982) 280–92.

A Magnificent Palanquin

Text

3:9 ab King Solomon made himself a palanquin
   c from the wood of Lebanon.
  10 a He made its posts of silver,
    b its back of gold,
    c its seat of purple;
    d its interior was inlaid with [(scenes of)] love.

Analysis

While the poem in 3:6-8 was marked by the lively exclamations of anonymous participants ("Who is this?" "Look"), this poem (3:9-10d) is a prosaic list. Thematically, 3:6-8 focused on the bride hidden in the litter, surrounded by columns of smoke and the jangling swords of mighty men, whereas 3:9-10d describes the most important preparations for this procession. This is the only text in the Song that is meant not as the speech of someone involved in the events but as an objective account. In the present context it has the character of an informative gloss. The two poems (3:6-8 and 3:9-10d) are held together by the catchword "litter" (or "palanquin") and by the legendary figure of Solomon (which might be a secondary addition to both).

Commentary

[3:8] Verse 3:7a spoke of a (portable) "bed" (cf. 1 Sam. 19:15); here the Hebrew text uses a loanword derived from the Greek φορεῖον, "litter," "stretcher" (cf. 2 Macc. 3:27). Litters were in use in Egypt from the third milleninum B.C. on, both open (portable chair) and closed (fig. 72). Workshop diagrams show that litters were made of wood and sometimes completely or partially covered with gold plate; for example, Papyrus Westcar mentions an ebony litter whose poles were made of fine wood and covered with gold.[1] Instead of such precious African varieties, the Song speaks of precious wood from Lebanon, thinking primarily of conifers, rich in resin (see the commentary on 1:17). Imported Lebanese wood is a regular feature of the splendor that the tradition associates with the name Solomon (cf. 1 Kgs. 5:6, 9, 14 [20, 23, 28]; 7:2; 10:17, 21).

[3:10a-c] The use of litters, particularly for women, increased during the hellenistic period with its passion for baroque pomp. In 167 B.C., at the opening ceremonies for the thirty-day games that Antiochus IV Epiphanes put on in Daphne (a suburb of Antioch), bearers carried in eighty richly dressed women on litters (φορείοις) with gold supports and five hundred litters with silver supports.[2] The same materials are mentioned here in the Song.

Although we know the raw materials, we cannot be certain which parts of the litter are being described. If we envision a litter like those found on the Esquiline hill in Rome in 1874 (fig. 73), we cannot be sure if the silver posts refer to the base or to the supports for the canopy. The term translated "back" could also be the bed of the litter or maybe even the canopy—actually any horizontal surface; and if מרכב means "seat," then we have to think more of a portable chair than a portable bed. But even if we cannot achieve clarity in these matters, it is nevertheless clear that this rather artless and probably late song (note the use of the Greek loanword) means to describe the magnificent ornamentation of Solomon's litter (3:7) in a way appropriate to the tastes of the Hellenistic period. Only the best was good enough for Solomon's beloved.

[3:10d] The last sentence of this poem is hard to understand. The "interior" (cf. Deut. 21:12; 2 Sam. 4:6; Ezek. 15:4) apparently refers to the inside of the chamber, closed off by curtains or panels. The latter is more probable (recall the wood from Lebanon in v. 9c), because the Hebrew text refers to inlay work or intarsia (cf. Esth. 1:6; Ezek. 40:17-18; 42:3), which requires a firm base. The technique of inlaying different kinds of wood and bone was known in Palestine in the Hellenistic period. A wooden sarcophagus from the first century B.C., found at En-gedi, is inlaid with circles, rosettes, and pomegranates (fig. 74).

Some scholars understand the phrase "inlaid with love" (NRSV) adverbially, in the sense of "lovingly inlaid," but that interpretation is philologically questionable. Some commentators (e.g., Krinetzki) correct the text, reading "inlaid with ivory tiles" (שנהנים) instead of "inlaid with love" (אהבה), but this change seems unnecessary. "Love" here probably describes the motif of the ornamentation on the inside of the litter. "Love" would then be used in a way similar to 2:4b, where it was a decoration on the banner raised over the woman in the wine hall. Under-

1. A. de Buck, *Egyptian Reading Book: Exercises and Middle Egyptian Texts,* 3d ed. (Leiden: Brill, 1970) 79.16–80.1.
2. Athenaeus, *The Deipnosophists* 5.195; tr. C. B. Gulick, *The Deipnosophists,* vol. 2, LCL (Cambridge, Mass.: Harvard Univ. Press, 1928) 385; cf. also 5.212 (litters with purple rugs), ibid., 461.

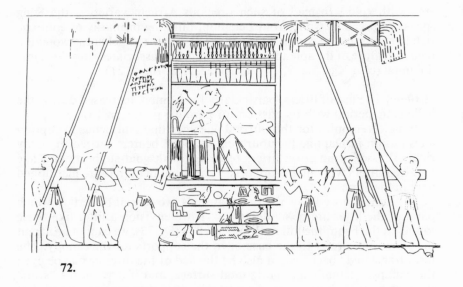

72.

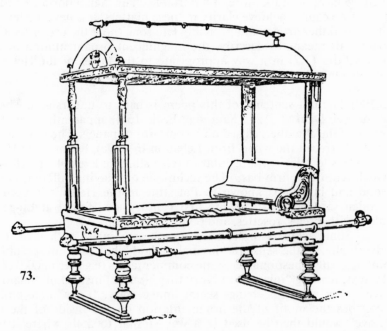

73.

Fig. 72. A distinguished official in a portable chair covered with a canopy. Four men with fans accompany the bearers. (Painting in tomb no. 12 in Deir el-Gebrawi; ca. 2200 B.C.)
Fig. 73. Litter with canopy, reconstructed from large fragments. (Found on the Esquiline hill, imperial Rome.)

132

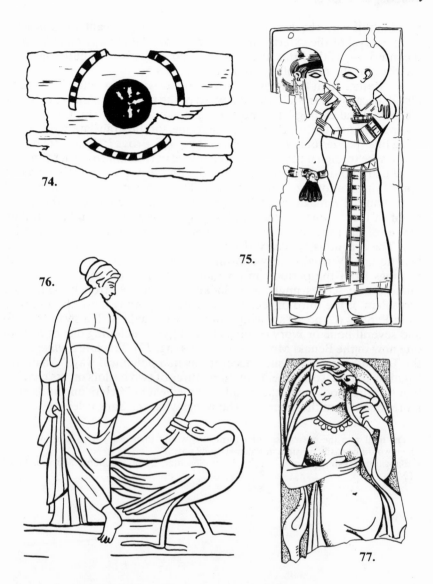

Fig. 74. Piece of a wooden sarcophagus inlaid with various kinds of wood and bone; the decorative motifs include pomegranates. (From a burial cave near En-gedi; first century B.C.)

Fig. 75. A princely couple in embrace. (Ivory carving decorating a bed [cf. fig. 40]; Ugarit, fourteenth century B.C.)

Fig. 76. Aphrodite or Leda with a swan. (Sketch based on a mosaic found in Paphos, Cyprus, near the temple of Aphrodite; third century B.C.)

Fig. 77. Aphrodite with necklace, her right hand on her left breast. (Ivory carving from Egypt; second/first century B.C.)

stood in this way, the last line of the brief song is significant; in contrast to the portrayal of the external features that describe the central element—the interior—of the litter, the concern is no longer for the building materials but for the motif of the whole thing.

Rather than the singular "love," the original text may have had a plural, because in front of the first word of the next song stands an מ—the Hebrew plural ending—that no one can adequately explain. If this plural ending belongs to "love" (אהגם),[3] then one should translate with something like "scenes of love" or "joys of love" (cf. Prov. 7:18). Erotic motifs in art were foreign neither to the Hellenistic period nor to earlier times. A royal bed found at Ugarit was covered with ivory tiles depicting, among other things, a loving couple (fig. 75). The upper portion of the base of Ashurbanipal's magnificent bed (fig. 40) is decorated with the erotic motif of the "women at the window." The same motif can be found on ivories of the ninth century B.C. from Samaria (cf. Amos 6:4-7 and 3:12, 15). The art industry received significant new impetus during the Hellenistic age. Virtually no wood-inlay work survives, but mosaics and carvings from the period can give an impression of what a litter with inlaid erotic scenes might have looked like in the strongly hellenized Jerusalem of the third or second century B.C.; among these are a mosaic from Paphos (Cypress) showing Aphrodite or Leda with a swan (fig. 76) and several bone or ivory carvings from Egypt, including one of Aphrodite now in the Benaki Museum in Athens (fig. 77). Tractate *Sanhedrin* of the Talmud caricatures such decorations in a polemical way: "Ahab was frigid by nature, so Jezebel painted pictures of two harlots on his chariot, that he might look upon them and become heated."[4] Here one finds once more the work of those scribes who reject what the Song celebrates.

3. The final ה in the present singular form אהנה would then result from a miswritten י, which would be easily possible in Paleo-Hebrew script.
4. Babylonian Talmud, *Sanh.* 39b; tr. Jacob Shachter, 2 vols. (London: Soncino, 1935) 1:252.

A Day of Gladness of Heart

Text

3:10 e-11 Daughters of Jerusalem, come out.
　　11 b Look, O daughters of Zion,
　　　　c at King Solomon, at the crown
　　　　d with which his mother crowned him
　　　　e on the day of his wedding,
　　　　f on the day of the gladness of his heart.

Analysis

The imperatives of 3:10e-11 are reminiscent of the direct style of 3:6-8 ("Who is this?" "Look"). One could regard 3:10e-11 as a continuation of 3:6-8, separated by the addition describing Solomon's magnificent litter. Then in 3:10e-11 the women of Jerusalem would be called on as ad hoc virgin companions of the bride, escorting the wedding procession (with the litter sent by Solomon) to the palace, where they would find the king in his wedding finery (cf. Psalm 45).

But such reconstruction is hypothetical. Perhaps this song is designed only to lure the young women outdoors. Like the singing in the vineyards in 2:10-13, wedding festivities like those described here would have been irresistibly attractive. Some such attraction was necessary to bring the young women out of their houses in large numbers (3 Macc. 1:17ff.). Whether the reference to King Solomon in his wedding garments was just a way to describe some ordinary happy groom or whether it portrayed one of the "little foxes" (Cant. 2:15) crowned to play the role of "Solomon-as-groom" for this occasion, the main point of the festivities was to lure young women outdoors. Joyous singing and dancing would naturally follow.

The poem is included here because of its festive atmosphere and the catchword "king" (Solomon). Its strictly parallel lines (daughter/

135

daughters; crown/crowned; day/day), which get shorter toward the end of the poem, develop an invitingly captivating rhythm.

Commentary

[3:10e-11b] "Daughters of Zion" here parallels the Song's usual expression, "daughters of Jerusalem" (cf. 1:5). This occurrence is unique in the Song. Zion was the most distinguished part of ancient Jerusalem, the site of the royal fortress (2 Sam. 5:7) and the temple mount (Isa. 29:8). Thus in Isa. 3:16 (cf. 4:4) the expression "daughters of Zion" calls attention to the women's haughtiness. But in later times Zion became nothing more than a somewhat solemn synonym for Jerusalem. That is the way it is used here. The young women of Jerusalem are called to come out and view the king with joy and happiness.

[3:11cd] Ps. 45:2-8 (3-9) describes the king, dressed in his festive wedding garments, as the very embodiment of beauty. The OT also speaks of the decorative adornment of nonroyal bridegrooms (Isa. 61:10), but crowns and wreaths for such nonroyal grooms are unknown until the postbiblical literature.[1] This text may describe a custom of rather late origin, but once begun the custom endured for a long time. Even now crowns are placed on the heads of the bridal couple in the Greek Orthodox marriage ceremony.

This text is the only reference in the Bible to being crowned by the mother. But the king's mother was known to have an important position at court, at least in Judah. She often seemed to play a decisive role in matters of succession to the throne, not the least in the case of Solomon (1 Kgs. 1:11-31). Along with such royal models of a mother's interest in her son's advancement, the psychosociological situation may have contributed to the beginnings of the custom described here. As other passages indicate (Cant. 3:4; 6:9; 8:2, 5), the Israelite mother was the one responsible for affairs of the heart. The Egyptian love songs reveal the same situation. As in Mesopotamia and Egypt, the mother was a strict protector of her daughter;[2] nevertheless, if the girl and her young man were to find understanding anywhere, it would be from the mother.

In an ancient Egyptian love poem, a young woman in love speaks (in her mind) to her friend, a young man who is attracted to her but not yet really smitten:

> If only [your] mother knew my heart— she would go inside for a while.
> O Golden One [love-goddess], put that in her heart![3]

---

1. 3 Macc. 4:8; Mishnah, *Soṭa* 9:14; Babylonian Talmud, *Soṭa* 49b; Str-B, 1:504–17.
2. C. Wilcke, "Die akkadischen Glossen in TMM NF3 Nr. 25 und eine neue Interpretation des Textes," *AfO* 23 (1970) 84–87; cf. U. Winter, *Frau und Göttin: Exegetische und ikonographische Studien zum weiblichen Gottesbild im Alten Israel und in dessen Umwelt*, OBO 53 (Fribourg: Universitätsverlag; Göttingen: Vandenhoeck & Ruprecht, 1983) 26–270; Schott, *Liebeslieder*, 51.
3. Papyrus Chester Beatty I, group A, no. 36; tr. Fox, 55.

In another song, the woman puts her trust in her own mother: "He does not know my desires to embrace him, / or he would send (word) to my mother."[4]

It is no different in Sumerian and Akkadian texts. For example, the mother of Inanna/Ishtar advises her to make herself ready for her lover: "Inanna, at her mother's command, / Bathed herself, anointed herself with goodly oil."[5]

Thus it is no surprise that the mother would adorn the son with a crown of gold or silver (Ps. 21:3 [4]); Zech. 6:11, 14) on his wedding day, even if Cant. 3:11 is the only reference to such a custom. According to Gen. 2:24, the wedding day marked the end of the close tie between a young man and his mother (and father); this tie was now exchanged for the one between the man and his wife (cf. Gen. 24:67). Crowning her son is the mother's crowning act of maternal care (for the time being). With it she sets him free, and along with the crown comes, no doubt, her wish that he be a king in his new household (Ps. 45:11 [12]) in the same way he has always been a king to her.

[3:11ef] The closing lines characterize the "day of his wedding" (an expression that appears only here in the OT) as the day of gladness of heart. The title of the collection of ancient Egyptian love poems in the Papyrus Chester Beatty I can be translated, "Poems of Great Gladness of Heart." In ancient Near Eastern and OT anthropology the heart is the personal center of the human being. Thus "gladness of heart" is a superlative kind of joy. It is a gladness that possesses a person completely, extending from the center to engulf every aspect of the human with happiness (cf. Eccl. 5:20 [19]; Isa. 30:29; Jer. 15:16).

4. Ibid., group A, no. 32; tr. Fox, 52.
5. Kramer, *Sacred Marriage,* 77.

All Beauty and Delight
Reside in You
(Descriptive Song I)

Text

4:1 a How beautiful you are, my love,
   b how very beautiful!
   c Your [glances] are doves
   d [out from] behind your veil.
   e Your hair is like a flock of goats,
   f moving down the slopes of Gilead.
  2 a Your teeth are like a flock of [(sheep) prepared for shearing]
   b that have come up from the washing,
   c all of which bear twins,
   d and not one among them is bereaved.
  3 a Your lips are like a crimson thread,
   b and your mouth is lovely.
   c [Like a slit in a pomegranate
   d is your palate(?) out from] behind your veil.
  4 a Your neck is like the tower of David,
   b built in courses;
   c on it hang a thousand bucklers,
   d all of them shields of warriors.
  5 a Your two breasts are like two fawns,
   b twins of a gazelle,
   c that feed among the [lotus blossoms].
  6 a [When] the [day (wind) begins to blow]
   b and the shadows flee,
   c I will hasten to the mountain of myrrh
   d and the hill of frankincense.

7 a You are altogether beautiful, my love;
   b there is no flaw in you.

Analysis

While the previous poem was governed by the two imperatives at the beginning ("come out," "look"), 4:1-5 is marked by a long series of nominal clauses (like "Your glances—doves"). The peculiar characteristic of these nominal clauses is their tentative comparisons and near approximations; much is left open. This feature is often lost in translation. Neither German nor English generally allows the bare juxtaposition of two quantities (parataxis) that is the mark of the nominal clause; these languages require a connecting link ("is," "are"), which lends this type of discourse a decisiveness that the Hebrew does not convey.

Almost every one of these equations is followed by a dependent clause that uses verbs (or other parts of speech) to emphasize some dynamic aspect of the metaphor, either of the receiver of meaning (your glance—or your palate—out from behind your veil) or the lender of meaning (a flock of goats, moving downward; a flock of ewes, coming up). These dependent clauses warn against a static understanding of the comparisons. Contrary to many interpretations, the issue here is not geometric shapes (shape of the eyes, shape of the neck, etc.); in Hebrew the meaning conveyed by these descriptions of the body is generally more dynamic, not static or geometric (see the commentary on the individual verses). The inherent powers of the beloved are the issue: the mystery of the attractive force of her beauty. The entire poem takes place within the framework of two assertions: "How beautiful *you* are," 4:1ab; and *"You are altogether beautiful,"* 4:7a. This framing emphasis on the partner is carried throughout the poem by the Hebrew possessive suffixes (*your* glances, *your* hair, *your* teeth, *your* palate, etc.). The person of the speaker (the "I") recedes in the face of the partner's splendor. Yet at some central points it steps out of the background and makes itself clearly known. The person of whom he sings is *"my* love" (4:1a and 4:7a). His admiration reaches its peak in a personal decision: I will enter this wonderland (v. 6c). In the entire song, only v. 6 contains no "you" or "your"; this phrasing gives the impression that the speaker wants to keep his decision to himself, at least temporarily. In another poem, 7:6-9 (7-10), a similar decision is introduced with "I say" (or better, "I think"—7:8a [9a]).

After the realistic sounding cry in 3:11 to look at the festively adorned King Solomon, the fantastic metaphors and similes of 4:1-7 come as a surprise. One can properly understand these images only by paying careful attention both to their dramatic nature (as already noted) and to the ancient Near Eastern custom of portraying the essential strength and significance of a deity or person (living or dead) by identifying his or her bodily features with the various powers and splendors of the surrounding world: You are altogether beautiful, for all beauty resides in you.

In the present context, this song functions as Solomon's welcoming greeting to his approaching bride (3:6-8); he receives her in front of

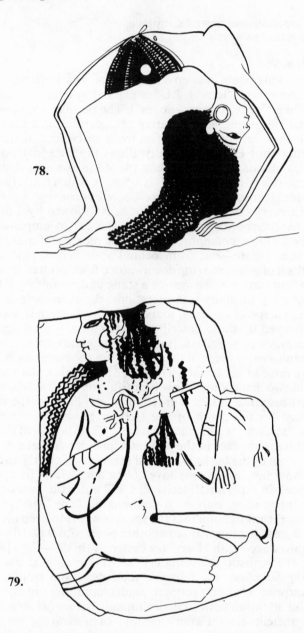

Fig. 78. Acrobatic dancer with luxuriant wig. (Painting on a limestone shard from Deir el-Medina; thirteenth century B.C.)

Fig. 79. A naked woman, kneeling, plays the lute; she holds a plectrum in her right hand. The long tresses of her wig are attractively arranged. (Sketch on a limestone shard from Deir el-Medina; thirteenth/twelfth century B.C.)

the palace, where he can be seen and heard by the "daughters of Jerusalem" addressed in 3:11. The "myrrh" and "frankincense" of 4:6cd relate back to 3:6c.

Commentary

[4:1a-c] This verse repeats verbatim 1:15, which is also the opening of a song (see the commentary there). Favorite songs still sometimes lead one to produce new poetic variations from their familiar beginnings.

[4:1d] The eyes-as-doves metaphor (i.e., glances as messengers of love) is expanded here with "out from behind your veil." The "veil" presents a problem, because Judean women were never veiled, neither before nor after the exile. An Assyrian relief from about 700 B.C. (fig. 116) shows the women of the Judean city of Lachish wearing a long scarf or shawl framing the face on both sides, but they are not veiled. Nevertheless, during the years of Assyrian and Babylonian domination, their customs may have had a temporary effect in Judah. In Assyria wives and daughters of free men were permitted outdoors only if they were veiled; prostitutes and slaves had to be unveiled (see the commentary on 3:3). In Isa. 47:2 Babylon is ordered to remove "her" veil, for "she" has become a slave. According to Gen. 24:65, a bride veiled herself before her wedding (at least in Judah); and, at least in its present context, Cant. 4:1-7 is a song of praise to the "bride of Solomon." Whatever the usual customs, the only purpose of the veil in v. 1d is to emphasize the shining intensity of the woman's glances—the veil is unable to hide them. The next comparison demonstrates again this function of the veil. Even if the glances of her eyes can penetrate the veil, it hardly seems likely that her hair could have an effect.

[4:1e] Yet here (repeated verbatim in 6:5c) that is just what happens—the hair works its full effect. The OT associates "hair" with things that are too numerous to count ("more in number than the hairs of my head," Ps. 69:4 [5]; cf. 40:12 [13]) and also with vital powers. Samson owed his supernatural power to never cutting his hair. When it was cut, his power was lost (Judg. 16:17); when it grew back, his power returned (16:22; cf. Num. 6:5). As an expression of their wildness, or perhaps even to increase it, warriors let their hair hang free (Judg. 5:2). Long bushy hair also characterizes the enemy of good order, the anarchist (Ps. 68:21 [22]), or the person who has returned to the wild (Dan. 4:33 [30]). The adjective is used as a noun ("the hairy [one]") to designate goats (Gen. 37:31) and goat-demons (Lev. 17:7; Isa. 13:21). The people of the OT associated hair with prolific power, with an unbridled, mysterious, even demonic vitality. In Cant. 7:5 [6] the poet sings about its erotic attraction (and danger): "Your flowing locks are like purple; / a king is held captive in the tresses." The singer of an ancient Egyptian love song feels the same about the hair of his beloved: "With her hair she lassos me."[1] Female Egyptian

1. Papyrus Chester Beatty I, group C, no. 43; tr. Fox, 73.

dancers and singers increase their erotic attraction by wearing wigs(?) with long wavy tresses, as shown by the shard drawing from Deir el-Medina (figs. 78–79; cf. figs. 131–32). Black hair symbolizes youth (see the commentary on 1:5).

The simile "like a flock of goats" strengthens associations already present in the Hebrew connotations of "hair." The notion of herd emphasizes the aspect of large numbers—too large to count. Along with their black color, goats are characterized by their impertinence and impudence (Dan. 8:5-7).

[4:1f] This verse is repeated almost verbatim in 6:5d. The term translated "moving down" means literally "to bubble" or "boil"; it refers to the continual movement within the flock. Mt. Gilead, from which the flock "bubbles down," is famous in the OT not only for its many flocks (Mic. 7:14; Jer. 50:19) but also—in the time of the judges (Judges 10–11; 1 Samuel 11) and kings (1 Kings 22; 2 Kings 8–9)—as a hotly contested eastern boundary. The flocks symbolize not only vitality but also the absence of urban civilization (Isa. 17:2; 32:14; Jer. 6:3); from the perspective of city culture, where there are goats there must surely be goat-spirits and goat-demons (Isa. 13:21; 34:14). Comparing the hair of the beloved to the impudent black goats in the wilds of Gilead reveals her vitality and her own wild, almost demonic, lust for life.

[4:2ab] The white teeth (cf. Gen. 49:12), here compared to sheep, stand in sharp contrast to the black goats. The words of Cant. 4:2 show up again in 6:6, except there the "sheep prepared for shearing" are replaced by "ewes." The sheep are washed before shearing to produce the proverbial "white wool" (Isa. 1:18; Ps. 147:16; Dan. 7:9).[2]

Separating the black rams from the white sheep apparently happens first in Ezek. 34:17-22 rather than in Matt. 25:32-33. This seemingly conventional contrast is the intention of Cant. 4:2. Although goats (rams) are known as wild and impudent, sheep, especially ewes silently accepting shearing, are a symbol of meekness (Isa. 53:7). In contrast to the goats flowing down the mountainside, the gleaming white sheep coming up from the watering hole all in a row resemble a festal procession (see the commentary on 3:6a). In fact, sheepshearing was celebrated as a festival (2 Sam. 13:23; 1 Sam. 25:4ff.).

[4:2cd] In their symmetry, the twins following each ewe emphasize the impression of order and blessed fertility. Twin births were not customary among sheep. Ishtar tries to win Gilgamesh for herself by promising him

---

2. The passive participle has to be translated "ready for shearing," not "shorn." See P. Joüon, *Grammaire de l'hébreu biblique* (Rome: Pontifical Biblical Institute, 1923) 342, § 121i; O. Loretz, *Das althebräische Liebeslied: Untersuchungen zur Stichometrie und Redaktionsgeschichte des Hohenliedes und des 45. Psalms,* Studien zur althebräischen Poesie 1, AOAT 14/1 (Kevelaer: Butzon & Bercker; Neukirchen-Vluyn: Neukirchener, 1971) 27.

that, if he agrees, "thy sheep [shall cast] twins."[3] That none of the sheep has lost a lamb to predators, disease, or anything else is another example of blessing and good fortune (note the contrast in Jer. 18:21). Thanks to this extended simile, the unbroken rows of the beloved's teeth, radiantly white and well formed, evoke the full blessing and the friendly and cheerful festivities of a sheepshearing.

[4:3ab] After playing with notions of black and white, the poet introduces a third color—crimson or scarlet. This bright red dye is extracted from the nests of a scale insect that lives on the Israelian oak *(Quercus calliprinos* Webb). Isa. 1:18 contrasts this red to the white of wool or snow. In Jer. 4:30, a woman seeking to entice a lover dresses in scarlet and paints her eyelids black. But like the comparisons of hair to goats and teeth to sheep, the comparison of lips to scarlet is undoubtedly not limited to color. Even in the fairy tale of Snow White, where the metaphors refer to actual colors ("white as snow," "red as blood," "black as ebony"), more is implied: snow connotes purity, blood the mysterious power of love, and ebony the sense of otherness or exotic treasures.

   A scarlet thread (or, better, a scarlet cord or scarlet fabric)[4] was used in Josh. 2:18 to mark the house of the prostitute Rahab in Jericho. When the Israelites arrived she was to place this symbol, which would normally hang on the door, in the window facing the front. Like Rahab's scarlet cord, the bright red lips of the beloved are an invitation to love (cf. Prov. 24:26). In the figurative sense, "lips" in Hebrew can also mean "language" (Gen. 11:1, 6-7). That sense may be implied here also, because the parallel term מדבר, which is used in this way only here, designates the mouth as the instrument of speech. Similarly, an ancient Egyptian descriptive song praises the seductive sweetness of the beloved's lips when she speaks.[5] Thus, the comparison of the lips to the scarlet cord would be like the metaphor comparing glances to doves, praising the ability both to articulate and to awaken the longing and readiness for love. The frequent German translation (e.g., in the Zürcher Bibel) of מדבר as *Plaudermund* (chatterbox) is a relic of a patriarchal belittling of the woman, who is thereby cleverly reduced to nothing but a dear child.

[4:3cd] The pomegranate *(Punica grantum* L.), often used decoratively in the ancient Near East (Exod. 28:33; 1 Kings 7:18), was regarded as an aphrodisiac (see the commentary on Cant. 2:5ab). But beyond that sense it became a Near Eastern symbol of life itself. In areas of Assyrian influence, the pomegranate functioned in the same way as the regenerative symbol of the lotus in the Levant, enriching and clarifying the symbolism of the tree of life (figs. 65, 66, and 89). On ivory inlays from Ashur (fig. 80), two pomegranate trees flank the "mountain of paradise,"

3. Gilgamesh VI.18; *ANET,* 84.
4. Cf. Akkadian *shinitu(m)* II, "dyed fabric"; *AHW,* 3:1242; J. P. Asmussen, "Bemerkungen zur sakralen Prostitution im Alten Testament," *ST* 11 (1957) 182.
5. Papyrus Chester Beatty I, group A, no. 31; tr. Fox, 52.

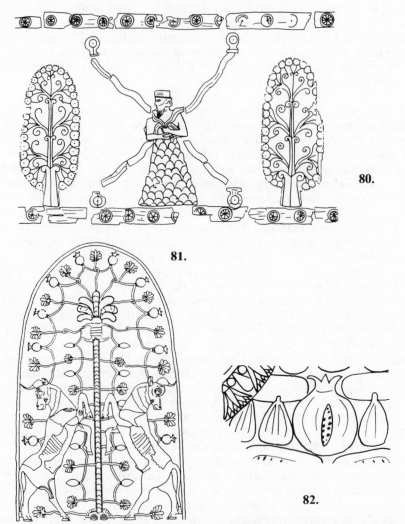

80.

81.

82.

Fig. 80. A mountain deity (identified by the scale patterns in the lower portion) holds a round vessel from which emanate the four rivers (cf. fig. 59). The figure reminds one of the garden of the gods on the mountain from which four rivers flow (Gen. 2:10; Ezek. 28:13-14; cf. fig. 100). The "mountain" is flanked by two pomegranate trees. (Ivory engraving from Ashur; thirteenth century B.C.)

Fig. 81. Two steers pull themselves up on an artificial tree whose identifiable elements are the palm crown and pomegranates. (Glazed faience tiles from Calah [modern Nimrud]; ca. 840 B.C.)

Fig. 82. Since the time of Thutmose III (1479–1426 B.C.), Egyptian portrayals of dining tables and sacrifices in the New Kingdom often include pomegranates; the vertical slit in the skin shows it to be ripe. (Portion of a painted relief in the mortuary temple of Seti I in Abydos; ca. 1280 B.C.)

83.

84.

Fig. 83. Ashursharrat, the wife of Ashurbanipal (cf. fig. 40), wearing a crenellated crown. (Fragment of a limestone stele from Ashur; seventh century B.C.)
Fig. 84. Female head with battlement crown. The round elements remind one of the shields that were hung on the battlements of the wall (Ezek. 27:11; 1 Macc. 4:57). (Limestone statuette from Makmish at Tel Michal near Herzliyya; between 450 and 400 B.C.)

from which emanate four rivers; and on a wall covering in Fort Shal-
maneser in Calah (modern Nimrud), pomegranates form part of the
palmette-shaped tree of life, which is flanked by steers (fig. 81).

In Egypt pomegranates are pictured for the first time in the "botanical garden" of Thutmose III (ca. 1450 B.C.; cf. fig. 108). In the ancient
Egyptian love songs of the Turin Papyrus, the pomegranate boasts:

> All [the trees]—except for me—
>   have passed away from the meadow.
>   I abide twelve months in the gar[den].
> I have endured: ⟨I⟩'ve cast off a blossom,
>   (but) next year's is (already) within me.[6]

This text demonstrates that the pomegranate was seen also in Egypt as a
tree of life, one that would "bear fresh fruit every month" (Ezek. 47:12;
Rev. 22:2). When the pomegranate tree says in the same Egyptian poem,
"my fruit resembles her breasts," the reference is not only to the external
form but also to the life-giving power of both the breasts and the tree.
Modern Arab love songs still often compare the breasts to pomegranates.[7]

The text speaks not merely of the pomegranate but of a "slit in the
pomegranate." One ought not speak of "slices," because the leathery fruit
contains chambers full of seeds surrounded by sweet pulp (thus the Latin
name *malum granatum,* "apple of seeds"). One cannot actually cut slices
of a pomegranate; one slits it open and picks or sucks out the sweet
berries. A good place to begin is the vertical fissure that forms in the fully
mature fruit. This fissure is virtually never absent in Egyptian portrayals
of the pomegranate (fig. 82). Here the slit in the pomegranate is compared
to the beloved's "soft" part (this is the sense of the Hebrew root). Most
often scholars have taken this "softness" as a reference to the woman's
temples (cf. Judg. 4:21-22; 5:26). The ancient Greek translation and
Jerome refer instead to the "cheek(s)"; Jerome's change from singular to
plural seems significant. One would expect a dual or a plural with
"cheeks." Greek and modern Arab love songs compare the cheeks to
apples.[8]

But the inviting slit in the pomegranate, revealing dark red and
bright red parts, seems most likely to refer to the beloved's open mouth,
to her palate. Compared to the softness of the inner mouth, the temples
and even the cheeks must seem hard (cf. Cant. 4:11ab). The reference to
the inside of the mouth strengthens and completes the references to the
gleaming rows of teeth and the scarlet lips; it forms an initial climax in
the poem prior to the retarding force of the tower image in v. 4. The erotic
effect of the open and yearning mouth (see the commentary on 1:2a), like

---

6. Turin Love Song 28; tr. Fox, 45.
7. Dalman, *Diwan,* 101, 214, 231, 235, 250.
8. Ibid., 101; LSJ, 1127; cf. also note 122.

that of the eyes or glances, is only heightened by the veil. The passion it betrays cannot be hidden.

[4:4] The comparison of the neck to a tower has led those authors who think first of form either to the notion of slenderness or, because ancient Near Eastern towers were as a rule not slender but massive, to the thought of a thick and powerful neck. But, Hebrew associates the neck with an attitude, not with a particular form. To speak "with neck" (Ps. 75:5 [6]) is to speak "with pride"; to run against someone "with neck" (Job 15:26) is to run against them "proudly" or even "presumptuously." The beloved's neck—her pride—is like "the tower of David." As a proud symbol of an old proud dynasty, the tower symbolizes her inviolability (Ps. 48:12 [13]). The addition "built in courses" refers to the easily visible rows of squared stones from which the tower was constructed and which emphasize its immovable solidity. The warriors' shields hung on the battlements proclaim the garrison's readiness to defend the tower (Ezek. 27:11; 1 Macc. 4:57). The comparison of the neck with a tower of large squared stones may be based on the "several storied" necklaces worn closely around a woman's neck (figs. 14–16, 44).

The crenellated crown worn by Assyrian queens in the seventh century B.C. (fig. 83) suggests that a woman might symbolize an unconquered city (or nation)—for example, see Ashursharrat at the celebration of her husband Ashurbanipal's great victory over the Elamites (cf. fig. 40). A 4-inch (10-cm.) stone head from the fifth century B.C. (fig. 84) wears a heavy crown that might symbolize a tower battlement. The neck and head of this figure, found in Makmish, give the appearance of a tower. In Hellenistic and Roman times, deities responsible for the protection and destiny of cities were given crenellated crowns.

The simile "your neck is like a tower" describes the beloved as a proud, unconquered city (cf. 7:4 [5] and 8:10). Pope thinks this interpretation contradicts the picture of the woman as an active seeker and aggressor (e.g., 3:1-5), but this same connection between proud reticence and provocative liveliness ("Your glances are messengers of love") occurs also in Isa. 3:16b, where the women of Jerusalem "walk with outstretched necks, glancing wantonly with their eyes." This attitude is clearly evaluated quite differently in the prophetic context than in the Song.

[4:5] Because the song moves down the body, the description of the neck is followed by the breasts, which have been emphasized by the outstretched neck. In 8:10 the breasts themselves are compared with towers. But 4:5 has something other than a boastful appearance in mind. Here is an extended form of the comparison of the breasts to the fawns of a gazelle. The addition "that feed among the lotus blossoms" is lacking in 7:3 (4), which makes the same comparison (breasts as fawns). Exegesis should work with the simpler version. Rudolph's oft-repeated interpretation presupposes the addition and seeks the point of comparison (yet again) in external form: "Two fawns graze in the flowered meadow with

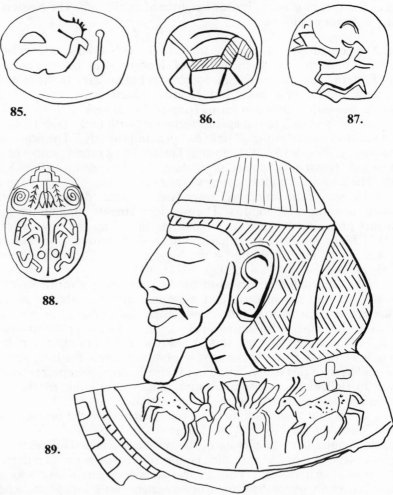

85.

86.

87.

88.

89.

Fig. 85. A gazelle on the back of a scarab; in front of the gazelle is the hieroglyph *nefer* ("beautiful" or "complete"). (Tell el-Farah [South]; tenth–eighth centuries B.C.)

Fig. 86. Ibex or wild goat on a typical Judean bone seal. (Lachish; eleventh-ninth centuries B.C.)

Fig. 87. Ibex on a mountain(?) with a lotus flower. (Bottom of a conical seal from Beth-shemesh; seventh century B.C.)

Fig. 88. Along with the branch and the lotus flower, the symbols of regeneration that frequently decorate the back of scarabs from the Middle Bronze Age IIB (1750-1550 B.C.), this one also includes two reclining ibexes or wild goats.

Fig. 89. The shoulder section of the garment worn by this Canaanite man is decorated with gazelles grazing at the "tree of life." The primary element of the artificial tree is a large lotus flower (cf. fig. 66). (Faience tile from the eastern Nile Delta; thirteenth/twelfth century B.C.)

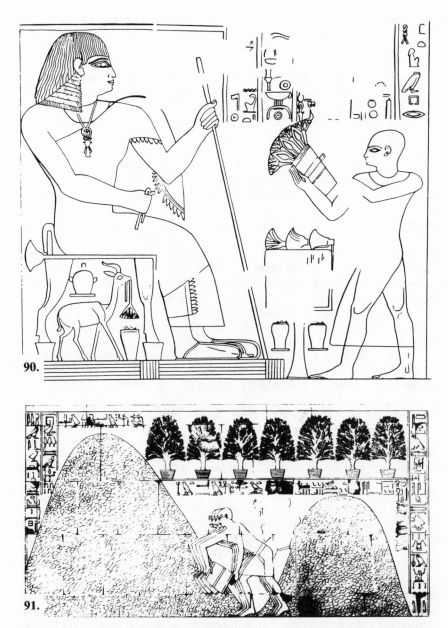

Fig. 90. Beneath the seat of the owner of this tomb, who is being presented with a lotus bouquet, is a gazelle with a lotus flower in its mouth. (Relief on the tomb of Pabasa, West Thebes, no. 279; ca. 650 B.C.)

Fig. 91. Four Egyptians use bushel baskets to measure a gigantic pile of myrrh resin; the seven myrrh bushes (*above*) are meant for the temple garden. (Relief on the mortuary temple of Hatshepsut in Deir el-Bahri; ca. 1460 B.C.)

only their backs projecting above the tall flowers. He compares her well-formed symmetrical breasts to the backs of these fawns—round, smooth, and glistening in the sun."[9] But this interpretation does not work with the shorter version in 7:3(4). Moreover, the flowers mentioned here are not just any kind of spring flowers but lotus blossoms. Hebrew literature does not attach notions of form to the term "breasts" but notions of blessing (Gen. 49:25), of kindness, nourishment, and trust building (Ps. 22:9 [10]; Job 3:12), of soft, warm security (see the commentary on 1:13)—in short, notions of full participation in life and of life's renewal.

As shown in the commentary on 2:9, the primary connotation of gazelles in Hebrew literature is their agile quickness. The catchword "fawns" adds the elements of playfulness and softness. The poet has two fawns to emphasize the parallelism with the two breasts. But the comparison may go even deeper than merely the sprightliness and softness common to the breasts and the young gazelles. Breasts are associated with life and renewal. Gazelles, goats, and similar animals inhabit the steppes and deserts—areas regarded in the ancient Near East as deadly and chaotic, like the world before creation and before the appearance of life (Gen. 2:5). Creatures that could not only survive amid such life-threatening desolation but even demonstrate a wonderful and inspiring sprightliness were appropriately regarded as carriers of a numinous power that could triumph over death itself; they were symbols of life and renewal.

According to E. Hornung and E. Staehelin, this symbolism explains the frequent appearance of goats and gazelles on Egyptian seal amulets, where they are often associated with vegetation.

We are convinced that these plant motifs are not meant to be a statement about the sparse vegetation in the desert; the branches are not meant to provide genre details. Rather, we believe that fresh plants *(rnpyt)* are used here to embody the idea of eternal youth *(rnpy)* or continual renewal. Combining wilderness fauna and branches expresses twofold the notion of regeneration that recurs so frequently on the seal amulets; of course, even by itself such an animal can already symbolize this notion.[10]

There are more than one hundred examples of gazelles and goats on scarabs and scaraboids from Palestine/Israel from 1150 to 586 B.C.; examples include a scarab from Tell el-Farah (South) and a scaraboid from Lachish (figs. 85–86). How well Hornung and Staehelin's interpretation applies in Palestine/Israel can be seen, for example, on a conical seal from Beth-shemesh (fig. 87), which combines a goat with the other classical symbol of regeneration, the lotus (figs. 33–38, 62–66). In addition to the symbolism of Egyptian origin, one dare not forget the connection of these

9. Rudolph, 147. This interpretation has been accepted by Krinetzki, Würthwein, and others.
10. E. Hornung and E. Staehelin, *Skarabäen und andere Siegelamulette aus Basler Sammlungen*, Ägyptische Denkmäler in der Schweiz 1 (Mainz: Ph. von Zabern, 1976) 138.

animals to love-goddesses (figs. 45–48) and their presence at the "tree of life" (figs. 8–11), which belongs in the sphere of the same goddesses; at the tree these animals appear as representatives of a joyful lust for life. In language very similar to that of the Song, the young man in Prov. 5:19 is advised to hold on to his own wife and not to go after others:

> [For she is] a lovely deer, a graceful doe.
> May her breasts satisfy you at all times;
> may you be intoxicated always by her love.

This text compares the woman as a whole to the nimble animals of the field, but it especially emphasizes her breasts as dispensers of life and joy.

Both breasts and fawns of a gazelle symbolize the warmth of life, an inspiring and victorious counterforce to death. But what about the addition, "that feeds among the lotus blossoms"? I have noted in the commentary on 2:1 and 2:16 how the lotus flower was used in the same way as the gazelle and other wilderness animals to symbolize the conquest of chaos—except that the lotus triumphs not over an arid chaos but over a turbid and watery one (cf. Gen. 1:2a). Thus combining gazelles or goats with lotus flowers—both symbols of life and the conquest of death—forms a superlative, just as the combination of two negative symbols—desert and chaotic floods—forms a negative superlative in Jer. 51:42-43: "The sea has risen over Babylon. . . . Her cities have become . . . a land of drought and a desert."

If one tries to envision young gazelles feeding among lotus blossoms as a photograph of nature, the result is as bizarre as trying to imagine Babylon being turned into a desert by a flood; the combination here is not natural but symbolic, and it is thoroughly traditional. The oldest iconographic example known to me comes from the Middle Bronze Age IIB (ca. 1750–1550 b.c.; fig. 88). The back of a scarab, itself a symbol of regeneration, is decorated with a lotus flower (flanked by two spirals and two branches) and two reclining goats or gazelles. An Egyptian faience tile shows a Canaanite whose robe is embroidered with two gazelles flanking a tree of life in lotus form (fig. 89; cf. fig. 66). On an Egyptian tomb relief from approximately 650 b.c., one can recognize a gazelle with a lotus flower in its mouth beneath the seat of the tomb's owner (fig. 90). At the same time, a bouquet of lotus flowers is being handed to the person who has died. The gazelle feeding on a lotus may be a symbol for the dead person, whose life should prove to be as capable of renewal as that of the gazelle with the lotus in its mouth.

[4:6ab] After this marvelous glorification of the woman, the blowing of the wind and the lengthening of the shadows summon the evening (see the commentary on 2:17).

[4:6cd] Thoughts of the evening and the idea of his beloved's life-giving and life-renewing breasts entice the lover to seek out the beloved. In 7:8 (9) the mention of breasts leads to a similar decision. The admiring

descriptions of the partner are left behind and the reactions of the admirer himself ("I") take center stage. Spurred on by theory (his med-
itations), he turns to praxis, going in quest of the "mountain of myrrh"
and the "hill of frankincense." If these metaphors were meant to refer to
particular parts of the body, they would probably be the cheeks (cf. 5:13b)
or the breasts. The Judeo-Hellenistic romance *Joseph and Aseneth* (first
century B.C./first century A.D.) contains a descriptive song derived from
the Song that says: "And her breasts (were) like the mountains of the
Most High God."[11] A comparison with Cant. 7:2(3) might lead one to
think of the belly instead, but such precision is hardly the text's intention.
The beloved as a whole, with all her "high places," becomes a landscape
(with mountains and hills)—more, a wonderland like Punt (eastern Sudan, northern Eritrea) in the Egyptian love lyrics (cf. 2:17). The expedition sent there about 1470 B.C. by Queen Hatshepsut is described as a
journey into wonderland. Her reliefs in Deir al-Bahri show how the
weight of huge piles of red myrrh was determined (fig. 91). The inscription over the people reads: "Measuring fresh myrrh in great quantities. . . . A wonder from the regions of Punt. Treasures of the land of the
gods."[12] A love song already cited (see the commentary on 2:17) says:

> I embrace her,
> and her arms open wide,
> I am like a man in Punt.[13]

The speaker in 4:6 also no doubt hopes to be "like a man in Punt" as he
makes his way to his "mountain of myrrh" and his "hill of frankincense."
The word pair "mountain / hill" in itself often evokes a mythic-cultic
landscape, filled with mysterious life-giving powers (Gen. 49:26; Deut.
33:15). The attraction of such places remained long after the prophets
had denounced the cult at the "high places" as a cult of Baal (cf. Hos.
4:13; Deut. 12:2).[14]

11. *Joseph and Aseneth* 18:9; tr. C. Burchard in *OTP*, 2:232.
12. K. Sethe, *Urkunden des ägyptischen Altertums,* vol. 4/2, 2d ed. (Berlin: Akademie;
Graz: Akademische Druck- und Verlagsanstalt, 1961) 335, lines 13-15.
13. Cairo Love Songs, group A, no. 20F; tr. Simpson, 310.
14. It seems unlikely that הר המור ("mountain of myrrh") is a play on הר מוריה ("Mount
Moriah") and גבעת הלבונה ("hill of frankincense") a play on לבנון ("Lebanon"), in order
deliberately to suppress the reminders of Baal with the addition of Yahwistic tones.
True, Jesus Sirach (ca. 180 B.C.) is still applying sacral connotations from the sphere of
Yahwism to the beloved when he says: "Like the shining lamp on the holy lampstand, /
so is a beautiful face on a stately figure" (Sir. 26:17). But an ancient Egyptian incantation
already has the word pair "myrrh/frankincense" in an erotic context, where a demon is
exorcised with the following words:

> Go, please, and sleep there
> where your beautiful wives are.
> Put myrrh on their hair
> and fresh frankincense on their members.

(A. Erman, *Zaubersprüche für Mutter und Kind: Aus dem Papyrus 3027 des Berliner*

Myrrh and frankincense are also combined in Cant. 3:6. The commentary on 1:13 showed that first and foremost the precious and exotic myrrh had erotic associations. In Egypt, Hathor, "the lady of myrrh," is the goddess of erotic joys and delights.[15] By contrast, in the OT "frankincense" suggests primarily a cultic atmosphere (see the commentary on 3:6). The combination of the two conjures up an intensity characteristic of something totally other or holy. "Mountain of myrrh" and "hill of frankincense" present the beloved hyperbolically as a landscape made up completely of these precious and intoxicating aromatic substances (cf. the "towers of ointments" in 5:13b). The decision to hasten to these hills promises experiences of previously unknown divine rapture.

[4:7] The last verse of the song affirms this conviction by rehearsing the theme of the first verse ("you are beautiful"), strengthening it with "altogether." This "altogether" is further explicated and emphasized by the announcement: "there is no flaw (מום) in you" (cf. 2 Sam. 14:25). The term מום is usually cultic, describing defects in priests or sacrifices (Lev. 21:17ff.; 22:20-21) that arouse the indignation of the deity and call forth his displeasure. But nothing about the beloved could displease her lover or disturb him in any way; nothing could make him reject her and send her away (unlike Deut. 24:1).

Museums, AKPAW.PH [Berlin, 1901] 19; Schott, *Liebeslieder,* 88.) On frankincense in an Old Akkadian love song, cf. Westenholz, "Help for Rejected Suitors," 202–3, lines 1–5.
15. Schott, *Liebeslieder,* 78.

Descend from the Peaks

Text

4:8 a [. . .] With me from Lebanon, [. . .] bride;
 b [with me you will come] from Lebanon.
 c [You will descend] from the peak of Amana,
 d from the peak of Senir and Hermon,
 e from the dens of lions,
 f from the mountains of leopards.

Analysis

The ancient Greek translation of the Bible, the Septuagint, reads אֶתִי ("come") instead of אִתִּי ("with me") in v. 8a. But because the old text-critical rule regards the more difficult reading as more probable, I have retained the אִתִּי of the Hebrew text.

The song in 4:1-7 is dominated by the rather static nominal clauses and the continued repetition of the admiring "you" and "your" that are appropriate to a descriptive song. The short song in 4:8, however, opens with the phrase "with me"—emphasized by its initial position, then imploringly repeated. Two imperfect forms ("you will come," "you will descend") constitute the song's center; its dynamic is controlled by the sixfold repetition of "from."

The connection with the preceding song is no doubt occasioned by the catchwords לבונה ("frankincense") in v. 6d and לבנון in v. 8a, as well as the "mountain" in vv. 6c and 8f.

This verse introduces a series of texts whose contents are marked by the catchwords "bride" and "Lebanon"; they are sometimes referred to as "Songs of Lebanon" (4:8—5:1). The delineation of individual songs within this complex is rather difficult. For example, one might regard 4:9-11, treated here as an independent song, as a continuation of 4:8 (see the commentary on 4:9-11).

154

In his 1898 commentary on the Song, Budde wrote of v. 8: "The
verse is completely unrelated to the context. . . . Even taken independently, it makes no sense." Seventy years later, Würthwein concurred:
"Budde's assertion that the fragment makes no sense is still true." What
drove the beloved to the mountains, to the leopards and lions?

Scholars have occasionally referred to a custom practiced early in
the twentieth century among the nomads of Hejaz and the southern
Sinai. The groom seeks the bride, who hides in the mountains. There they
sleep together, and she remains in her mountain hideaway until her
pregnancy is well advanced.[1] Yet this custom does not explain why the
beloved in Cant. 4:8 is so urgently summoned to come down from the
mountains; and it is not at all certain that such a custom ever existed in
Israel.

Commentary

[4:8ab] It is much more likely that here again is the phenomenon of giving
the beloved the form and attributes of a goddess. Goddesses enthroned
on mountains are not found with great frequency in ancient Near Eastern
art, but they are hardly out of the ordinary, as seen in figure 11, in the
impression of a cylinder seal from Ur (fig. 92), or on a cylinder seal
depicting Ishtar as a wild mountain dweller energetically climbing a
mountain (or stepping on a mountain god?) (fig. 93). The woman addressed in 4:8 is not atop just any mountain but the highest mountains
known to Hebrew experience (cf. Deut. 3:25). The Lebanon range, mentioned first, rises in the north (Qurnet as Sauda) to a height of 10,131 feet
(3,088 meters) above sea level. The ancients regarded it as a mountain of
the gods (Ezekiel 31) whose cedars had been personally planted by Yahweh (Ps. 104:16; regarding the cedars, see the commentary on Cant. 1:17
and 4:11c). The Gilgamesh Epic celebrates Lebanon as "the cedar mountain, abode of the gods, Throne-seat of [Ishtar]."[2] Jeremiah characterizes
Jerusalem's pride with these words: "O inhabitant of Lebanon, nested
among the cedars" (Jer. 22:23).

The aloof pride of Lebanon and of the beloved who sojourns there
is matched by the equally proud claim of the speaker, expressed through
his use of the term כלה. The כלה is not only the "bride," beaming in her
opulent and precious finery (Jer. 2:32; Isa. 49:18; 61:10; 62:5), but also
the woman who is promised, legally bound to her contractual partner and
to her father-in-law (Gen. 38:24; Hos. 4:13-14). In the Song, כלה never
has a possessive pronoun and, other than here and in 4:11, always occurs
along with "sister" (4:9, 10, 12; 5:1)—even though the marriage of siblings was forbidden in the OT (Lev. 18:9). This usage probably means
that the Song employs both כלה and "sister" as honorary titles rather than
as legal terms—especially because legal affairs generally play no role in
the Song (note the total absence of the father).

1. G. Jacob, *Das Hohelied aufgrund arabischer und anderer Parallelen* (Berlin: Mayer &
Müller, 1902) 22–23.
2. Gilgamesh V.i.6; *ANET,* 82; cf. note 34.

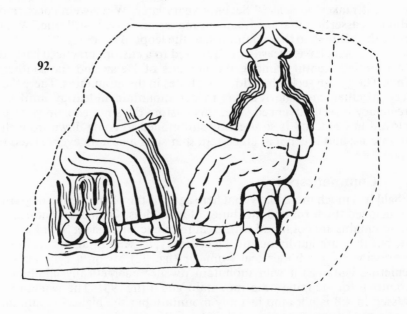

Fig. 92. A goddess enthroned on a mountain range. (Cylinder seal impression from Ur; ca. 2000 B.C.)

Fig. 93. With a broad, swinging step, Ishtar climbs a mountain, at the same time kicking a fleeing god in the back; to her left are the palms regularly associated with her (cf. figs. 59, 95, and 135–46). To the left of the palms are two gods waving. (Cylinder seal from the Akkad Period; ca. 2200 B.C.)

Fig. 94. The warlike Ishtar puts her foot on a lion, which she has on a leash; to her left is a star, which is typical of her. Across from the goddess stands an adoring deity. (Cylinder seal of the Akkad Period; ca. 2200 B.C.)

Fig. 95. The warlike Ishtar with bow and arrow, quivers and swords, stands on a lioness or leopard; a worshiper stands in front of her. The palms also belong to the sphere of the goddess (cf. fig. 93), as do the crossed ibexes or wild goats (cf. figs. 45–50). (Neo-Assyrian cylinder seal; seventh century B.C.)

[4:8cd] Senir, Amana, and Hermon probably designate the northern, middle, and southern parts of the Anti-Lebanon mountain range, although Deut. 3:9 uses two of these names to refer to the same peak ("the Sidonians call Hermon Sirion, while the Amorites call it Senir"). The modern name for Hermon is Jabal ash-Shaykh or "piebald mountain," because for the greater part of the year the top is white with snow. Rising 9,040 feet (2,759 meters) above sea level, it can be seen from large parts of Galilee. The older name is related to the word for the "ban" (חרם; cf. "harem"). Several sanctuaries, with temples and altars, were found on Hermon into Roman times.

[4:8ef] References to leopards and lions as attributes of female deities date back to the neolithic age (seventh/sixth millennium B.C.). This attribution applied especially to the warlike Ishtar. Her dominion over predatory animals illustrates her wild, unbroken, unapproachable, and virgin power. Her icons enjoyed undiminished popularity from the Akkad period (ca. 2200 B.C.; fig. 94) to the Neo-Assyrian period (ca. 700 B.C.; fig. 95; cf. also figs. 47 and 59). In the meantime, the image also arrived in Egypt (fig. 96). It retained its popularity into the Greco-Roman period; indeed, erotically attractive women in the company of leopards and lions are still a favorite theme of contemporary posters. The eastern Mediterranean region also has several references to a goddess who was associated with a mountain and a lion at the same time—see, e.g., a Cretan seal from the palace of Minos (fig. 97) or a stone relief from the Hittite stone sanctuary of Yazilikaya (fig. 98). In a highly schematized form, the motif is found on a seal impression from Tell en-Nasbeh (Mizpah?) at a level from the period between 1100 and 700 B.C. (fig. 99).

Purpose and Thrust

The brief song offers an expressive presentation both of the woman's aloofness or unapproachability and of the man's power as he overcomes these things. He wants to compel her to come down from her godlike pedestal—a proud request of a proud woman!

96.

Fig. 96. At the center of this composition, a goddess, naked except for her bracelets, stands frontally displayed on a lion. The goddess, designated Qodshu ("holiness"), wears her hair in the style of Hathor. With one hand she holds a snake, with the other she holds flowers to the nose of Min, the fertility-god with an erect phallus (cf. fig. 63). To her right stands the warlike Resheph; in the lower register are a male and female worshiper. (Painted limestone stele from Deir el-Medina; thirteenth century B.C.)

159

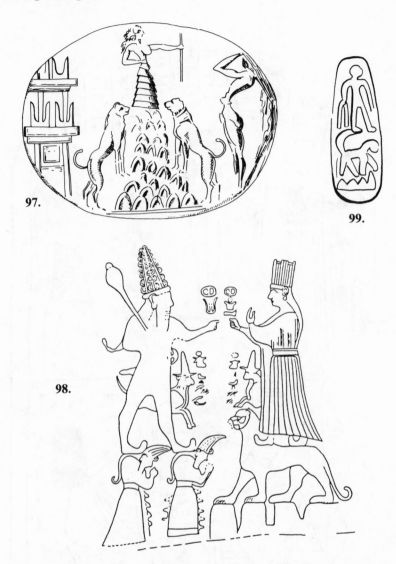

Fig. 97. A goddess with bare breasts stands on a mountain peak, flanked by two lions; to her left an altar, to her right a worshiper. (Stamp seal from the palace of Minos in Knossos; ca. 1500 B.C.)

Fig. 98. The weather-god Teshub (*left*) encounters the sun-goddess Chebat, who is standing on a lion. The lion's four paws rest on mountains. (Relief in the stone sanctuary of Yazilikaya; ca. 1250 B.C.)

Fig. 99. A goddess with a cloth(?) in her hand above a lion who walks on mountains. (Seal impression from Tell en-Nasbeh [Mizpah?], between 1100 and 700 B.C.; the impression is printed here in mirror image in order to display the "normal" orientation of the original.)

You Drive Me Crazy!

Text

4:9 a   You [drive me crazy], my sister, [. . .] bride,
   b   you [drive me crazy] with a [single one of your glances],
   c   with [a single sparkle] of your necklace.
10 a   How sweet is your love, my sister, [. . .] bride!
   b   how much better is your love than wine,
   c   and [(how much better is)] the fragrance of your
     [ointments] than [all balsam fragrances]!
11 a   [Liquid honey drips from your lips, . . .] bride;
   b   honey and milk are under your tongue;
   c   the scent of your garments is like the scent of Lebanon.

Analysis

The song in 4:8, with its two imploring imperfects (each with a future
sense), attempts to change a situation. By contrast, 4:9-11 uses perfects
and nominal clauses to describe a situation of supreme bliss, one that is
incomprehensible, even crazy (see the commentary on v. 9ab). The three
repetitive parallelisms, each with three members, produce a rhythmic
undulation, bringing one new high point after another: v. 9, "You drive
me crazy . . . , you drive me crazy with a single one of your glances, with a
single sparkle . . ."; v. 10, "How sweet is your love . . . , how much better is
your love than . . . , (how much better) . . . than . . ."; v. 11, "Liquid honey
from your lips . . . , honey . . . under your tongue. . . ." One should note
that the Hebrew words for "liquid honey" and "honey" are different and
that the third member of the third couplet departs completely from the
rhythmic pattern; by its repetition of "scent" it achieves its own striking
character, which forms the closing accent of the song.

    One could ask whether 4:9-11 ought not be connected with 4:8.
The description of supreme bliss in 4:9-11 would then be understood as

the basis for the urgent entreaty of 4:8. In 1:2-3, whose theme is closely related to the present song, one also finds a jussive form ("Let him kiss me") followed by nominal clauses ("your love is better than wine," etc.) and a perfect. There (as in 2:14) the two parts are connected with a causal "for" כִּי. Such a connecting "for" would be conceivable at the beginning of v. 9, but it is simply not there. In addition, the parallelism in 4:8 always has two members, whereas in 4:9-11 it consistently has three; finally, there is an immense discrepancy in content between the beloved's unapproachable appearance on the highest mountain peaks (v. 8) and the enjoyment of the "honey" under her tongue (v. 11). Thus it is probably more appropriate to interpret 4:8 and 4:9-11 separately as independent songs. The combination of the two songs is perhaps based on the catchwords "bride" in v. 8a and again in vv. 9a and 10a and "Lebanon" in v. 8a and in v. 11c.

Commentary

[4:9a] The Hebrew word translated here "to drive crazy" ("to enchant") is a verb derived from the noun לֵבָב, "heart." The meaning of the verbal form (the *piel*) is ambiguous. It can be privative ("you have stolen my heart") or intensifying ("you make my heart beat faster," "you excite my heart"). In any case, she affects his heart so that it no longer functions normally. As used in an erotic context, "you drive me crazy," includes both meanings of the verbal form.

The Hebrews ascribe different functions to the heart than modern Westerners do. For the latter, the heart is the seat of the emotions; for the former, it is the seat of understanding, thought, and planning (Deut. 29:4 [3]). In English to be "heartless" is to be "without feeling," but in Hebrew it would mean something like being "dull" or "foolish" (Hos. 7:11). Westerners think with the head and feel with the heart; Hebrews think with the heart and feel with the belly or the intestines (Lam. 2:11). The Hebrews knew nothing of a "cool" way of thinking, disconnected from all emotion (cf. Hos. 11:8; Jer. 20:9). Thus, when the beloved touches the man's heart, both thoughts and feelings are equally enchanted, disconcerted, and stolen away. The motif of the beloved who renders her admirer senseless is also found in the love poetry of ancient Egypt. In the first song of Papyrus Chester Beatty I, the man sings: "She has captured my heart in her embrace."[1] The second song on the same papyrus begins with this sentence in the mouth of the woman: "My brother roils my heart with his voice."[2] Then she adds:

> (Yet) my heart is vexed when he comes to mind,
> for love of him has captured me.
> He is senseless of heart—
> and I am just like him![3]

1. Papyrus Chester Beatty I, group A, no. 31; tr. Fox, 52.
2. Ibid., no. 32; tr. Fox, 52.
3. Ibid.

The fourth song on this papyrus begins with the strophe:

> My heart quickly scurries away
>> when I think of your love.
> It does not let me act like a (normal) person—
>> it has leapt ⟨out⟩ of its place.[4]

The motif is also common in modern Arab love poetry from Palestine. "Her wink terrifies the heart of the lion, / O, how much sense has she stolen!"[5]

In v. 9 the man calls the one who drives him senseless "sister." In virtually all ancient Egyptian love songs the lovers address one another as "sister" and "brother." Under the influence of the sibling marriages practiced by the Greco-Egyptian ruling house of the Ptolemies to maintain the purity of the royal blood, interpreters thought the use of "brother" and "sister" in poetic address indicated that sibling marriage was widespread in Egypt. In actuality, however, sibling marriage apparently occurred among the common people only rarely. The "sister/brother" address is found often in early Sumerian love poetry; it did not originate in Egypt.[6] It is a metaphor, meant to express the intense feeling of relatedness and solidarity that has animated lovers in every age.

This same feeling is expressed in the relational formula used by Adam in his initial greeting to Eve (Gen. 2:23): "This at last is bone of my bones / and flesh of my flesh." This formula is interchangeable with the designation "brother" or "sister": "You are my [brother], you are my bone and my flesh" (2 Sam. 19:12 [13]). Goethe still uses the term "sister" to express the feeling of deepest unity in his famous poem of 1776 that begins "Wherefore did'st thou grant us knowing glances" ("Warum gabst du uns die tiefen Blicke"); in the poem he addresses Charlotte von Stein with these words:

> Speak, what are the fates for us preparing?
> Tell me how they matched us accurate?
> Ah, some former life you have been sharing
> As my sister or my wedded mate.[7]

Such deep unity is closely associated with equality and solidarity. The "sister" greeted with the formula of relatedness in Genesis 2 is described by Yahweh as a "helper" in the face of loneliness, a role that accords her the status of equal partner (Gen. 2:18, 20). Someone who is not an equal cannot be a remedy for another's loneliness.

One should not understand "sister" merely as a metaphor for

---

4. Ibid., no. 34; tr. Fox, 53.
5. Dalman, *Diwan*, 134.
6. Kramer, *Sacred Marriage*, 99–100, 104–5.
7. tr. Helen Kurz Roberts, in Goethe, *The Eternal Feminine: Selected Poems of Goethe*, ed. Frederick Ungar [New York: Frederick Ungar, 1980] 35.

163

"tenderness," as is often the case. It is a metaphor of relatedness and togetherness. These feelings can lead to tender contact, and the metaphor functions at the same time to legitimize this contact. One can kiss a brother or sister in public (Cant. 8:1). The continuation of the poem makes clear that the "sister" metaphor is not meant to exclude sexual and erotic themes. (For more on the term "bride," here combined with "sister," see the commentary on 4:8ab.)

[4:9b] The beloved has made him senseless or driven him crazy with just one of her eyes or glances (see the commentary on 1:15b). The admirer reports the disconcerting power of the woman's glances in 6:5: "Turn away your eyes from me, / for they make me crazy." The metaphor describing glances as messengers of love (eyes as doves; 1:15b; 4:1cd) shows that it is the flash of affection and love in the glances that disconcerts and unravels the one they touch.

[4:9c] One עֲנָק of the woman's necklace has the same effect as one of her loving glances. This Hebrew word occurs only two other times in the OT (both in the plural) and designates objects which hang around the necks of people (Prov. 1:9) or of camels (Judg. 8:26): decorative pearls, necklaces, pendants, or amulets. The translator can choose among these four possibilities or perhaps others. In the present context the word is used for a part of a necklace. Thus to translate the term itself with "chain" or "necklace" would make sense only if one were thinking of part of a larger necklace composed of several strands (cf. figs. 14–16, 44). Because the parallel term (literally, "eye") is translated with the more dynamic "glance," and because a single part of a necklace would scarcely have a special effect, I have translated עֲנָק with the dynamic "sparkle." The fact that many ancient Near Eastern goddesses were pictured naked or nearly naked yet opulently adorned with jewelry shows the great erotic effect ascribed to jewelry and its glitter (cf. figs. 11, 45, 47, etc.; cf. also 1:10 on the erotic effect of jewelry). The intoxicating effect of eyes and jewelry is also the theme of an ancient Egyptian love song: "With her eyes she catches me, / (and) with her necklace she causes me to bow down."[8]

[4:10ab] The commentary on 1:15a shows that the Hebrew term יָפֶה, "beautiful," also includes the notion of "desirable." That connotation is clear in Ezek. 16:13, which portrays Jerusalem as a young woman gradually growing mature and beautiful—in other words, desirable (cf. also Cant. 7:6 [7]). See the commentary on 1:2b for "love that is better than wine."

[4:10c] The word translated here "ointments" is the plural of "(olive) oil"; the term refers to oil or fat mixed with various fragrant substances and

8. Papyrus Chester Beatty I, group C, no. 43; tr. White, 184; cf. O. Keel, *Deine Blicke sind Tauben: Zur Metaphorik des Hohen Liedes,* SBS 114/115 (Stuttgart: Katholisches Bibelwerk, 1984) 55, note 127.

smeared on oneself or one's guests on festive occasions as an ointment (cf. Amos 6:6; the commentary on Cant. 1:3a; and figs. 4–6). Verses 1:3a and 4:10c use similar words to say very different things. In 1:3a the love of the man is preferred to his "scent"; in 4:10c the "fragrance" of the woman is praised more highly than all balsam fragrances.

The Hebrew word בשׂם appears here for the first time in the Song but then turns up six more times (4:14, 16; 5:1, 13; 6:2; 8:14). Like the Arabic *bisham*, it probably referred originally to any pleasant fragrance (cf. Exod. 30:23); later its meaning was narrowed to balsam alone, the pleasant fragrance par excellence. The balsam bush (*Commiphora opobalsamum* Foureau) is native to southern Arabia. It is similar to the dwarf birch, and the tips of its sap-filled branches secrete a pale yellow fluid. Immanuel Löw describes its aroma as "fine and pleasing, spicy, similar to lemon or rosemary, comparable to the fresh resin of the silver fir."[9] Flavius Josephus (first century A.D.) writes that the בשׂמים brought to King Solomon by the queen of Sheba (1 Kings 10:2, 10) were balsam bushes.[10] According to Josephus the sap of the balsam was the most valuable of all the products of Judea.[11]

Pliny the Elder (first century A.D.) reports that Roman society preferred the fragrance of balsam to all other fragrances—and that the price showed it! He also thought balsam came only from Judea.[12] Balsam was raised in En-gedi and Jericho in carefully guarded royal or imperial fields. Excavations in En-gedi seem to indicate that the balsam plantings there were laid out at the end of the seventh century B.C. (Josiah) or in the Persia era (sixth century B.C.). The references in the Song no doubt already have genuine balsam in mind.

But in 4:10c the man prefers the aroma of the perfumed oils of his beloved to all the fragrances of balsam. Every perfume combines with the natural odor of the wearer to make an individual and distinctive aroma (cf. Gen. 27:26-27). It is this fragrance that makes him happy. At the same time, the oil and its fragrance function metaphorically to describe the intoxicating bliss that the woman brings her lover.

[4:11ab] With its threefold repetition of the combination of פ and ת (נפת תשׂפנה שׂפתותיך), v. 11a is nicely onomatopoeic. One can hear the thin liquid honey dripping from the honeycomb. This liquid honey (1 Sam. 14:26) is used here to symbolize lips when kissing (see Prov. 24:26 and the commentary on Cant. 4:3a and 13cd). In an Assyrian incantation, a woman seeking love speaks these words: "May my lips be liquid honey . . ., / may the lip of my vulva(?) be a lip of honey!"[13] The image is still found among Palestinian love songs of the modern era: "Her saliva is like

9. I. Löw, *Kryptogamae, Acanthacae, Graminaceae,* vol. 1 of *Die Flora der Juden* (1928; reprint, Hildesheim: G. Olms, 1967) 300.
10. Josephus *Ant.* 8.74.
11. Josephus *J.W.* 4.469.
12. Pliny the Elder *Natural History* 12.111.
13. H. Zimmern, Der Schenkenliebeszauber Berl. VAT9728 (Assur) = Lond. K.3464 + Par. N.3554 (Nineve)," *ZA* 32 (1918–19) 174, lines 48–50.

crystal sugar!/ O, how sweet is the sucking of her lips, / sweeter than sugar or honey!"[14] Or, again: "Her mouth is sweet to me, / within it a comb of honey."[15] Milk and honey are the foods of paradise (Deut. 32:13-14; cf. also Isa. 7:15; Job 20:17). The paradisiacal land promised to Israel by God flows with milk and honey (e.g., Exod. 3:8). The lover finds these paradisiacal foods under the tongue of his beloved.

Words can also be found under the tongue (Ps. 10:7; 66:17). But this text, which speaks of the scent of the beloved and of love more intoxicating than wine, is certainly thinking of a nonverbal form of communication. In the same context, 1:2 speaks explicitly of kissing. Thus the honey under the tongue of the beloved must refer to tongue kissing. This kissing is apparently mentioned already in a Sumerian love song:

> The brother brought me into his house,
> Laid me down on a fragrant honey-bed.
> My precious sweet, lying by my "heart,"
> One by one "tongue-making," one by one,
> My brother of fairest face, did so fifty times.[16]

"Tongue-making" is obviously a metaphor for intercourse in this poem.

[4:11c] But the Song does not go that far, not even metaphorically. Instead it returns to the motif of the woman's all-encompassing scent, which so disconcerts the speaker. This scent is as overwhelming as the proverbial fragrance of mighty Lebanon (Hos. 14:6 [7]), whose many flowers and extensive, resin-rich conifer forests (cf. Isa. 40:16) made it a wonder, a garden of the gods.

14. S. H. Stephan, "Modern Palestinian Parallels to the Song of Songs," *JPOS* 2 (1922) 214.
15. Dalman, *Diwan*, 134.
16. *ANET*, 645; this translation is from Kramer, *Sacred Marriage*, 104; regarding honey, cf. ibid., 92, 94, 96.

The Paradise of Love

Text

4:12 a A garden locked [(are you)], my sister, [. . .] bride,
     b a garden locked, a fountain sealed.
 13 a Your ["canals" (are) a park of pomegranate trees]
     b with all choicest fruits,
     c henna with nard,
 14 a ⟨nard and [turmeric], calamus and cinnamon,
     b with all trees of frankincense,
     c myrrh and aloes,⟩
     d with all the best [balsam bushes]—
 15 a [fountain of the gardens,]
     b a well of living water,
     c [as it flows from Lebanon.]
 16 a Awake, O north wind, and come, O south wind!
     b [Let my garden be fragrant! May (the fragrance) of its balsam shrubs] be wafted abroad.
     c Let my beloved come to his garden,
     d and eat its choicest fruits.
5:1 a I come to my garden, my sister, [. . .] bride;
     b I gather my myrrh with my [balsam.]
     c I eat my honeycomb with my honey,
     d I drink my wine with my milk.
     e Eat, friends, drink, and be drunk with love.

Analysis

The previous song, 4:9-11, described the woman's effect on her lover; her glances, her scent, her kisses rob him of his senses. This "you/me" relationship is already clearly evident in the first two verbs. A first-person suffix occurrs no fewer than four times in the three verses, a second-person suffix ten times. But 4:12-15—a unit of approximately the same

167

length—has only one first-person suffix ("my sister") and only one of the second person ("your canals"). Without these two words we would have a purely objective description of an unknown bride, using only nominal clauses. Five verbs occur in 4:9-11, none at all in 4:12-15 (except for the participles, which express conditions rather than decisive actions). Indeed, most of this unit does not even have nominal clauses. Instead, it has a simple listing of what can be found in the "park." Interestingly, the list is structured by a fourfold use of עִם, meaning "together with," "in communion with," "in the company of," or "at the same time as". Here it evokes a picture of thick, intertwined vegetation. Because v. 14 seems a bit excessive and begins by repeating (in the singular) the last word of v. 13, v. 14a-c might be a secondary addition. In any case, the listing of objects in v. 14 is like an early form of science, especially prevalent in Sumer, that sought to produce an inventory of the world. As shown by the beginning of the Egyptian Onomasticon of Amenemope[1] or by Psalm 148 and the song of the three youths in the fiery furnace (Pr. Azar. 28-68), such inventories can easily be turned into hymns. Here an inventory of spice plants is transformed into praise not of God but of the "sister bride"; one sees yet again how the lover perceives everything wonderful through and in reference to his beloved.

The motifs of Cant. 4:12-15 are as different from 4:9-11 as the form. In place of the intoxicating glances, fragrances, and kisses, is a static picture of the bride as a miraculous garden and fountain, nourishing an incredible variety of plants.

Along with the catchword "Lebanon," which closes both 4:9-11 and 4:12-15, and the address "my sister, bride," it is primarily the "balsam fragrances" in 4:10c and the "balsam bushes" in 4:14d that tie 4:12-15 and 4:9-11 together and that are probably responsible for the inclusion of 4:12-15 at this point.

Although the division between 4:9-11 and 4:12-15 seems clear to me, I am not sure whether 4:16—5:1 should be read with 4:12-15 (Gerleman and Rudolph) or whether these passages should be separated and read as two poems (Krinetzki).

In contrast to 4:12-15, 4:16—5:1 is formally distinguished by a number of verbal clauses. Verse 16ab begins with three imperatives which are followed by three imperfects expressing wishes (4:16b-d). Verse 5:1a-d promises the fulfillment of these wishes in four perfects. The section closes in 5:1ef with three more imperatives. The still life described in the nominal clauses of 4:12-15—the enclosed garden with its waters, maturing fruit, and many fragrant plants—is followed in 4:16—5:1 by a rush of movement (though expressed solely in demands, wishes, and promises).

The content of this requested, desired, and promised movement is, for the most part, drawn from 4:12-15. The winds in 4:16ab are to spread abroad the fragrance of the balsam bushes of 4:14a. The beloved

---

1. A. H. Gardiner, *Ancient Egyptian Onomastica: Text Vol. I* (1947; reprint, Oxford, 1968) 1*–2*.

Fig. 100. The small temple on the hill is surrounded by a park with trees. From the right comes an aqueduct that divides into several canals. Thus, the temple is located in a paradisiacal environment (cf. fig. 80). (Relief from the palace of Ashurbanipal in Nineveh; ca. 640 B.C.)

of 4:16d is to come into the garden of v. 12 and taste of its choicest fruits (mentioned also in v. 13b).

This passage seems to be much more than the loose connection of songs joined by catchwords that one often finds in the redactional work of the Song. Verses 4:12-15 and 4:16—5:1 are related to one another in so many ways that one can hardly understand the desires and wishes of 4:16—5:1 without the still life of 4:12-15. We should probably regard the two parts as an original unity. The combination of nominal and verbal clauses is found, though to a lesser degree, also in the classical descriptive songs of 4:1-7 (cf. v. 6cd) and 7:6-9 (7-10) (cf. v. 8 [9]).

Commentary

[4:12] One of the most beautiful things and one of the greatest pleasures known to the ancient Near East was a garden—a carefully enclosed and heavily watered plot of ground planted with fragrant plants, blooming bushes, and trees filled with choicest fruits. The inner court of every house had some kind of garden. A few herbs for the kitchen, a grape vine, or a fig tree usually had to suffice. To sit under these trees in peace and to enjoy their fruits without disturbance was the highest form of happiness (1 Kgs 4:25 [5:5]; Mic. 4:4).

Fig. 101. To the right, a priest of Amon hands a sacred bouquet of flowers to Neferhotep, a deserving official, while another priest anoints him. In front of the first flag-topped pylon, Neferhotep hands the bouquet to his wife; this group is in a garden that surrounds the temple buildings. The park includes a pond, fed by a canal from the Nile. The pond contains the usual water lilies. (Painting in the tomb of Neferhotep, West Thebes, no. 49; ca. 1320 B.C.)

A real garden required more space and, above all, more water than was available in the courtyard of the average house.

According to one of the sayings of Balaam:

> How fair are your tents, O Jacob,
> . . . .
> like palm-groves that stretch far away,
> like gardens beside a river. (Num. 24:5-6)

The fictitious king in Eccl. 2:3ff., to whom all possibilities were open and who attempted the best that humans could attempt, says: "I made myself gardens and parks, and planted in them all kinds of fruit trees. I made myself pools from which to water the forest of growing trees." Such a royal garden was a necessary part of every royal palace (Jer. 39:4; 52:7; Neh. 3:15). When most moderns think of a garden, they think first of flowers and vegetables, but the ancient Near Eastern garden was usually more like a small park with shrubs and trees (Jer. 29:5; Amos 9:14).

What made human beings happy could surely not be withheld from the deity. The "house of Yahweh" was surrounded by the "garden [or park] of Yahweh" (Gen. 13:10), where the finest trees grew (Ps. 52:8 [10]; 92:12-15 [13-16]). Ancient Near Eastern depictions, for example, a relief from the palace of Ashurbanipal in Nineveh (fig. 100), show temples in the middle of luxuriant parks, traversed by canals (cf. also fig. 101). With its fragrant conifers, Lebanon was regarded in large parts of the Near East as a prototype of these "gardens of the gods." An Assyrian text of the seventh century B.C. describes a temple park as "the Garden of Plenty, the image of Lebanon"[2] (see the commentary on Cant. 1:17 and 4:8ab). The OT also calls Lebanon the "garden of God" (Ezek. 31:8). The relation between this geographically identifiable "garden of God" and the primeval "Garden of Eden" cannot be fully explained. "Eden" is sometimes used as a geographical term (Gen. 2:8; Ezek. 28:13), but often it means simply "garden of delights" (עֵדֶן = "delight"; cf. Gen. 2:15; Ezek. 36:35; Joel 2:3). More important than the geographical location are Eden's characteristic rushing waters, its shady trees and pleasant fruits, and its comfortable intimacy between God and humans.

Both the descriptions of the blessed primeval time and those of the coming age of salvation are impossible without "gardens" and garden metaphors: "The Lord will . . . satisfy your needs in parched places . . . ,

2. *ANET,* 110.

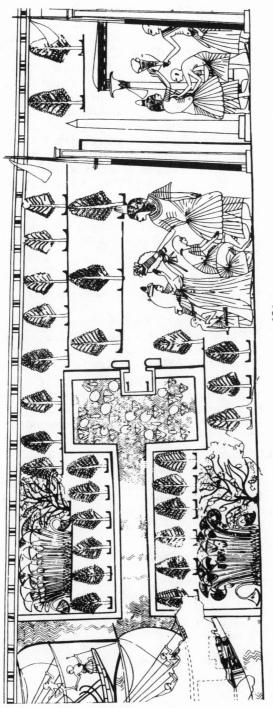

101.

and you shall be like a watered garden, like a spring of water, whose waters never fail" (Isa. 58:11; cf. Jer. 31:12). A river flows perpetually from the visionary temple of Ezekiel 40–47; the innumerable trees on its banks bear fruit every month (Ezek. 47:1, 7, 12; cf. Rev. 22:1-2).

Sir. 24:13-24 forms a link between the description of the primeval or future garden of paradise and the Song's description of the beloved as a garden. Sirach introduces Lady Wisdom both as a bride of the wise teacher and as a garden with paradisiacal features.

In the face of the broad and manifold significance of the "garden," it is no wonder that no collection of ancient Near Eastern love songs was complete without this metaphor. Sumerian songs connected to sacred marriage describe the beloved as a "well-stocked garden."[3] In another song, Inanna, the great Sumerian goddess of love and fertility, sings:

> My brother has brought me into the garden.
> Dumuzi has brought me into the garden. . . .
> By an apple tree [cf. Cant. 2:3] I kneeled as is proper.
> Before my brother coming in song,
> Before the lord Dumuzi who came toward me, . . .
> I poured out plants from my womb,
> I placed plants before him, I poured out plants before him.[4]

This poem introduces Inanna as the power whose womb brings fertility to the garden. The holy garden, associated with the Dumuzi-Adonis cult, continued to play a role in OT Israel—even though it was ridiculed (cf. Isa. 1:29; 65:3; 66:17). The Akkadian translation of the "Message of Lú-dingir-ra" describes a woman as "a garden of delight, full of joy."[5]

The temple garden of the sun-god in Heliopolis serves as the place for a rendezvous in an ancient Egyptian love song: "(And) you may take my heart to Re's Heliopolis. / When I retire with you to the trees of the garden house."[6]

Figure 101 shows the park belonging to the temple of Amon in Karnak. In the Turin Love Song Papyrus, several trees of the orchard, including the pomegranate, the fig, and the sycamore, boast of sheltering the lovers.[7] But, as in the Sumerian songs and the Song, in Egypt the garden was not only the setting for love—the beloved herself was a garden:

> I am your favorite sister.
> I am yours like the field
> planted with flowers
> and with all sorts of fragrant plants.

---

3. Kramer, *Sacred Marriage,* 96.
4. Ibid., 101.
5. M. Civil, "The 'Message of Lú-dingir-ra to his Mother' and a Group of Akkado-Hittite 'Proverbs,'" *JNES* 23 (1964) 3, line 35.
6. Papyrus Harris 500, group A, no. 8; tr. White, 171.
7. Fox, 44–47.

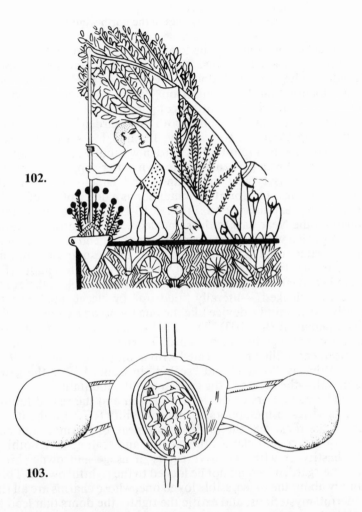

102.

103.

Fig. 102. A gardener dips water out of a lower canal into a higher one, using a
container hanging from a horizontal pole balanced on a pillar. The lump of clay at
the end of the horizontal pole serves as a counterweight, making it easier to lift
the filled container. This contrivance, called a shaduf, is still used in Egypt. A
blooming pomegranate bush can be seen behind the gardener (cf. figs. 80–82);
under the right end of the shaduf is a mandrake (cf. figs. 149–52). The canal is
filled with the ever-present lotus flowers (cf. figs. 31–38, 62—66, 87–90, 129–30).
(Painting from the tomb of Ipui, West Thebes, no. 217; thirteenth century B.C.)
Fig. 103. Each of two swinging cabinet doors is fitted with a knob. These knobs
are tied together with a cord. The knot is encased in a lump of clay impressed with
a seal so it cannot be surreptitiously opened. (Cabinet from the tomb of
Tutankhamen; ca. 1325 B.C.)

> Pleasant is the canal within it,
> which your hand scooped out,
> while we cooled ourselves in the north wind.[8]

The "canal" scooped out by the lover's hand can hardly be anything but the deflowered vagina, because "hand" probably serves as a euphemism for phallus in Egyptian as it does in Ugaritic and in Hebrew (cf. Isa. 57:8, 10). In modern Arab love songs from Palestine, a nocturnal visit to the beloved is like entering the gardens of paradise.[9]

The sister bride is extolled both as a "garden" and as a "fountain" or "spring" in Cant. 4:12-15. As vv. 13a and 15a show, the text has in mind a garden with a fountain. A garden without water is unthinkable in the Near East, but a garden with its own water supply is very precious, even though it is typical in Lebanon and Israel with their relatively abundant springs. The fountain metaphor as a description of the beloved woman, used extensively in Prov. 5:15-18, is apparently not found throughout the Near East to the same degree as the garden metaphor.

A garden with its own spring does not depend on canals or another external water supply, as did the gardens of Mesopotamia (cf. fig. 100) and Egypt (fig. 101); their frequent watering, using the shaduf (fig. 102), required great effort. A garden with its own water is self-sufficient and can be securely "locked"—literally "tied up" or "laced up." The text apparently has in mind a device like the one found on a cabinet in the tomb of Tutankhamen (fig. 103). Two knobs, one on each of two swinging doors, are tied together with a cord. To guard against unauthorized or unnoticed entry, the knot is sealed with a lump of clay (cf. Job 9:7; Deut. 32:34). What is "locked" and "sealed" in Cant. 4:12 is the gate in the garden wall—the access to the garden and the fountain.

The metaphors of the locked garden and the sealed fountain belong to a series of metaphors of inaccessibility (cf. 2:14, the dove in the clefts of the rock; 4:8, the bride on the peak of Hermon among lions). Contrary to frequent claims, the locking and sealing have nothing to do with chastity or with exclusive rights of usage and ownership, under which the "garden" would not be locked to the rightful owner. This image is simply about the inaccessible loved one, whose charms are all the more wonderful, mysterious, and exotic the tighter the doors that lead to them are locked.

[4:13ab] The word translated "canals" is a noun from the verb שלח, "to send." The noun can mean "spear" (Neh. 4:17, 23 [11, 17]) or "gutter / canal" (Neh. 3:15; cf. the related שלוח [Isa. 8:6] or Σιλωάμ [John 9:7]).

---

8. Papyrus Harris 500, group C, no. 18; tr. Fox, 26. On the Ugaritic use of "hand" (יד) to mean "phallus," cf. *KTU* 1.23:33-35 (J. Aisleitner, *Die mythologischen und Kultischen Texte aus Ras Schamra*, BOH 8 [Budapest: Akadamiai Kiadó, 1964] 60; A. Caquot et al., *Textes Ougaritiques*, vol. 1, *Mythes et Legendes: Introduction, traduction, commentaire*, Littératures anciennes du Proche-Orient 7 [Paris: Cerf, 1974] 374); *KTU* 1.4.IV:38 (Aisleitner, 40; Caquot, 205).
9. Dalman, *Diwan*, 93, 135, 260.

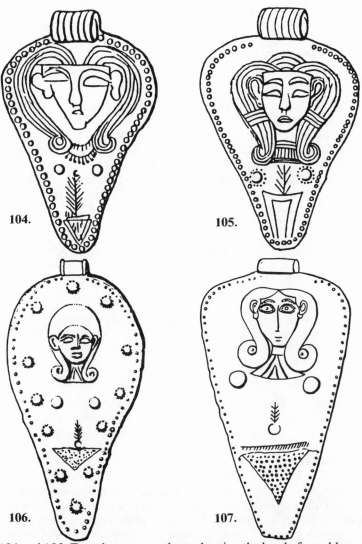

104.

105.

106.

107.

Figs. 104 and 105. Two electrum pendants showing the head of a goddess with a necklace and a Hathor hairstyle (cf. figs. 47 and 96). The breasts are barely indicated, but the pubic region is prominent; in fig. 105 it takes the shape of a "canal." A branch (stylized tree) grows from the pubic area. (Ugarit; fourteenth/thirteenth century B.C.)

Figs. 106 and 107. Two pendants of the same type as those in figs. 104 and 105. In each of these pendants the stylized tree grows out of the navel instead of the pubic area; on the interchangeability of navel and genitalia, cf. Cant. 7:2 (3) and fig. 127. (Fig. 106: gold pendant from Minet el-Beida, the harbor of Ugarit, fourteenth/thirteenth century B.C.; fig. 107: gold pendant from Tell el-Adshul, south of Gaza, fifteenth century B.C.)

Fig. 108. A section of a relief showing plants and animals that Thutmose III brought from Palestine-Syria and introduced into Egypt; in the upper register are several varieties of iris, in the lower register (*far left*) is a bunch of pomegranates. (Relief in the banquet hall of Thuthmose III in Karnak; ca. 1450 B.C.)

Because the parallel term is "pit" in Job 33:18 (cf. Job 33:28; 36:12 [in the Hebrew text; most English translations have "sword"]), it can also designate a vertical excavation or shaft. In Arabic *shalch* can mean "vagina." The Sumerian and Egyptian poems quoted previously associate "garden," "canal," "womb," and "vagina." Even legal texts (Lev. 12:7; 20:18) use "fountain" or "spring" as a metaphor for the female genitalia. In a modern Arab poem a young woman attests to her virginity with the words: "No bucket has been lowered into me."[10] These modern Arab poems frequently raise the virginity issue.

The plural form in this verse ("canals") is similar to the use of "springs" in Prov. 5:15-18, which admonishes the young husband:

> Drink water from your own cistern,
>> flowing water from your own well.
> Should your springs be scattered abroad,
>> streams of water in the streets?
> Let them be for yourself alone,
>> and not for sharing with strangers.
> Let your fountain be blessed,
>> and rejoice in the wife of your youth.

The use of the plural in Cant. 4:13a ("canals") and Prov. 5:16 ("springs" and "streams") forbids rigorously ascribing a single meaning to the metaphor and, at the same time, expresses the strength of the feelings related to this subject (see where the Hebrew uses plural forms to intensify the importance of things related to the deity in Ps. 43:3; 46:4 [5]; 84:1, 3 [2, 4]; 87:1; 132:5, 7; 133:3). The nominal clause "Your canals [are] a park ..." makes sense only when one understands "canals" euphemistically.

The Hebrew word for "park" (פרדס) is a loanword from Persian (*pairidaeza*). It has come into English ("paradise") by way of Greek (παραδεισος). Its primary use in Hebrew is to designate the (royal) orchard (Eccl. 2:5; Neh. 2:8), and, indeed, v. 13a speaks of pomegranate trees (see the commentary on 4:3cd for more on pomegranate symbolism). The poet describes the yield of the pomegranate trees as a precious harvest or gift, using a carefully chosen archaic term (Deut. 33:13-16). The metaphor of the vulva as a pomegranate orchard, which at first glance seems rather strange, is probably based ultimately on the notion of the earth as a woman (cf. Cant. 2:17c-f) from whose womb all vegetation springs forth (cf. the Sumerian song quoted on p. 172). Canaanite pendants depict a stylized plant growing from the pubic area or from the navel of a goddess

10. Ibid., 107.

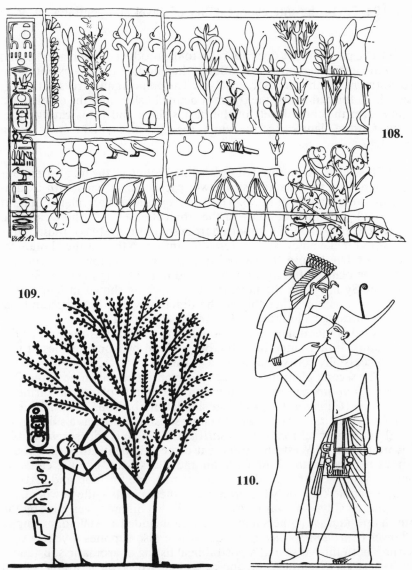

Fig. 108. A section of a relief showing plants and animals that Thutmose III brought from Palestine-Syria and introduced into Egypt; in the upper register are several varieties of iris, in the lower register (*far left*) is a bunch of pomegranates. (Relief in the banquet hall of Thuthmose III in Karnak; ca. 1450 B.C.)

Fig. 109. The goddess Isis in the form of a tree (cf. fig. 142) nurses the dead Thutmose III in order to give him new life. (Painting in the tomb of Thutmose III in the Valley of the Kings; ca. 1430 B.C.)

Fig. 110. A goddess in human form nurses the dead king Seti to give him new life. (Part of a painted relief in the mortuary temple of Seti I in Abydos; ca. 1280 B.C.)

177

(figs. 104–7. On the interchangeability of navel and genitalia, cf. 7:2a
[3a]).

[4:13c] The plural of כפר does not refer to the product of the plant (henna)
but to the individual bushes; similarly, the plural of nard does not mean
the ointment but the plants themselves. The pomegranate trees with their
beautifully formed fruits, the fragrant henna bushes, and the exotic nard
plants form the three levels of the park's thick and intoxicating vegetation. On the significance of henna, see the commentary on 1:14; on
nard, 1:12.

[4:14] This verse is composed of two parallel couplets, the first listing four
fragrant plants, the second listing two; each couplet ends with a sum-
marizing formula ("with . . ."). The verse mentions eight plants that, at
best, could grow in Israel only in the tropical oases near the Dead Sea;
more likely, they had to be imported from southern Arabia or India. Thus
they would make an exotic impression, similar to that of the "botanical
garden" of Thuthmose III, carved in stone in the temple of Karnak; it
depicts the plants "that his majesty found in the foreign land of Retenu
[Palestine-Syria]."[11] In the portion of the carving shown in figure 108,
one can see, among other things, the different varieties of iris and the
pomegranates that Thuthmose III introduced into Egypt.

  Nard is mentioned again (now in the singular) as the first of the
eight plants. It originated in India, but, at least by Roman times, it was
being successfully cultivated in Syria as well.[12]

  The second plant in v. 14, כרכם, is mentioned only here in the OT.
In Arabic, *kurkum* can refer to at least two different plants: (a) turmeric
or curcuma (*Curcuma longa* L.)—a slender, herbaceous plant native to
Southeast Asia; its roots contain a yellow substance used as a spice and a
dye; (b) crocus or saffron (*Crocus sativus* L.), which is widespread today,
blooming even in Western gardens; it came originally from the moun-
tainous regions south of the Caspian and Black Seas; like the curcuma
root, its yellow color is used as a spice and a dye for food and textiles.
Because people knew only the products of these plants—the powder used
as a spice or a dye—it was possible to call two different varieties by the
same name, *kurkum*; others may have been included as well, for example,
safflower (*Carthamus tinctoribus* L.), which also supplies a yellow dye.
Because both this verse and a postbiblical listing of aromatic substances
for the Jerusalem temple[13] include כרכם along with typical products from
India and Southeast Asia, and because the garden of delights is meant to
be as exotic as possible, it is preferable to relate כרכם to curcuma or
turmeric.

11. W. Wreszinski, *Atlas zur altägyptischen Kulturgeschichte,* vol. 2 (Leipzig: Hinrichs'sche, 1935) pl. 31; cf. also pl. 26.
12. Pliny the Elder *Natural History* 12.121; Horace *Carmen* 2.11.16.
13. Cf. I. Löw, *Iridaceae, Papilionaceae,* vol. 2 of *Die Flora der Juden* (1924; reprint,
Hildesheim: G. Olms, 1967) 8-9.

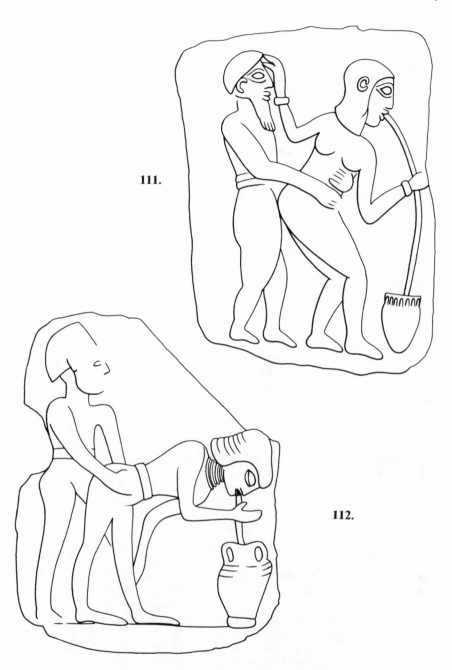

111.

112.

Figs. 111 and 112. A naked woman (or, in fig. 112, a woman wearing only necklaces and a belt) drinks beer through a straw while a man approaches her from behind. (Old Babylonian terra-cotta reliefs; ca. 1750 B.C.)

The third plant, קנה, actually means "cane," "reed," or "tall reedy grass"; but קנה is only a shortened form of קנה-בשם, "aromatic cane" (Exod. 30:23). According to Jer. 6:20, it, like frankincense, was imported from distant lands for cultic purposes. It was expensive (Isa. 43:24); Ezek. 27:19 lists it along with cinnamon. The term probably refers to palmarosa (*Cymbopogon martinii* Stapf), a tall reedlike grass still cultivated in India for the sake of its aromatic oil (palmarosa oil).

The fourth plant, קנמון, is the cinnamon tree, whose bark is used for its famous aroma. The term includes not only Chinese cinnamon (*Cinnamomum cassia* Blume), the source of the spice known in antiquity, but also *Cinnamomum zeylanicum* Nees, native to India and Sri Lanka (Ceylon), whose product, despite reports to the contrary, was exported to the West prior to the fourteenth century A.D. According to Exod. 30:23, cinnamon was used along with myrrh and palmarosa (NRSV "aromatic cane") to perfume the holy oil. It was also used along with myrrh by the "wily" harlot in Prov. 7:17 to perfume her bed.

The fifth plant is the frankincense bush, native to southern Arabia and East Africa (see the commentary on Cant. 3:6c); the sixth is the myrrh bush or myrrh tree, which comes from the same regions (see the commentary on 1:13). The seventh name, אהלות ("aloes"), seems to have been a collective term for various kinds of aromatic woods of the ancient world—the most important of which was no doubt aloes (*Aquillaria agallocha* Roxburgh), a slender tree found in both northern India and eastern Africa. The oil of this aloes tree was used to perfume the king's wedding garments in Ps. 45:8 (9) and the woman's bed in Prov. 7:17. This pleasant-smelling wood is unrelated to the succulent *Aloe vera* L., whose oil was used in embalming (cf. John 19:39-40). Finally, mention is made of the balsam shrubs of southern Arabia, whose products were regarded as the crown of all fragrances (see the commentary on Cant. 4:10c).

The plants in the garden described here are impressive not only because they are wonderfully exotic (Chinese, Indian, southern Arabian, and eastern African imports grow alongside one another) but even more because of their variety. The four aromatic plants used to produce holy oil are named in Exod. 30:23-24 (myrrh, palmarosa, and two kinds of cinnamon); the king's garments are perfumed for his wedding with myrrh, aloes, and one variety of cinnamon (Ps. 45:8 [9]); the harlot (as already noted) uses the same recipe to try to make her bed attractive (Prov. 7:17). But in comparison to the abundance of fragrant plants mentioned in Cant. 4:14, meager indeed is the number used for the holy oil, the royal wedding garments, and the bed of the harlot.

[4:15] Following this grand excursus on the woman's infatuating splendor, v. 15a joins the separate images of the "garden" and the "fountain" (v. 12) by speaking of a "fountain of the gardens" (the plural has an intensifying function). This fountain or spring supplies water for not just one but many widely distributed gardens filled with botanical treasures. In contrast to a cistern, which preserves only collected rainwater, a well of "living water"—the literal phrase—is a shaft with a bubbling spring at the bottom (cf. Gen. 26:19; John 4:10-15). This water is as clear, fresh, and rejuvenating as the brooks flowing down from the majestic Lebanon mountain range; these are the "snow of Lebanon . . . the mountain waters . . . the cold flowing streams," which according to Jer. 18:14 do not "run dry." Nor does the beloved—a garden of wonders with a miraculous fountain—ever lose her power to refresh and enchant, even in the Near Eastern heat.

[4:16ab] A new tone begins here. The still life of the garden is replaced by three commands to the north and south winds to awaken and come into the garden. The text no longer speaks of the fountain, the figurative principle of life, but only of the garden and its splendors. On the one hand, the refreshing north wind, which appears also in an Egyptian love song already cited (pp. 172ff.), augments the cool shadows of the garden (cf. 2:3). On the other hand, the warm south wind stimulates the slumber-inducing fragrances of the garden. As in Isa. 43:6, "north" and "south" form a merism (expressing a totality through opposing poles or contrasting parts), which leads into the series of merisms in 5:1. Merisms are typical of hymns (cf. "heaven," "earth," and "sea" in Ps. 96:11; "young" and "old" in Ps. 148:12); there is something exuberant and expressive in their urge toward completeness, their yearning for totality.

The emotional effect of the sudden awakening is also expressed in the fact that it is not at all clear who speaks the imperatives in v. 16ab. Many commentators think it is the woman (Gerleman, Rudolph, Krinetzki); but when it becomes clear that she is the speaker in v. 16cd, she calls herself "his garden." According to Ginsburg, Schneider, and Pope, the use of "my garden" in v. 16b still sounds like an address used by the man: "A garden locked are you, my sister bride" (v. 12a). The garden seems like a "sleeping beauty" that the man does not dare to awaken. Thus he calls on the winds, the breath and spirit of life that can turn dead bodies into living creatures (Ezek. 37:9; cf. also Ps. 104:30). The winds are to turn the slumbering garden into one that wafts abroad its fragrance, just as Lebanon sends forth its flowing streams (the same Hebrew word occurs in vv. 15c and 16b).

[4:16cd] The woman whom the man had seen as "sleeping beauty" responds quietly to the imploring imperatives addressed to the winds, saying that the lover himself—not the south wind—should come into his garden. In the OT, to "come" or "go into" a woman frequently means to sleep with her (Gen. 16:2; Ps. 51:title [2]). The man is to "come" and eat of the highly praised fruits (cf. Cant. 4:13b). "Eating fruit" appears in 2:3d as a metaphor for erotic pleasures. Even by itself, "to eat" can be a metaphor for intercourse. Of the adulteress, Prov. 30:20 says: "She eats, and wipes her mouth, / and says, 'I have done no wrong'" (cf. Sir. 23:17).[14] The "choicest fruits" offered in Cant. 4:16 are reminiscent of the "choicest fruits" of v. 13b and 2:3cd and of the pomegranate park as a

14. Cf. Qur'an, Sura 2:183.

metaphor for the vulva. In other places, e.g., in an ancient Egyptian love song from the Turin Papyrus,[15] pomegranates are used as models for the beloved's breasts. In Jewish love songs of the intertestamental period and in modern Palestinian Arab love songs the comparison of the breasts to apples or pomegranates has become stereotypical.[16]

> Your breast, O you, is like a pomegranate fruit. . . .
> How sweet to pluck it in the morning
> and to open the garden.[17]

Prov. 5:19b says that the breasts satisfy the lover at all times (cf. Cant. 2:5b). One should also note here the frequent portrayal of the breasts on naked female figures in Syrian and Palestinian handiwork.

[5:1ab] The admirer responds to the woman's surprisingly direct invitation to come into his garden and to eat its fruits with the firm promise to come, to gather, to eat, and to drink. Each of the seven objects of his activity is modified with a first-person possessive suffix ("my"). As in 2:16a, this suffix does not express pride of ownership (see the commentary there); instead it shows that the man passionately reciprocates the feeling of belonging signaled by the woman ("Let my beloved come to *his* garden"; 4:16c). The passion is expressed in the three merisms and in the three uses of עִם ("with") that join the two parts of each merism.

"Myrrh" and "balsam" relate back to the fragrant garden of spices (v. 14cd). One should probably understand the gathering or plucking in the same way as in a modern Arab song from Palestine: "Are you a virgin, or has someone plucked your rose?"[18] —although, significantly, the Song never raises the question of whether the woman is still a virgin (certainly not with this directness).

[5:1cd] "I eat" responds to the woman's invitation ("[let him] eat" in 4:16d). With "honeycomb" and "honey," "wine" and "milk," however, the poet leaves the metaphorical language of the garden. The previous song (4:11ab) used "honey" as a metaphor for the sweetness of love's pleasures, mostly in reference to lips and tongue (note the commentary there and on 5:16). But what is surprising here is that the man eats not only the honey but also the honeycomb from which the honey drips (1 Sam. 14:27). That image corresponds perhaps to the German "Ich fress' dich mit Haut und Haar" ("I eat you with skin and hair") or the English "I could eat you up"; it expresses a passion without restraint. The word order ("honeycomb/honey") is peculiar.

---

15. Turin Love Song, no. 28; Fox, 44.
16. *Joseph and Aseneth* 8:4; tr. Burchard in *OTP,* 2:211; Dalman, *Diwan,* 101, 214, 231, 250, 253 (cf. note 82).
17. Stephan, "Modern Palestinian Parallels," 214; cf. 215, 222, 243, 275.
18. Dalman, *Diwan,* 69.

Parallel to "eating" comes "drinking." Drinking milk naturally evokes the beloved's breasts. In an ancient Egyptian love song, the beloved asks her friend:

> Is it because you are hungry that you would leave? . . .
>   (Then) take my breasts
>   that their gift may flow forth to you.[19]

A modern Arab love song from Palestine sounds like an echo of the old poem when the young woman addresses her lover (whose name is "Wolf"):

> I don't know if you (are) thirsty or hungry, O Wolf.
> If you are hungry, I announce your supper;
> If you are thirsty, the drink of my breasts (is there);
> They are like buckets.[20]

Portrayals of the pharaoh at his birth, coronation, or death often show a goddess nursing him. On one occasion the goddess is entirely in the form of a tree, including even the hands and breast (fig. 109); sometimes she takes animal form (a cow), but more often she appears as a human (fig. 110). The nursing signifies election, participation in the world of the gods, and a lengthening or regeneration of life. This poem resonates to all of that, though in a somewhat subdued manner—even the man's special election is included when one thinks of how strongly the beginning of the poem emphasized that the garden was locked.

As with the honeycomb and honey, it is again a surprise that the lover wants to drink "my wine with my milk." Apart from Longus's "Daphnis and Chloe"[21] (second century B.C.), this combination is hardly customary. It seems out of place, especially given the OT's negative reactions to other mixtures (Lev. 19:19; Deut. 22:9-11). On the one hand, along with honey, "milk" stands for that which is sweet and soft (Cant. 4:11); on the other hand, "wine" symbolizes the intoxicating element of love (cf. 2:4). Old Babylonian clay tablets show the female partner drinking from a pitcher of beer during coitus (figs. 111 and 112). Alongside these and similar pictures one can rightly consider a Neo-Sumerian text in which the woman addresses her partner with the following words:

> My god, sweet is the drink of the wine-maid,
> Like her drink sweet is her vulva, sweet is her drink,
> Like her lips sweet is her vulva, sweet is her drink.[22]

Eating and drinking are metaphors for the lovers' erotic pleasures, but that metaphor does not exhaust the meaning of these terms. Eating and

19. Papyrus Harris 500, group A, no. 1; tr. Fox, 8.
20. Dalman, *Diwan,* 106; cf. 83.
21. Longus *Daphnis and Chloe* 1.23.3.
22. Kramer, *Sacred Marriage,* 94.

drinking imply appropriation in the fullest sense (Jer. 15:16; Ezek. 2:8; 3:1ff.; 23:33-34). The object of a person's love becomes part of that person. That point is expressed with rare clarity and total openness in a love poem by Ricarda Huch:

> I never get enough of your heart,
> Never enough of your fiery kisses.
> I want you the way the Christian has the Savior:
> Allowed to enjoy the Lord's body as a meal.
> O my divine one, that is how I want you.[23]

[5:1e] In a series of imperatives that close the poem, the man (apparently) turns to his companions and invites them to eat and drink. The move to the plural is reminiscent of 1:2-4, which, also at the high point, changes suddenly to plural forms. This shift is a way to express or to legitimize the escape from business as usual. The final imperative, "be drunk with love," shows that this line is a call to break loose from everyday restrictions, an occasion for intoxication; this call is an explicit expression of what was already implied by the indiscriminate drinking of wine and milk (using a perfect to anticipate the future).

Purpose and Thrust

The "Songs of Lebanon" (4:8; 4:9-11; 4:12—5:1), which speak of Lebanon and in which the beloved is addressed as "sister" or "bride," come to a close with this third poem. With their images of inaccessibility (peaks of Lebanon, locked garden) on the one hand and their metaphors of utmost intimacy (sister, eating, drinking) on the other, they define the broad polarities of every significant romantic relationship. These songs form a high point in the Song, marked not only by their content but also structurally by their central location in the collection.

23. Cf. E. G. Rüsche, "Über ein Liebesgedicht von Ricarda Huch," *TZ* 13 (1957) 42–60.

A Missed Opportunity

Text

5:2 a I [am (already) asleep], but my heart [is (still)] awake.
   b Listen! my beloved is knocking.
   c "Open to me, my sister, my love,
   d my dove, my [all];
   e for my head is wet with dew,
   f my locks with the drops of the night."
  3 a I [have] put off my garment!
   b [What? Should] I put it on again?
   c I [have] bathed my feet!
   d [What? Should] I soil them?
  4 a My beloved thrust his hand [through] the opening [(in the door)],
   b and my inmost being yearned for him.
  5 a I arose to open to my beloved,
   b and my hands dripped with myrrh,
   c my fingers with [genuine] myrrh,
   d ⟨[from] the handles of the bolt.⟩
  6 a I opened to my beloved,
   b but my beloved had turned and was gone,
   c [I was completely stunned by his retreat.]
   d I sought him, but did not find him;
   e I called him, but he gave no answer.
  7 a [The sentinels found me,
   b making their rounds in the city;]
   c they beat me, they wounded me,
   d they took away my mantle,
   e those sentinels of the walls.
  8 a I adjure you,
   b O daughters of Jerusalem,
   c if you find my beloved,
   d tell him this:
   e I am [sick] with love.

185

Analysis

No argument is necessary for beginning a new section with 5:2; the theme clearly changes. The talk of gardens is over. Instead of imperatives, invitations, and promises, the woman delivers a first-person narrative; it is enlivened by sections of direct discourse, but the woman always returns to her first-person narrative, speaking of her beloved in the third person. The form and content are strongly reminiscent of 3:1-5, although, in contrast to 5:2-8, that section ends positively; the connections to 2:8-9 and 7:13 (14)—8:2 are less clear. Like 3:1-5, this poem ends with an entreaty to the "daughters of Jerusalem" (cf. 1:5), although here its function differs from its usual one. In 2:7; 3:5; and 8:4, the entreaty strengthens the request not to stir up love. But here it takes up again the finding motif (vv. 6d, 7a) and obligates the women of Jerusalem, if they find the woman's beloved, to act as messengers between him and her, because she has not been able to find him herself.

It is more difficult to determine this poem's place in the collection than its delineation and structure. One can point to a series of catchwords common to 4:12—5:1 and 5:2-8—e.g., "myrrh" (4:14c; 5:1b; 5:5bc), the address "sister" (4:12a; 5:1a; 5:2c), and "awake" (imperative in 4:16a; adjective in 5:2a). Beyond the simple use of catchwords, the theme common to both poems (i.e., the movement from reserve to awakening) may have played a role in the redaction.

Whereas the woman in 3:1-5 passionately seeks and finds her beloved, the woman in 5:2-8 is more reminiscent of the one in 1:7-8, who hesitates in seeking the beloved and opening herself to him; as a result, because the lover is impetuous and impatient, she misses the opportunity.

Like 3:1-5, as a love poem this passage does not intend a realistic description of an actual event or dream (for details, see the commentary on 3:1-5). Even the notion that a girl or woman would sleep in a room with a door opening onto the street is improbable. Both texts are lyrical formulations of a typical relational fantasy describing the missing of the opportune moment, the painful recurrence of feelings out of phase: when he wants to, she does not; when she wants to, he does not (any longer).

Commentary

[5:2a] A naked woman (cf. v. 3a) lying in bed was a motif of Egyptian painters both when they were free to follow their own imaginations (i.e., when practicing or sketching on shards, fig. 68) and when they were illustrating erotic papyri (fig. 69). But in addition a series of small Egyptian sculptures, especially from the time of the Ramessides (ca. 1300–1100 B.C.) and the Third Intermediate Period (ca. 1100–700 B.C.), depicts a naked young woman or erotic scenes or a mother in bed with a child. These scenes were frequently placed in graves, especially of women, to wish for or magically to enable love, conception, birth, and nursing even in the world to come. The custom found its way to Canaan in the thirteenth century B.C. One limestone example comes from Deir el-Belah

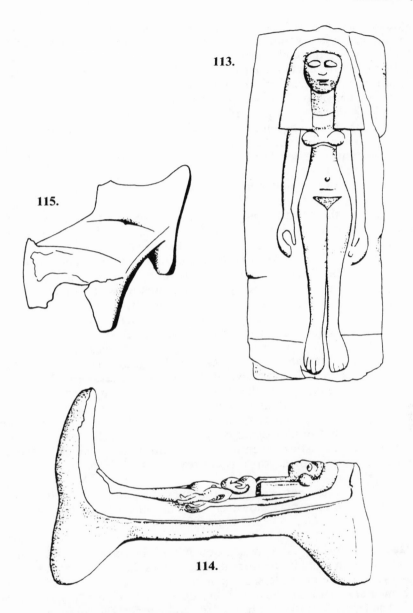

113.

115.

114.

Fig. 113. A naked girl lying on her bed. (Limestone sculpture from Deir el-Belah, south of Gaza; thirteenth century B.C.)

Fig. 114. A young woman lies in bed with a child at her left breast. (Terra-cotta from Egypt; thirteenth century B.C.)

Fig. 115. Small votive bed; like the fuller examples in figs. 113–14, the bed represents a desire for love that is willing to make use of all kinds of magical practices. (Terra-cotta from Beer-sheba; seventh century B.C.)

south of Gaza (fig. 113). The slender, overly long arms and legs indicate that the figure is a young girl. The contrast between the erotic nudity, emphasized by the collar around the neck and the wig, and the rigid posture make the figure seem to hover between sleep and consciousness, a condition characteristic of this motif. Among the carefully finished lime-stone pieces are also a few clay figures, mass-produced in molds. A typical example of the latter is in the National Collection of Egyptian Art in Munich (fig. 114). The motif was carried over from the Canaanite era into the time of the Israelites. The empty clay votive bed, found at the seventh-century B.C. level in Beer-sheba, almost certainly belongs to this tradition (fig. 115).

How can one understand the idea in v. 2a of being awake and asleep at the same time? "Heart" is the organ of thought (see the "thoughts of their hearts" in Gen. 6:5 and the commentary on Cant. 4:9a); it stands for the innermost self, for the center (cf. "in the heart of the sea" in Exod. 15:8, which means "in the midst of the sea"). "To steal someone's heart" (Gen. 31:20) is to lull his or her attentiveness to outwit the person. The "heart" is the first thing to awaken and the last to fall asleep. Does this text mean that the heart is already awake or that it is still awake? Probably the latter. The poem apparently envisions the lover's coming late in the evening. The objection, "I have [just] put off my garment," makes little sense in the morning.

Earlier interpreters, who could not imagine this scene to be real, saw v. 2a as an unambiguous reference to dreaming (the notion that the piece was poetic fiction lay beyond them). They referred to a line from Cicero: "For though [when dreaming] the sleeping body then lies as if it were dead, yet the soul is alive and strong."[1] But the Song never speaks of dreams or dreaming. When dealing with poetry like that collected in the Song, one should think instead of poetic fiction that draws its material primarily from artistic conventions—conventions fed as much by events in the real world as by daydreams or dreams during sleep.

[5:2b] The Hebrew words seem to imitate the knocking at the door (קוֹל דּוֹדִי דוֹפֵק). The term דוֹפֵק, however, does not mean "to knock" but "to push" or "force" (Gen. 33:13; Judg. 19:22).

[5:2cd] This pushing is expressed not only in the imperative ("Open to me!") but even more in the torrent of addresses that follow; each has the possessive pronoun, underscoring solidarity and commitment. See the commentary on 4:9 for the use of the address "sister"; for "my love," see 1:9. The terms "dove"—the bird of the goddess (see the commentary on 1:15b and 2:14ab)—and "my all" no longer emphasize solidarity but the divine status accorded the beloved. Pushing has become prayer. Here the possessive pronoun does not at all express possession or claims of owner-ship but rather dependence (on the goddess/beloved).

1. Cicero *De Divinatione* 1.30.63; in Cicero, *De senectute, de amicitia, de divinatione*, tr. W. Falconer, LCL (Cambridge, Mass.: Harvard Univ. Press, 1959) 295.

[5:2ef] These lines describe the man's need. "Dew" appears often in the OT, almost always as a "blessing" (Gen. 27:28, 39, etc.). But here the man's hair soaked with chilly dew describes an unpleasant situation— like the description of Nebuchadnezzar cut off from human society in Dan. 4:25, 28 (22, 25); 5:21. Palestinian dew could occasionally be as heavy as rain, as indicated by the story of Gideon (Judg. 6:33-40), who was able to squeeze a bowlful of water from a fleece spread out on the threshing floor overnight. Rabbinic and Palestinian Arab sources even speak of harmful dew.[2]

In Gen. 31:40 Jacob complains of the sharp contrast between the heat of the day and the cold of the night. The petitions and complaints of v. 2c-f are the Song's only real example of the somewhat whiny genre of the "door complaint" (*Paraklausithyron*), which is well known in Greco-Latin love poetry (in 2:8-9 and 2:10-13 the man does not complain). In a creatively modified example of this genre, probably originating in Alexandria and falsely passed down under the name Anacreon, Eros says:

> "Fear not," said he, with piteous din,
> "Pray ope the door and let me in.
> A poor unshelter'd boy am I,
> For help who knows not where to fly.
> Lost in the dark, and with the dews,
> All cold and wet, that midnight brews."[3]

[5:3] Some exegetes understand this verse as part of the man's speech (e.g., Buzy), but most rightly ascribe it to the woman. As was customary, she had undressed completely for sleeping (1 Sam. 19:24; cf. Neh. 4:23 [17]). The כתנת mentioned here is a close-fitting, ankle-length, shirtlike undergarment. In warm weather it could also be worn by itself, as shown by the portrayal of Judean women on an Assyrian relief (fig. 116; cf. 2 Sam. 13:18-19). The outer garment, needed in cold weather, was also used as a blanket (cf. Exod. 22:25-26; Deut. 24:13). The same relief shows that people usually went barefoot (less often they wore sandals; cf. Cant. 7:1 [2]). Before preparing for an evening at home or going to bed, one washed one's feet (Gen. 24:32; 2 Sam. 11:8). The woman has made her detailed preparations (perhaps accompanied by a sense of longing and waiting?), has gone to bed, and is already half asleep. The Hebrew word translated "What?" is an extraordinary form of the interrogative particle, otherwise occurring only in Esth. 8:6 (also twice); it expresses astonishment and indignation. The lover (arriving late?) has apparently all too easily taken for granted that she would once again get dressed and dirty her feet.

Many exegetes are puzzled by the woman's reaction. They think they need allegory, mythology, or depth psychology to explain her be-

---

2. *Midrash Rabbah*, Genesis 13:9 (on Gen. 2:6); tr. H. Freedman and M. Simon, *Midrash Rabbah Genesis I* (London: Soncino, 1939) 105; Stephan, "Modern Palestinian Parallels," 215.
3. *Pseudo-Anacreon* 3.10; quoted by Ginsburg, 165; and Pope, 513.

Fig. 116. Judean men and women from Lachish are led away by an Assyrian soldier. The woman and the older girls on the cart are wearing shirtlike garments and a long scarf. They are barefoot. (Portion of a relief from the palace of Sennacherib in Nineveh; ca. 700 B.C.)

they need allegory, mythology, or depth psychology to explain her behavior. But what she does is hardly out of the ordinary.

An ancient Egyptian love song already reports the complaint of a locked-out lover:

> See what the lady has done to me!
> Faugh! Shall I keep silent for her sake?
> She made me stand at the door of her house
> while she went inside.
> She didn't say to me, come in, young man,
> but deaf to me remained tonight.[4]

This Egyptian poem gives no reason for the woman's refusal to let the man enter. In Cant. 5:2-3, her semiconsciousness may explain why she did not get up right away. Or perhaps the detailed description of her preparations for bed implies reproach: Why didn't he come sooner? Now it is too late. She may be exacting a little revenge or teasing a bit. Or perhaps she deliberately delays in order to slow down his late (she was already asleep!) and boisterous pushiness, to get him more in tune with her own drowsiness. These are only conjectures; unlike the allegorists and depth psychologists, the poet does not want to explain anything but merely to describe situations and events typical of love.

[5:4] This verse describes the lover's second attempt to achieve his goal—this time without words. Above the door bolt was apparently a barely fist-sized hole (the Hebrew term is also used for the hole in the lid of the offering chest in 2 Kgs 12:9 [10]); this hole permitted the person inside, before opening the door, to view someone who wanted to enter.[5] Keyholes were apparently rare and were made in such a way that it was not possible to put a hand through them.

The text does not say exactly what the man intended to do with his hand in the peephole. He was most likely trying to open the bolt. In an ancient Egyptian love song, the impatient lover addresses the bolt itself. He promises abundant sacrifices to the various parts of the door (just as sacrifices are offered to the door deities of the underworld in Spell 125 of the *Book of the Dead*):

> I passed by her house in the dark,
> I knocked and no one opened.
> . . . .

4. Papyrus Chester Beatty I, group C, no. 46; tr. Simpson, 324–25.
5. Cf. G. Dalman, *Arbeit und Sitte in Palästina*, vol. 7, *Das Haus, Hühnerzucht, Taubenzucht, Bienenzucht* (1940; reprint, Hildesheim: G. Olms, 1964) 69–70.

116.

> Open, door bolts!
> Door leaves you are my fate, you are my genie.
> Our ox will be slaughtered for you inside.
> Door leaves do not use your strength.
>
> A long-horned bull will be slaughtered to the bolt,
> a short-horned bull to the door pin,
> a wild fowl to the threshold,
> and its fat to the key.

But then the pseudo-religious atmosphere is left behind as the man recognizes the possibility of using the sacrifices to bribe a young worker.

> But all the best parts of our ox
> shall go to the carpenter's boy,
> so he'll make us a door of grass
> and a door bolt of reeds.
>
> And any time when the lover comes
> he'll find her house open,
> he'll find beds made with linen sheets
> and in them a lovely girl.[6]

It is frequently assumed that the hand is put through the hole in v. 4a in order to drip myrrh on the bolt. But only the gloss in v. 5c suggests this interpretation, and therefore it cannot be the original meaning.

Finally, it is possible that squeezing his hand through the hole says something about the purpose of the nocturnal visit. "Hand" is occasionally used in the OT (Isa. 57:8, 10) and in Ugaritic (cf. the text cited in relation to Cant. 4:12 in note 114) as a euphemism for "phallus." The "hole" could then be understood as a symbol for the vagina. Thus this gesture would silently express the lover's desire.

But whether this gesture is a sexual pantomime or merely a helpless hand pushed through the hole in the door in an attempt to open the bolt, the result is a strong stirring of the woman's emotions as she watches (in darkness?) from inside.

The word translated "inmost being" literally means the abdominal organs, e.g., the intestines (cf. 2 Sam. 20:10), or more often the female (Isa. 49:1; Ps. 71:6; Ruth 1:11) or male (Gen. 15:4; 2 Sam. 16:11; 7:12) reproductive organs. In the OT, emotional experiences are not separated from the body; they are described in relation to particular bodily parts. The "yearning" or "heaving" of the inmost being can betray maternal compassion (Jer. 31:20) or passion and desire (Isa. 63:15).

[5:5] The Hebrew verbs at the beginning of vv. 5 and 6 not only have a first-person suffix, but each is also followed by the first-person pronoun (even though this pronoun is grammatically redundant). Thus the "I" is

---

6. Papyrus Chester Beatty I, group C, no. 47; tr. Simpson, 325.

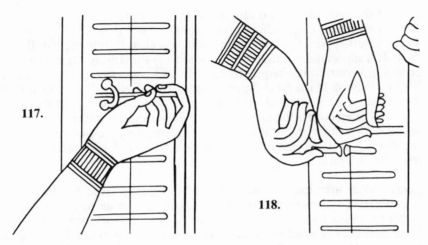

Figs. 117 and 118. The pharaoh's hands open the shrines of various deities for the morning rituals. The widened ends of the bolts can be seen easily in fig. 117, though the mounts are unrealistically omitted; in fig. 118 at least one mount can be seen easily, although the bolt fits in it much too loosely. (Sections of a painted relief in the mortuary temple of Seti I in Abydos; ca. 1280 B.C.)

strongly emphasized: *I* arose; *I* opened. Also emphasized is the woman's willingness to fulfill the lover's wish of v. 2c: "I arose to open. . . . I opened. . . ."

In the present version of the text, the myrrh is on the handles of the bolt used to lock the door. But the text has no parallel to the phrase "upon the handles of the bolt," which, for that reason alone, appears to be a gloss. The gloss could arise from the expression מֹר עֹבֵר in v. 5c, which I have translated "genuine myrrh." The participle עֹבֵר means "moving on," "passing over," etc.; but here it may well be used as in Gen. 23:16 with the sense of "current," "going" (as in "the going rate"), "favorite," or "genuine." Someone who understood the expression literally, rather than in this idiomatic sense, and who therefore missed an indication of where the myrrh was "coming from," added the speculative gloss that it flowed "from the handles of the bolt" that the woman was preparing to open. The "handles" (literally, "hands") may be the widened ends of the wooden bolts (fig. 117) that prevent them from sliding out of their mounts, or perhaps the mounts themselves (fig. 118). Actual bolts found in the tomb of Tuthankhamen show that the mounts fit much tighter than those on the relief from the mortuary temple of Seti I shown in figure 107. In figure 106, from the same temple, the mounts are unrealistically missing altogether.

Before the unfortunate gloss made the myrrh flow from the handles of the bolt, the woman's hands or fingers dripping myrrh (see the commentary on 1:13) probably meant to signify her receptivity to love (cf. 5:13; Esth. 2:13; Ps. 45:8 [9]). A literal interpretation, which would support the symbolic one, is also possible: now fully awake and aroused, she quickly prepares herself, pouring expensive myrrh oil over her hands. Taken together with the hand in the hole, the gloss ("from the handles of the bolt") allows the myrrh to be understood as something left by the man or as a gift from him. Frequently cited in this connection is a section of the fourth book of the great didactic poem of Lucretius, *De rerum natura* (first century B.C.), which deals with psychology: "But the lover shut out, weeping, often covers the threshold with flowers and wreaths, anoints the proud doorposts with oil of marjoram, presses his love-sick kisses upon the door."[7] But the man in 5:2-7 is not this kind of infatuated and tenacious admirer.

[5:6ab] After arriving late and waking his beloved from her half-sleep with his passionate urgency, the man responds to her hesitation by trying to get in on his own; when that attempt does not work, the inconstant lover changes his mind and leaves. This poem has been titled "Punished Coyness" (Rudolph) or "Love's Sorrow through Rejection" (Schneider), but this view is biased from the man's perspective, thinking the woman should always be at his beck and call without delay. One could just as well entitle the poem "The Inconsiderate Lover" or "Love's Sorrow through Impatience"; this view would also be biased, ascribing fault to the man, just as the other titles did to the woman. But the poem is not about determining guilt; it is about a recurrent and painful experience of people in love: their feelings do not always match.

When she opens the door, he has changed his mind and left. The word used here in Hebrew, חמק, is rare; it means "turn aside," "be inconstant," "vacillate" (Jer. 31:22). The related Arabic word *chamiqa* means "be foolish."

[5:6c] What I have translated "I was completely stunned" means literally "my נפש went out." For the meaning of נפש see the commentary on 3:1-5. The departure of the נפש means a complete disappearance of the will to live. It is a condition that immediately precedes death (Gen. 35:18); one might say death has already begun. The woman is not in this condition because of what the man *says* (דבר II; as in the NRSV translation) but because of his *retreat* (דבר I).*
(Other words related to דבר I are דביר, "the back room," "the holy of holies," and מדבר, "the hinterland," "the steppe," as well as Arabic *dabara*, "to turn one's back.") The man's impatient, hasty retreat made him miss the opportunity offered by the woman once all her feelings were awake. But now he is gone and knows nothing of the woman's situation. Thus, unless everything is to be lost, she must go after him.

---

7. *De rerum natura* 4.1177–79; tr. W. H. D. Rouse (Cambridge: Harvard Univ. Press, 1966) 331.
*[KB, 199, lists the two different roots of דבר—TRANS.]

[5:6de] These lines describe a classic situation in the circumstances of ancient Near Eastern love (see the commentary on 3:1-5). "I sought him, but did not find him" duplicates 3:2d; here it parallels "I called him, but he gave no answer." These themes from the language of human love are transferred to the relationship between Yahweh and Israel by the prophets (Hos. 2:7 [9]; 5:6; Jer. 7:27; 29:13; Isa. 65:1, 12) and the wisdom teachers (Prov. 1:28). But to assume, with the allegorizers, that seeking and not finding in the Song also refers to Israel and Yahweh is to get the dependence backward.

[5:7] As in the poem of 3:1-5 (especially v. 3a), here too the woman, during her search, runs into the sentinels on patrol. But whereas the woman of chap. 3 treats the patrols as colleagues from whom she can request information, this scene proceeds much more realistically. The guards would treat a woman wandering the streets at night as a roving adulteress (Prov. 7:11-12) or as a prostitute. According to a Middle Assyrian law book from the twelfth century B.C.: "A prostitute dare not veil herself; her head remains uncovered. Anyone seeing a veiled prostitute should arrest her, gather witnesses, and bring her to the entrance of the palace. Her jewelry may not be taken, but the one who arrests her receives her clothing. She should be given 50 blows with a club and have asphalt poured over her head."[8] This mentality might have spread into Israel under the influence of Assyrian domination. But even if Israel's practice were less brutal, the Assyrian background helps explain the rough treatment of the woman and, above all, the fact that they took away her mantle (cf. fig. 116 and Isa. 3:23). The "sentinels of the walls" are the same as the sentinels who patrol the city. The part (the walls) stands for the whole (the city); cf. Lev. 25:29.

[5:8] Whereas at the end of 3:1-5 the woman adjures the daughters of Jerusalem (the stereotypical public) not to disturb her in the happiness of her love, here with equal urgency she asks them to tell her beloved of her misfortune, to tell him she is sick with love (on this theme, see the commentary on 2:4-5). The only one able to cure this type of illness is the one who caused it.

8. See Borger et al., *Rechts- und Wirkschaftsurkunden*, 87–88 §40.

Distinguished among Ten Thousand (Descriptive Song II)

Text

5:9 a ⟨What is your beloved more than another beloved,
   b O fairest among women?
   c What is your beloved more than another beloved,
   d that you thus adjure us?⟩
10 a My beloved is [shiny and red],
   b distinguished among ten thousand.
11 a His head is the finest gold;
   b his locks are [date panicles(?)],
   c black as a raven.
12 a His eyes are like doves
   b beside [streams full] of water,
   c [(like doves)] bathed in milk,
   d [sitting over the full (basin)].
13 a His cheeks are like beds of [balsam],
   b [(like) towers of ointments.]
   c His lips are [lotus blossoms,
   d dripping with genuine] myrrh.
14 a His arms are [gold (arm) bands]
   b [strewn] with [garnets].
   c His [abdomen is burnished ivory],
   d encrusted with [lapis lazuli].
15 a His [calves] are alabaster columns,
   b set upon bases of gold.
   c His appearance is like Lebanon,
   d choice as the cedars.
16 a His [palate] is most sweet,
   b and he is altogether desirable.
   c ⟨This is my beloved and this is my friend,
   d O daughters of Jerusalem.⟩

Analysis

The words "that you thus adjure us" in v. 9d refer back to v. 8a ("I adjure you"). But the twofold occurrence of "What is your beloved more than another beloved?" in v. 9a and 9c points forward to the following descriptive song in vv. 10-16b. The closing "This is my beloved" in v. 16c and the renewed address to the "daughters of Jerusalem" in v. 16d form the end of a parenthesis begun with the question to the "daughters of Jerusalem" in v. 9 ("What is your beloved . . . ?"); these bracketed comments mark the external limits of the unit and also hold it together internally. But there is no radical break with the context. The catchword "adjure" in v. 9d connects 5:9-16 with 5:2-8, and both the additional question and the offer by the "daughters of Jerusalem" to help find the missing lover make 6:1-3 seem to be a continuation of 5:2-16.

The question "What is your beloved more than another beloved?" makes the following descriptive song seem more an expression of enthusiastic admiration than an aid in the identification of the lover. But the latter is what the "daughters of Jerusalem" would have needed in order to pass on the information that the woman is "sick with love." The question should have been "Who is your beloved?" rather than "What is your beloved more than another?" As a result, v. 9 is not a completely smooth and organic link between 5:3-8 and 5:10-16; therefore scholars often regard it as the work of a redactor. At the same time, however, it must be clear that what is "smooth and organic" in classic Western art cannot be expected in ancient Near Eastern art (and poetry), which tended to work with traditional components, loosely juxtaposing individual elements. A widely distributed Sumerian poem (fragments of an Akkadian and a Hittite translation have been found in Hattushash, Turkey, and in Ugarit in Syria) already used a long, highly poetic "descriptive song" to identify to a courier the woman he was supposed to greet.[1] Thus it is conceivable that 5:2-16 was originally composed as a unit. But because one can understand 5:2-8 and 5:10-16 as clearly distinct units, I interpret them separately.

Because the text is styled as a conversation between the woman and her companions, the beloved partner is not directly addressed (just as in 4:1-7); instead he is discussed in the third person. Only the references to "my beloved" in vv. 10a and 16cd (which open and close the description) identify the magnificent man as the lover of the woman who is speaking.

Verses 10-16 are the only descriptive song in the book about the man. Arab love songs from modern Palestine still sing of the man's beauty much less frequently than the woman's.[2] For a discussion of the genre of "descriptive song," see the introduction; regarding the nominal clauses in vv. 10b-16b, see the commentary on 4:1-7. It is noteworthy

---

1. Civil, "Message," 2, lines 22—23; cf. Keel, *Deine Blicke*, 95.
2. Dalman, *Diwan*, XII.

that, in contrast to 4:1-7, 5:9-16 has no verbal clauses. The verbal mod-
ifiers in Hebrew are all participles. This fact, along with the predomi-
nance of metaphors over similes (cf. the introduction to 7:1-5 [2-6]) and
the concentration on colors and precious materials (gold, ivory, jewels),
give the impression of unexpected, colorful, precious, but somewhat
barbaric splendor. One might explain this impression by the fact that
essential elements of this portrayal derive from descriptions of the statues of gods. I shall return to this point in the exegesis of vv. 14-15.

Commentary

[5:9] As already discussed, v. 9 joins 5:2-8 and 5:10-16. The repeated
question, "What is your beloved . . . ?" is asked by the "daughters of
Jerusalem," who in v. 8 were adjured by the lovesick woman to tell her
beloved about her illness. Her passion leads the women of Jerusalem to
ask about the qualities of her lover. Their question seems to have an
ironic tone, like the address "O fairest among women" (for this form of
the superlative, see Judg. 6:15 and Luke 1:42). The address appears in a
similar form also in Cant. 1:8 and 6:1; it probably alludes to the increased
feeling of self-worth induced by passion and the freer expression of one's
own needs. Passion makes one beautiful!

[5:10a] The opening line, "my beloved is shiny and red," seems rather
distasteful to modern Westerners. The rare word חח does not mean
"white" (that would be לבן) but "sparkling," "shiny." It is used twice of
heat, shimmering above the land (Isa. 18:4; Jer. 4:11). Lam. 4:7 is also
thinking more about something shiny than something white:

> Her princes were purer than snow,
> [more shiny] [צחו] than milk;
> their bodies were [redder] than coral.

There is apparently a traditional connection between shiny and red. This
expression is probably a case of hendiadys ("one [thing] by means of
two"), meaning "shiny red." The prose description of David's beauty,
however, says only that he was "red" or "ruddy" and had beautiful eyes (1
Sam. 16:12; cf. 17:42). Both features are signs of liveliness and intensity.
The human being is אדם, "the red (one)." In Egyptian art the traditional
color of the male body is a dark red-brown. A red-painted limestone stele
from the temple of Arad in ancient Israel is the only symbol of the
presence of Yahweh yet found by archaeologists. The "shiny red (one)" is
the ideal man. Contrary to the opinion of Rudolph, the Song's aesthetic
standards are not the same as those of the German folk song, which
speaks of cheeks that "gleam like milk and purple."

[5:10b] His sparkling, vital appearance makes the beloved stand out like a
banner. The participle translated here as "distinguished" is very probably
related to רגל, "banner" (see the commentary on 2:4b and figs. 17, 41, and
42). On the uniqueness of the man, see also 2:1-3.

[5:11a] Although the descriptive song in 7:1-5 (2-6) works up from the feet to the head, this one describes the man from head to foot (2 Sam. 14:25; cf. also Cant. 4:1-7). Beginning with the head follows logically on the description of the beloved as "distinguished." For the Hebrews, the head was above all the part of the body that made the individual recognizable in a crowd (Exod. 16:16; Judg. 5:30; cf. also 1 Sam. 10:23). The Hebrews localized thinking in the heart (see the commentary on Cant. 4:9a). But the head was supreme, the summit, comparable to a mountain (7:5 [6]). The metaphor comparing the head to smelted gold, gold that is proved and refined, indicates that the beloved towers over all others in splendor and value. The gold metaphor amplifies the idea of shininess in v. 10a.

[5:11bc] These lines raise the intensity of the color "red" (v. 10a) into the realm of the demonic. The "date panicles," 20 inches (half-meter) long even without the stem, testify to the wild and unruly character of his hair. Or if the Hebrew word, found only here, refers to the palm spathe (cf. Gerleman), then the comparison is chosen for the color, because these spathes are usually completely black on the outside. At any rate, the raven simile emphasizes the blackness, which contrasts sharply with the gleaming gold. While gold, as the purest and most cultured material known to humankind, is the stuff of which the gods are made (see the commentary on 5:14), the black raven belongs to the realm of the hairy goat-spirits and the wild demons (Isa. 34:11; Zeph. 2:14). In the context of the descriptive song, it depicts the mysterious and uncanny side of the beloved (cf. "I am black and beautiful" in Cant. 1:5 and the commentary on hair in 4:1ef).

[5:12] For more on the "eyes like doves"—eyes that radiantly exhibit love—see the commentary on 1:15 and 4:1. This verse includes an addition relating the eyes to streams full of water. Most streambeds in Palestine/Israel are dry and empty for almost the entire year; they are filled with water for only a short time during the rainy season. "Streams full of water" evoke a happy time of abundance (Joel 3:18 [4:18]). Thus the man's eyes are like doves in pleasant surroundings.

Bathing in milk also suggests fortunate circumstances, because it is possible only when milk is abundant (Job 29:6; Exod. 3:8, 17). The milk baths indicate that the poet is talking about white doves (cf. Gen. 49:12; Lam. 4:7). The white variety of the rock dove was particularly sacred to the goddess; this relation was clear already in the eighteenth century B.C., as shown by the well-known wall painting at Mari that depicts an overly large white dove on a palm tree to the right of the temple of Ishtar (fig. 59). As late as the first century B.C. Tibullus says that the Syrians of Palestine revered the white dove.[3]

The language of the third addition, "sitting over the full basin," is somewhat ambiguous. The Hebrew word here translated "full basin"

---

3. Tibullus 1.7.18; tr. J. P. Postgate in *Catullus, Tibullus, and Pervigilium Veneris*, 229.

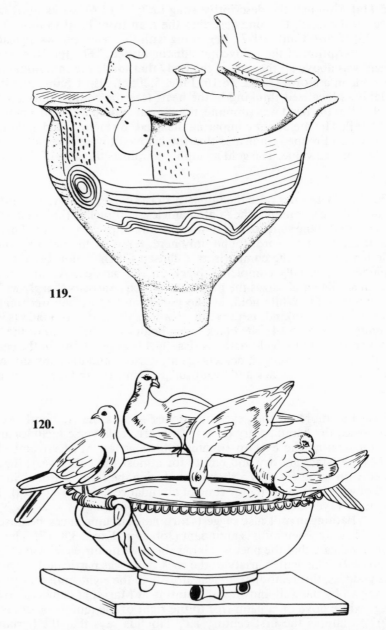

119.

120.

Fig. 119. Two large birds, probably doves, sit on the rim of a large vessel; a small drinking bowl is in front of each. (Clay vessel from Vounos, Cypress; ca. 2000 B.C.)

Fig. 120. Four doves sit on the rim of a water basin; one of them is drinking from it. (Painting from Hadrian's villa near Rome; ca. 125 A.D.)

certainly designates a full container of some kind. At least since 2000 B.C., the fine arts depict a basin with doves sitting on its rim. An example from this period was found in Vounos, Cypress (fig. 119). The theme is seen in a famous painting from the villa of the emperor Hadrian (fig. 120), where the basin is an obvious copy of much older Hellenistic models. All three additions to the dove metaphor emphasize the freshness, radiance, and happiness characteristic of eyes that proclaim love. Their brightness stands out all the more in contrast to the raven-black hair.

[5:13ab] With v. 13 the description moves from visual sensations—an imposing rhythm of light and darkness—to the realm of odors. Here too the comparisons are fantastic hyperboles and superlatives that imply that the woman's beloved evokes notions of divinity. His cheeks are compared not merely to balsam (see the commentary on 4:10c) but to entire beds of balsam, like the ones planted by the last kings of Judah at Jericho and En-gedi; these beds were jealously guarded by their heirs up to the time of the Roman Empire. Rudolph's suggestion that the beds of balsam are a play on the man's perfumed whiskers (rather than the cheeks per se) seems doubtful. To be sure, this interpretation would make the picture more realistic, with less distance between the metaphor's lender of meaning (the balsam beds) and the receiver of meaning (the cheeks or whiskers), especially with regard to external form. But the receiver of meaning in this text is, after all, the cheeks, not the whiskers, and neither realism nor the priority of form is typical for the metaphors in the Song. Therefore I also find no reason to replace the Hebrew "towers (מגדלות) of ointments" with the ancient Greek translation, "pouring forth (*megad-delot*) perfumes." Reminiscent of the mountain of myrrh and hill of frankincense of 4:6cd, the bold metaphor may have been inspired by the Egyptian cones of ointment—headpieces made of fat mixed with aromatic substances (primarily myrrh) that were placed on the heads of Egyptian guests as part of festive amenities from the fifteenth century B.C. on (see the commentary on 1:3a and fig. 6). It was worth some stains on the clothes to allow the exquisitely perfumed oil to saturate the hair and upper body.

[5:13cd] Commentators have generally thought the metaphor of the lips as "lilies" refers to their form (Krinetzki) or to the red color of flowers like tulips or anemones (Rudolph, Würthwein). But I have shown in the commentary on 2:1b (cf. figs. 31–38) that שׁושׁנים means "lotus flowers" and nothing else, and that the metaphor expresses not the form or the color of the lips but the enlivening effect of their kisses (Prov. 24:26; cf. the commentary on Cant. 2:16b and figs. 62–66). The man has this effect, which is the subject of the whole v. 13 and its various fragrance metaphors. An ancient Egyptian love song says of the beloved woman: "her fingers are like lotuses."[4] The comparison would not make much sense if

4. Papyrus Chester Beatty I, group A, no. 31; tr. Fox, 52.

it were based on form, but here too the idea is probably the new, exciting life set in motion by the woman's fingers or the man's lips. This meaning is strengthened by the next line, "dripping with genuine myrrh." The addition apparently applies to the lips, not the lotus flowers. In 4:11a the honey dripping from the woman's lips symbolizes the sweetness of erotic pleasures. Just as in 1:13-14, which compares the man to a bag of myrrh, the myrrh of 5:13 indicates that the man's kisses are like life-giving amulets. Furthermore, myrrh always connotes great value, which is particularly emphasized here by the adjective "genuine" (see the commentary on 5:5c).

[5:14-15a] These lines take up the gold metaphor of v. 11a once again. To the gold are added precious stones and ivory, producing a picture of a figure who is extraordinarily valuable, even though an artificial construction. Descriptions of this kind probably applied first to statues of gods, which were made of the most expensive materials (cf. Jer. 10:9 and Dan. 2:32-33, where the description also begins with the golden head). In analogy to these statues, whose bodies, according to an ancient Egyptian text, were "made of stone and constructed of metal,"[5] people began to imagine the actual bodies of the gods, especially the sun-god, in the same way. For example, the Myth of the Cow of Heaven (fourteenth/thirteenth century B.C.) says of the sun-god: "His bones were of silver, his limbs were of gold, his hair was genuine lapis lazuli."[6] A hymn to Amon-Re from the twelfth century B.C. (a later copy from the Persian period, fifth century B.C., is found on the walls of the temple at the oasis of Hiba) says almost the same thing: "His bones are of silver, his flesh is of gold; that which was on his head is of genuine lapis lazuli."[7]

The golden light of the sun and stars and the blue of the sky (the "ocean of heaven") certainly contributed to this image. Reversing this (actual) relationship, a hymn to the sun that appears in four Theban tombs says: "The heaven is gold because of the beauty of your [the sun-god's] face, / the primal ocean is lapis lazuli because you rise in it."[8] In analogy to the sun-god, the Egyptians also pictured his earthly representative, the pharaoh, made of these same materials. According to a story from the twentieth/nineteenth century B.C. about the first king of the Fifth Dynasty, who was described as a son of the sun-god, "His limbs were inlaid with gold, his head covering was lapis lazuli."[9] In one of the harem scenes from Medinet Habu, one of the princesses praises Ramses III (fig.

5. A. Volten, *Zwei altägyptische politische Schriften: Die Lehre für König Merikare (Pap. Carlsberg VI) und die Lehre des Königs Amenemhet*, Analecta Aegyptiaca 4 (Copenhagen: Einar Munksgaard, 1945) 67-69, 125; cf. also 70ff.
6. E. Hornung, *Der ägyptische Mythos von der Himmelskuh: Eine Ätiologie des Unvolkommenen*, OBO 46 (Fribourg: Universitätsverlag; Göttingen: Vandenhoeck & Ruprecht, 1982) 1/37, 5–7; cf. 52, note 6.
7. J. Assmann, *Ägyptische Hymnen und Gebete*, BAW (Zurich and Munich: Artemis, 1975) 300.
8. Ibid., 232; cf. 561.
9. De Buck, *Egyptian Reading Book*, 84.15; cf. M. T. Derchain-Urtel, "Die Schlange des 'Schiffbrüchigen,'" *Studien zur altägyptischen Kultur* 1 (1974) 85–89.

Fig. 121. The princesses sing to their royal father Ramses III on his visit to the harem. Their song describes his bodily features, picturing him as a fantastic composite statue. (Relief from the "High Gate" in Medinet Habu, Upper Egypt; ca. 1160 B.C.)

121; cf. fig. 152): "Your hair (is) lapis lazuli, your eyebrows (are) *qaʻ*-stone, your eyes (are) green malachite, your mouth (is) red jasper."[10]

The Near East does not seem to have described living gods and kings in this manner. But statues made of different materials have been found dating back to the third millennium B.C. (cf., e.g., fig. 8). In the Gilgamesh Epic (twelfth century B.C.), the hero has a statue of his friend Enkidu made after the latter's death:

> "O smith, [. . .],
> Coppersmith, goldsmith, engraver! Make my friend [. . .]!"
> [Then] he fashioned a statue for his friend,
> [The friend whose stature [. . .]:
> "[. . .], of lapis is thy breast, of gold thy body. . . ."[11]

10. University of Chicago, Oriental Institute, epigraphic and architectural survey, *Medinet Habu*, vol. 8, *The Eastern High Gate*, OIP 94 (Chicago: Univ. of Chicago, 1970) pl. 648; cf. p. 14.
11. Gilgamesh VIII.ii.25–29; *ANET*, 506.

The main concern here is not the body of the god but, as the list of artistic craftsmen shows, the artistry. In Cant. 7:1 (2), the thighs and hips of the woman are expressly praised as the work of an artist's hands.

In the Near East these valuable materials are also highly praised for their purity. In an Akkadian incantation the magician/priest says over a sick man:

> Like lapis lazuli I want to cleanse my body,
> Like marble his features should shine,
> Like pure silver, like red gold,
> I want to make clean what is dull.[12]

The main interest in 5:15-16 is not the purity, the divinity, or the artistry of these materials but their value. At the same time, however, one must realize that although these various aspects may be individually emphasized at different times, one cannot separate them. The traditions about the most famous composite artworks in antiquity—the statues of Zeus at Olympia and of Athena Parthenos, made by Phidias about 450 B.C.— demonstrate this principle. The two colossal statues, each 39 feet (12 meters) tall, made of wood, gold, ivory, and precious stones, were famous not only because of the value and artistry of their construction but also because contemporaries regarded them as the most perfect representation of divinity.[13] One might well say the same thing about this section of the Song.

[5:14ab] The object with which the arms of the beloved are compared in v. 14a cannot be identified with certainty. In one case the Hebrew word seems to designate the pivots of a door (1 Kgs. 6:34), in another the rods or rings on which curtains are hung (Esth. 1:6). The accent here is not on the shape but on the sheen and value of the materials, as shown by the fact that the rings(?) or rods(?) are set with precious stones—which makes little sense with either door pivots or with curtain rods or curtain rings. Perhaps the poet is thinking of the bracelets that sometimes completely covered the arms of high-ranking people in the ancient Near East. These bracelets were set with a stone known in Hebrew as תרשיש. The translation "garnet" depends on the Greek version (Exod. 28:18; Ezek. 10:9), although that version too does not seem to be completely certain, because sometimes (as in this text) it leaves the term untranslated, and sometimes it translates it differently.

[5:14cd] The word translated "abdomen" usually refers to internal organs—the intestines, the reproductive organs (or, metaphorically, compassion; see the commentary on 5:4b). Here, as in the description of the statue in Dan. 2:32, it means the abdomen, the belly, the loins, which are equated with a luxurious object of carefully polished, dully gleaming

12. Ebeling, "Liebeszauber," 36; cited in Pope, 547.
13. *Der Kleine Pauly: Lexikon der Antike*, vol. 4 (Munich: Deutsche Taschenbuchverlag,

ivory (Amos 3:15; 6:4). Solomon had a throne made of ivory (1 Kgs. 10:18). The inlaid lapis lazuli is not meant to indicate tatoos or blood vessels (Rudolph) but, like the garnets on the "golden arms," costliness. This costliness is also the point of the participles, here translated "strewn" and "encrusted."

The gleaming yellow gold and the dark blue lapis lazuli (brought in ancient times from Afghanistan to the Levant) were not only costly but also heavenly materials—the stuff of the bodies of the gods, as the texts cited previously have shown. In Israelite tradition, the place where God's feet rested (Exod. 24:10) and the throne on which he sat (Ezek. 1:26) were made of lapis lazuli. These costly, divine materials are used in a discreet way to describe the area of the hips, the belly, and perhaps indirectly the genitals of the beloved.

[5:15ab] Burnished ivory, encrusted with lapis lazuli, contrasts sharply with the columns of fine alabaster (cf. 1 Chron. 29:2; Esth. 1:6) used metaphorically to describe the calves (cf. Ps. 147:10 RSV). But then the "bases" are said to be made of the same material as the head (Cant. 5:11a): (fine) gold. This point effectively does away with the order of precedence implied earlier. The woman's beloved is gold from head to foot. Krinetzki mistakenly translates "thighs" instead of "calves," thinking that "thighs" refer to the "male genital area" and "serve as a phallic symbol." The "columns," he thinks, symbolize the "stretched-out character of the male body, which finds its fullest expression in the erect penis." His interpretation is contradicted, however, by—among other things—the fact that the metaphor can also be applied without question to the feet of a beautiful woman, as in Sir. 26:18: "Like golden pillars on silver bases, / so are shapely legs and steadfast feet." The use of depth psychology to interpret the Song easily tends to become just as monotonous and monomaniacal as the use of allegory; the variety of experiences and formulations are papered over again and again with the same few words: animus and anima, penis and vagina—a litany that becomes as monotonous as the earlier one about the heavenly Solomon and the believing soul.

Over against Krinetzki, the impartial observer notices how little sexual specificity occurs in the descriptive songs. The primary sex characteristics are never mentioned directly (on the use of euphemism, see the commentary on 4:13 and 7:2 [3]). Some metaphors are used of both sexes—for example, eyes as doves. Sometimes different metaphors are used to point to the same peculiarity—for example, the wild, black hair (cf. 4:1 and 5:11). The only sexually explicit characteristic given great emphasis are the female breasts. The Song presents the kind of restrained eroticism found in the handicrafts of the Iron Age (as opposed to those of the Bronze Age) and in the love songs of Egypt (as opposed to those of the Sumerian sacred marriage); it concentrates more on the secondary sex characteristics (especially the breasts) than on the primary ones (see the commentary on 7:8 [9]).

[5:15c] This line sums up the appearance or vision (Exod. 24:17; Num. 12:8) of the beloved by comparing him to mighty Lebanon, whose highest peak reaches 10,000 feet (3,000 meters) (see the commentary on 4:8ab) and whose resin-rich forests, flowers, and fragrant plants make it seem a garden of the gods. See the commentary on 4:11c, where, as here, "Lebanon" serves as a closing superlative.

[5:15d] Just as the description of the feet as bases of gold in v. 15b refers back to the golden head in v. 11a, so the reference to "choice as the cedars" alludes to "distinguished among ten thousand" in v. 10b. The choiceness of the "cedars of Lebanon" (Ps. 29:5) is expressed in their designation as "trees of God" (the literal reading of the Hebrew in Ps. 80:10 [11]) and as "trees of Yahweh . . . that he planted" (Ps. 104:16).

[5:16ab] In these songs the description of the beloved normally ends with a decision to enjoy the splendors that have been portrayed (cf. 4:6, following 4:1-5; 4:16—5:1, following 4:12-15; 7:8 [9], following 7:6-7 [7-8]; etc.). In every case, the songs have a formal change at this point: a series of nominal clauses is followed by a verbal clause. In this poem, however, which has no verbs at all (see the introduction to the poem), the clauses in v. 16ab have the same function as the verbal clauses in the other examples. That connection is the only way to explain the return to the "palate" after the description has arrived at the feet and drawn a summary conclusion. Verse 16 is no longer "description"—no metaphors or similes occur here. The reference to the man's sweetness forms the basis for the statement that "he is altogether desirable" (cf. Ezek. 24:16). The mouth or the palate is given special emphasis because love play (also in the Song) normally begins with kissing (cf. 1:2a; 2:3d).

[5:16cd] This sentence is the last in the series of references back to the opening of the poem that began in v. 15b. These connections can be diagrammed as follows:

> *a* v. 8b O daughters of Jerusalem, . . . tell him . . .
> *b* v. 9ac What is your beloved more than . . .
> *c* v. 10b distinguished among . . .
> *d* v. 11a His head is the finest gold
> *d'* v. 15b [his feet are] gold
> *c'* v. 15d choice as . . .
> *b'* v. 16c This is my beloved
> *a'* v. 16d O daughters of Jerusalem

This literary style is called chiasm, after the Greek letter χ $\begin{smallmatrix} a & & b \\ & \chi & \\ b' & & a' \end{smallmatrix}$. A chiasm expresses correspondence: "just as . . . so . . ." In the center of this chiasm are the golden head and feet (*d, d'*). Like his head, so are his feet made of gold. From top to bottom he is magnificent, pure, costly, divine—like gold. He is superior to all others. In answer to the question from the daughters of Jerusalem, this magnificence is what is special about the beloved *(b, b')*. With this announcement the poem comes to a close—but only after having reached great heights of enthusiasm.

Confidence

Text

6:1 a Where has your beloved gone,
  b O fairest among women?
  c Which way has your beloved turned,
  d that we may seek him with you?
 2 a My beloved has gone down to his garden,
  b to the beds of [balsam],
  c to [graze] in the gardens,
  d and to gather [lotus blossoms].
 3 a I am my beloved's and my beloved is mine;
  b he [who grazes] among the [lotus blossoms].

Analysis

The question in 6:1 is constructed similarly to the one in 5:9. The first line of 5:9a ("What is your beloved more than another?"), which is repeated in 5:9c, is matched by the question of 6:1a ("Where has your beloved gone?"), repeated in 6:1c. In both cases, the address "O fairest among women" comes between the two repeated questions. Although in 5:9 the question closes with the surprised and ironic clause "that you thus adjure us," the ending in 6:1 is a statement by the daughters of Jerusalem expressing their willingness to help: "that we may seek him with you." This phrasing refers back to 5:6d: "I sought him, but did not find him." She did not find him because she did not know where he went—hence the question in 6:1 is a surprise, and even more so the answer in 6:2. Not only does she suddenly know where he went; she knows that he has gone nowhere else than to her, to his beloved—because, as 6:3 says, they belong together. Verse 6:3 is a literal repetition of 2:16, except that there the order is "he—I," rather than "I—he" as here (and in 7:10 [11]).

Several factors combine to make 6:1-3 seem to be a carefully constructed, rather deliberate continuation of 5:2-8 and 5:9-16: the parallelism of the questions in 6:1 and 5:9, the set piece in 6:3 (which is like a refrain), and the fragment in 6:2 (which also resembles a set piece); the fragment is strongly reminiscent of the garden metaphors in 4:12—5:1. But if one naively reads the whole construct of 5:2—6:3 as one unit, then the "daughters of Jerusalem," who in 5:9 were still skeptically asking "What is your beloved more than another beloved?" have been transformed by the enthusiastic descriptive song of 5:10-16 into people who want to help find him. Furthermore, the woman's answer to the question about the whereabouts of her beloved makes the whole painful episode of missed opportunity and frantic searching in 5:2-8 seem a mere misunderstanding; in the bright light of the solidarity formula in 6:3 it becomes a fleeting cloud that only briefly overshadows the couple's love. No matter how artificial the literary composition of 5:2—6:3 (of which 6:1-3 is the third and final section), the experience described there is genuine and common. Thus one can truly say that the "delightful confusion," which, according to Goethe in the "West-Eastern Divan," characterizes the Song, is not altogether unintentional and without artistic sense; it adds an enigmatic and inscrutable element, giving these few pages charm and personality.

Commentary

[6:1] For the meaning of the question in its context, see the preceding **Analysis** to this unit. It is asked by the daughters of Jerusalem. The content is reminiscent of the question that El, the father of the gods, instructs the goddess Anat to ask in Ugaritic mythology. After noting several signs that Baal is alive again, following his absence during the dry period, Anat asks the sun-goddess, Shapash, where Baal has gone; Shapash promises her that she will seek him.[1] But although this lover's search may first have found literary form in the cosmic realm of mythology, Cant. 6:1 has no trace of any such thing. On the address "O fairest among women," see the commentary on 5:9b.

[6:2] I see no reason to follow Pope here and seek the lover in the garden of the netherworld. The Ugaritic myth just cited does not look for a Baal who has been exiled to the world of the dead but one who has returned from it.

Just because the lover has "gone down" to the garden does not mean this is a *descensus ad inferos*, a "descent into hell." Up until the Greco-Roman era, settlements in Palestine/Israel were exclusively on the hills; thus the gardens were in the valleys, along the streams and beside the springs found there. If "going down" has any metaphorical connotation, it is most likely a reference to going in contrition and humility (Exod. 11:8). In the Hebrew text "my beloved" stands emphasized at the beginning of the sentence, contrary to all rules of word order. He himself will again come down to his garden, and neither the woman nor the

1. Baal and Mot 6.iii.10ff.; tr. Gibson, 78.

daughters of Jerusalem need to look for him. As in 4:16 and 5:1, "his garden" can only mean the woman herself, his beloved (who is speaking). On the beloved partner as a garden, see the commentary on 4:12.

In 6:2b the "beds of balsam" parallel the garden. The man's cheeks were compared with balsam plantings in 5:13a (see the commentary there). Once again, the same metaphor can serve to describe female charms in one place, male in another.

The "gardener" of 6:2ab is not suddenly transformed into a shepherd in 6:2c (contrary to Gerleman); the new image is that of a gazelle or a stag grazing in the gardens (regarding the plural, cf. the commentary on 4:15). The man is compared to a gazelle or stag in 2:9, 17 and 8:14. Cant. 4:5 applies the metaphor of the gazelle grazing among lotus blossoms to the woman's breasts. Figures 66, 88–90, and similar pictures show that the gazelle among lotuses, eating the lotus flowers, is a firmly established theme. This superlative symbol (see the commentary on 4:5) of mysterious liveliness, of an unconquerable will to live and a triumphant lust for life, shows why the speaker can be certain that her beloved will again come down to his garden. He will not be able to resist returning to graze, to gather the lotus flowers. Whether it is the "gardener" or the "gazelle" that picks or "gathers" the flowers makes no difference ("gather" is used in Ps. 104:28 of both humans and animals). What we do know is that the expression describes the most intense enjoyment (cf. Cant. 5:1), the highest pleasures (cf. 5:13; 7:2 [3]). The lotus flowers are by no means out of place here. As Eccl. 2:3ff. shows, following Egyptian custom, ponds were included in the gardens of Israel, and these were never without lotuses (cf. figs. 101–2).

[6:3] Her confident certainty is strengthened by the solidarity formula (see the commentary on 2:16). Indeed, the deepest basis for their solidarity appears to be the gazelle's (or the lover's) grazing among the lotuses and consuming the blossoms. From her he receives ever anew "love's sweet breath—a new-born life" (cf. 2:1-3); thus she can be as certain that he belongs to her as he is that she belongs to him.

Tremendum et fascinosum* II

Text

6:4 a You are beautiful as Tirzah, my love,
   b comely as Jerusalem,
   c [terrifying] as an army with banners.
5 a Turn away your eyes from me,
   b for they [make me crazy].
   c Your hair is like a flock of goats,
   d moving down the slopes of Gilead.
6 a Your teeth are like a flock of ewes,
   b that have come up from the washing;
   c all of them bear twins,
   d and not one among them is bereaved.
7 a [Like a slit] in a pomegranate
   b [is your palate(?) out from] behind your veil.]

Analysis

This poem leaves behind the sequence of three loosely connected poems about the man's disappearance or absence (5:2—6:3); now he addresses his beloved directly with an admiring description, confirming in her at the same time the confidence that was the theme of the poem in 6:1-3.

Six pronouns ("you" and "your") express direct address; three ("me" and "mine") demonstrate the speaker's own perplexity. The latter is expressed in the imperative of v. 5ab with an intensity that markedly breaks the calm rhythm of the nominal clauses that precede and follow it: "Turn away your eyes from me, / for they make me crazy!" The nominal sentences that describe the hair, teeth, and palate (or mouth) in vv. 5c-7b are, apart from a few small variations—identical to those in 4:1d-3d. Only the lines in 4:3ab are missing. But the similarities between 6:4-7 and

*Eng. trans. is "fear and fascination."

211

4:1-4 extend beyond the literal repetition of this passage. The first metaphor in the descriptive song of chap. 4 says: "Your glances [literally, eyes] are doves." The commentary there shows that the doves are to be understood as messengers of love. The request to turn away the eyes, formulated as an imperative in 6:5a, returns to the same phenomenon with even greater force (see the commentary). As the exegesis shows, the comparison of the woman to two royal cities in 6:4 belongs in the same conceptual field as the metaphor relating the neck to the tower of David in 4:4. The same juxtaposition of proud appearance and seductive glances is found also in Isa. 3:16. Nevertheless, even though it is evident that not only these two themes themselves but also their use in combination are traditional elements, Gerleman sees a tension "between the heroic character of the introduction (Cant. 6:4-5b) and the idyllic tone of the following detailed description." Rudolph, however, has noticed a chiasm in the text (regarding chiasms, cf. the commentary on 5:16cd) that clarifies the situation. The poem begins by praising the woman's comeliness and beauty (*a*)—even though, by comparing her to mighty cities, it induces a level of awe at the same time. This awe is expressed again in her glances, which both betray and arouse passion (*b*). The dark and unruly hair is similarly alarming (*b'*; see the commentary on 4:1c). But then the sheep—washed clean, gentle and fertile—bring one back to the friendly comeliness with which the poem began (*a'*). The chiastic arrangement of these two qualities emphasizes that the beloved woman is equally fascinating (*a, a'*) and—with her passion and her easily vulnerable pride—frightening (*b, b'*).

The poem closes with praise of her delicate palate (or open mouth). Many scholars have thought this ending abrupt, in comparison with that of 4:1-7, and have seen the whole piece as only a torso. But one should note that the praise of the man in 5:10-16b also closes with a reference to his palate or open mouth. I tried to show in the commentary on 5:16ab that this ending hinted at the expected transition from theory to praxis—a practice that would begin with kisses. The same intention could exist here, in which case the text would not be a torso but a carefully planned unit, albeit one in which the clarity of the plan has been somewhat obscured by the author's use of set pieces. But the original audience may not have found this abruptness to be a problem at all; for them the connotations of the various similes and metaphors may have been completely self-evident, strictly normed by established tradition.

Commentary

[6:4ab] The OT sometimes presents cities as virgins—for example, Jerusalem/ Zion (Isa. 37:22; 52:1-2) or Babylon (Isa. 47:1-2). Among other things, the title "virgin" carries with it the idea of being intact; this idea is especially clear when, for example, the virgin daughter Zion ridicules a retreating Sennacherib who has failed in his attempt to violate her (Isa. 37:22 = 2 Kgs. 19:21).

In the Hellenistic era, cities (or their fates) were personified by city goddesses. There are innumerable imitations of the statue of Tyche, personifying Antioch, created by the sculptor Eutychides in 300 B.C. The sculpture depicts a female figure, sitting atop a mountain, wearing a crown in the form of a city wall; at her feet is the Orontes River (fig. 122). The mountain reminds one of Cant. 4:8, as does the lion whose head appears alongside the head of a goddess, also wearing a crenellated crown, on a Roman coin from the year 67 B.C. (fig. 123).

The Song does not compare the city to a woman but—the other way around—the woman to a proud city or fortress, defined by its wall (Lev. 25:29). In Cant. 8:10, however, the young woman is less certain of her inviolability:

> I am a wall,
> and my breasts are like towers;
> yet in his eyes I am
> as one who has surrendered.

The verses comparing the woman's neck and nose with a tower (4:4; 7:4 [5]) express her pride more convincingly. But these similes would be incomprehensible without the fuller comparison of the woman to a city.

Walls and towers symbolize more than pride and inviolability, however; the OT also greatly admires their aesthetic qualities, which v. 4ab has in mind. The point of comparison between the woman and the city is their common "beauty." The city name Tirzah also occurs as the name of a woman (Num. 26:33; 27:1); it means "pleasing" or "lovely." The ancient Greek translation rendered Tirzah with εὐδοκία, "contentment, object of desire." But the result ("You are beautiful as contentment") sounds rather strange, especially because the name of a city, Jerusalem, stands parallel to "contentment." Yet using Tirzah as the name of a city also raises some questions. In Josh. 12:24 Tirzah appears as a Canaanite city, which is almost certainly identifiable with Tell el-Farah (North), 6 miles (10 km.) north of Shechem. Its reputation in the OT comes from the fact that it was used from the time of Jeroboam I through Omri (ca. 930–880 B.C.) as the residence of the kings of Israel, after they had declared their independence from the Davidic dynasty (1 Kgs. 14:17; 16:17-18, 23). Samaria became the capital of the Northern Kingdom about 880 and played that role for almost 160 years until Israel's fall. Why doesn't Cant. 6:4 parallel Jerusalem with Samaria instead of the relatively short-term capital of Tirzah? Did the song originate in the tenth/ninth century B.C. when Tirzah was the capital? But such a reference would be difficult to imagine during that period given the extremely tense relations between the two capitals (cf. 1 Kgs. 15:6, 16). With its temple to Baal (1 Kgs. 16:32), Samaria was from the beginning a symbol of apostasy (Hos. 13:16); at a later time, however, Tirzah—because of the meaning of its name and the transfiguring power of its early history—may have taken on a reputation matching that of the attractive capital of its sister kingdom (cf. the two sisters in Ezekiel 16 and 23).

Similar problems do not exist with Jerusalem, because this city

122.

123.

Fig. 122. The female figure sitting atop a mountain is characterized by her crenellated crown as a goddess representing the fortunes of a city—in this case, Antioch (cf. figs. 40 and 83–84 for forerunners of this type). The river, represented by the male bust at her feet, is the Orontes. (Roman copy of an original sculpture by Eutychides from ca. 300 B.C.; second century A.D.)

Fig. 123. This goddess on a Roman coin is adorned with a Roman crenellated crown; the accompanying lion identifies her as Cybele, the great mother of the gods. She is no doubt presented here as the guardian of Rome, because the holy stone symbolic of her presence had been brought to Rome in 204 B.C. (Coin of Plaetorius Cestianus; 67 B.C.)

was one of the most beautiful things known to the people of Judah. Psalm 48 celebrates Jerusalem as "beautiful in elevation, . . . the joy of all the earth"; visitors are urged to go all around Zion and to count its towers (Ps. 48:2, 12 [3, 13]). Ps. 50:2 praises Zion as "the perfection of beauty." Both psalms are apparently cited in Lam. 2:15:

> All who pass along the way . . .
>
> . . . .
>
> . . . wag their heads
>   at daughter Jerusalem;
> "Is this the city that was called
>   the perfection of beauty,
>   the joy of all the earth?"

[6:4c] Something that truly fascinates humans also engenders respect and awe—even anxiety; in the same way something that inspires respect and awe almost always fascinates humans. Both elements are contained in the picture of the city and its mighty walls and towers. Verse 4c now unfolds the other side, saying of the beloved that she is as "terrifying as an army with banners." The adjective translated "terrifying" occurs only one other time in the Hebrew Bible—in Hab. 1:7 it characterizes the chariot forces of the Babylonians. The noun from the same root is used to describe the "divine terror" by which Yahweh confuses his enemies in battle (Exod. 15:16; 23:27). The term translated "an army with banners" means an army organized into groups under banners. The word contains the same root used for the "banner" in Cant. 2:4. This hauntingly beautiful woman commands respect, for she exhibits the inner order, the strict discipline, of an army grouped around banners in battle formation; the loving admirer is rendered shy and reserved in her presence (see the commentary on 6:10).

[6:5ab] The three nominal clauses in 6:4 are now surprisingly and dramatically followed by a plea in imperative form: "Turn away your eyes from me." "Eyes" or "glances" appear regularly in the Song as messengers of love (in light of the dove metaphor; cf. 1:15; 4:1; 5:12). According to 4:9 a single glance can ravish a man's heart. The traditional combination (cf. Isa. 3:16) of the woman's proud bearing (evoked by the city similes in Cant. 6:4) and glances that betray her love and arouse her lover make the man's confusion complete. The root of the Hebrew word translated here "to make crazy" is related to the noun רהב, which designates a chaotic power that, according to Hebrew thought, called the ongoing existence of a sound and ordered world into question (Isa. 51:9; Ps. 89:10 [11]; Job 9:13; 26:12). Every great love is a new cosmos, whose birth is accompanied by life-threatening manifestations of chaos, for the birth of a new world calls into question that which already exists.

[6:5cd] The dangerous, even demonic aspect of the beloved is symbolized by the comparison of her hair to a herd of black goats in the wild forests of Gilead (see the commentary on 4:1ef).

[6:6] The comely and attractive aspect of the city (or the woman) is again brought to the fore by comparing her teeth to a festive procession of newly washed ewes (see the commentary on 4:2).

[6:7] The palate or open mouth, which is compared to a slit in a pomegranate, builds the transition from the man's admiring (but theoretical) observation of his equally terrifying and attracting beloved to his actual enjoyment of her gifts of love (see **Analysis** of this section and the commentary on 4:3cd). Their intimate encounter is an expression of love before which both fear and fascination fade into the background.

Like a Goddess

Text

6:8 a There are sixty queens
    b and eighty concubines,
    c and maidens without number.
  9 a My dove, my perfect one, is the only one,
    b the darling of her mother,
    c flawless to her that bore her.
    d The [daughters see] her and [call] her happy;
    e the queens and concubines [praise] her.
10 a "Who is this that looks [down] like the dawn,
    b fair as the ["white" (disk)],
    c [pure] as the [glowing fire],
    d [terrifying] as an army with banners?"

Analysis

A clear break occurs between the previous poem and this one. In 6:8-10 the woman is no longer addressed directly; instead her lover speaks about her in the third person. In terms of content, the language is no longer scenic, comparing the woman to cities and flocks; in this poem her value is measured on the scale of social categories. As in 3:6-11, the setting is the court, where relative social status is particularly important.

The twofold occurrence of the courtly pyramid of rank (queens, concubines, young ladies at court) divides the poem into two strophes of six lines each. The first strophe contrasts the many women at the court with the one preferred by the lover—a woman who was already recognized by her mother as very special. In the second strophe the woman appears at the top of the pyramid; those beneath look up to her as to a heavenly being.

Krinetzki calls 6:8-9 and 6:10 two independent poems. In that

217

case, the praise from the queens mentioned in v. 9e would relate back to the exclusivity of the monogamous relationship enjoyed by the woman but not by the queens themselves. But putting so much weight on the difference between objective status and subjective value is a modern, moralizing tendency, as Krinetzki's commentary shows when, contrary to the OT's own perspective (cf. 1 Sam. 1:4-8; Isa. 4:1), it claims that "a man can genuinely love only one woman without denigrating her to an object." This view might be more believable if the poem were placed in the mouth of a woman, but the speaker quite clearly seems to be the man. My interpretation is also based on the contrast between quality and quantity—not on the quality of the subjective relationship but on the quality of the woman herself; this quality is manifested in the high estimate of her not only by her lover (which is to be taken for granted) but also by her mother and by the whole court. The last would have been seen as particularly convincing.

Verse 10 can be seen as an originally independent song. But because it is now built into the context to provide a climax to the preceding material, it makes little sense to treat it in isolation—especially because the reasons advanced, say, by Rudolph for its separation are not convincing. He argues that, even though "flawless" in v. 9c and "pure" in v. 10c are the same word in Hebrew, they do not mean the same thing. Verse 9 emphasizes innocence, v. 10 beauty. But his distinction divides something that the people of the OT regarded as a unity.

The similarity between v. 10 and v. 4 may be the reason that 6:8-10 follows 6:4-9. This explanation would mean that 6:8-10 was already available to the redactor as a unit.

Commentary

[6:8] The three categories of women designate different ranks at the royal court. What is surprising in the list is the multitude of queens. Whether at the court of Egypt or Assyria or Persia, the king had only one "great royal wife" at a time, one "queen" (Esth. 2:17). The OT never speaks of a queen in relation to Judah and Israel but always only of the "king's wives" (2 Sam. 12:8; Jer. 38:23). These wives are called "princesses" in 1 Kgs. 11:3. One of them could have been the favorite wife (2 Chron. 11:21), but this status apparently never resulted in an official rank or title. The reference to "queens" in this verse may well be simply a rather lofty designation for those who otherwise are normally called the "king's wives" or "princesses."

In addition to these women with the full rights of wives, kings had concubines. The Hebrew word פִּילֶגֶשׁ seems to be related to the Greek παλλακίς and the Latin *pellex*, both of which have the same meaning.

The third category, the maidens, turn up in v. 9 as "daughters" (cf. Ps. 45:9 [10]). They are probably young girls at court, daughters who provide various services, gaining in turn an education that will enable them to marry well.

The numbers given here are most similar to those mentioned for the harem of King Rehoboam of Judah: 18 wives and 60 concubines (2

Chron. 11:21). Each wife and concubine would have had a number of court maidens at her disposal.

The much larger harem of Solomon—700 wives and 300 concubines (1 Kgs. 11:3)—was no doubt primarily a diplomatic instrument of the first order; it probably included daughters of all the princes and kings with whom he had diplomatic relations. In addition, the gigantic harem also served to illustrate Solomon's legendary splendor. The "queens" represent legitimately obtained rank and honor, the concubines the prerogatives gained by individual lovemaking skills and household proficiency (cf. 2 Sam. 15:16), and the maidens the beauty of youth.

I think Rudolph is in error when, following Delitzsch, he calls this group a "stable of wenches" (*Weiberstall*). Unlike Cant. 2:1-3, 6:8-10 does not intend to extol the beloved (a lotus flower) at the expense of other women (brambles). Some OT voices are raised against an overly large royal harem. The basis for this polemic is the fear of foreign religious influence (Deut. 17:17; 1 Kgs. 11:1-10). But the harem described here is quite modest in comparison with the thousand foreign wives of Solomon. Upgrading the "king's wives" to "queens" argues against a negative interpretation. Above all, it would hardly do honor to the beloved to be praised by a "stable of wenches." The label is rather an example of a puritanism totally foreign to the Song.

[6:9a-c] Here the lover compares his beloved, his dove, his perfect one (cf. the commentary on 5:2cd) to all the resplendent ranks of women at the court. In the structure of the Hebrew text, this 60 to 1 ratio retards the dramatic action. It reminds the reader of the parable told to David by the prophet Nathan: "The rich man had very many flocks and herds; but the poor man had nothing but one little ewe lamb, which he had bought" (2 Sam. 12:2-3). In the parable too the large number of flocks represents the royal harem; the one lamb is the wife of Uriah the Hittite.

Just as the value of the little lamb in the parable is enhanced by the love with which it was raised by its owner, so here the significance of the beloved is enhanced by the standing she enjoys with her mother. The Hebrew text does not make clear whether she is celebrated as her mother's only daughter in fact or as the only one who mattered—recall, for example, how old Jacob had eyes only for Joseph (Gen. 37:3-4). The one who has known her from birth regards her as flawless—almost like an immaculate conception, with purity and superiority from the very beginning. (On the role of the mother in the Song, see also the commentary on 3:4 and 11.) This clear priority within the family circle is, however—as in the case of Joseph—not merely a subjective preference but a preeminence that holds up to public scrutiny.

[6:9de] The royal household demonstrates her public preeminence. It is appropriate that recognition comes first from the lowest rank. It is less difficult for them than for those higher in the establishment to praise someone else (cf. Gen. 30:13). The lowest rank is called "daughters" here (cf. Ps. 45:9 [10]), not "maidens" as in v. 9c. But even the higher-ranking ladies, the queens and concubines, can not help being impressed. The word used for their praise, הלל, is known primarily from the cultic praise of God (Hallelujah!). It refers originally to a high-pitched tone that is converted to a rousing rhythmic trill by lightly beating on the chest, throat, or mouth. In the OT it often stands for enthusiastic praise, like the description of Sarai's beauty by pharaoh's courtiers (Gen. 12:15). In a properly ordered world, not only the majesty of God but also the beauty of women is extolled (cf. Ps. 78:63).

[6:10] This praise is illustrated by a brief song that opens with a cry of amazement: "Who is this?" (cf. Cant 3:6-8). The context puts it in the mouth of the queens, thereby giving the object of their praise an absolute, superlative status, alone atop the pyramid of maidens, concubines, and queens. The Hebrew word translated here "look down" is used especially of God, looking down from heaven (Deut. 26:15; Ps. 14:2; 85:11 [12]; 102:19 [20]; Lam. 3:50). The downward-looking woman is first compared to the dawn—a divine being in Canaanite mythology. OT poetry still has traces of this connection—for example, when it speaks of dawn's eyelids (Job 3:9; 41:18 [10]) or wings (Ps. 139:9) or awakening (Ps. 57:8 [9]; 108:2 [3]). In the ancient Near East, moon and sun were manifestations of the highest deities. Despite all the prophetic instruction, even in the post-exilic period the people of the OT had to make a supreme effort to free themselves from the suggestive power of such manifestations (cf., e.g., Job 31:26-28).

This text does not give sun and moon their usual names but rather poetic paraphrases. Like frankincense (לבונה) and the mountains of Lebanon (לבנון), the full moon (לבנה) is paraphrased by a variant of "white" (masc., לבן; fem., לבנה; cf. Isa. 24:23; 30:26). The noonday sun appears as a glowing fire that no one can escape (cf. Ps. 19:6 [7]). The "glowing fire," which purifies and refines, is itself described here as "pure" (ברה). The same word was already used in v. 9c: "flawless [ברה] to her that bore her." What was declared true there in the realm of human affairs is now given a cosmic dimension. In the face of this limitless radiance, there is nothing surprising about the next statement with its catchword "terrifying." Although the context in 6:4c did not make fully clear what was meant by the "army with banners," here, in the context of the sun and moon, the army can only be the "host of heaven," the world of the stars (cf. the stereotypical expression "sun, moon, and host of heaven" in Deut. 17:3; Jer. 8:2; etc.). Nowhere is the circle of stars more "terrifying" in the cosmic realm than when it surrounds Ishtar, the mistress of heaven, wearing her sword and accompanied by the sun and moon. She is portrayed on innumerable cylinder seals and stamp seals of the eighth/seventh century B.C., appearing along with the sun (which is carried by a being who is part human, part animal) and the moon (fig. 124), or alone (fig. 125) before a male or female admirer. The author of this poem may have had this picture of the goddess of heaven in mind as he described the different ranks of the women at court looking up in admiration at his beloved, the queen of queens.

124.

125.

Fig. 124. The warlike Ishtar, surrounded by a wreath of stars, appears to an admirer; she has a sword at her side and a goat as her symbolic animal (cf. figs. 50, 95). On the top edge (*from right to left*) can be seen a horned cap (a symbol), the Pleiades (Seven Sisters), the moon, the heaven and sun(?) carried by a figure who is part human, part scorpion, and the symbols of Marduk and Nabu above a dragon. (Neo-Assyrian cylinder seal; eighth century B.C.)

Fig. 125. Ishtar surrounded by the same symbols as in fig. 124 (except the horned cap and the goat) plus a few more (crescent moon on a stand, the lightning of the weather-god, two fish, etc.; the goat at her feet is replaced by a pomegranate). (Neo-Assyrian cylinder seal; eighth century B.C.)

Patient/Impatient Checking

Text

11 a I went down to the nut orchard,
   b to look at the [shoots by the stream],
   c to see whether the vines had budded,
   d whether the pomegranates were in bloom.

Analysis

After the song of admiration in 6:8-10, which was kept strictly in the third person, the section beginning with v. 11 again finds the singer or poet speaking of himself in the first person. The content of this brief song, with its metaphors of garden and field, also plainly differs from the world of courtly ranks in 6:8-10. I can find no clear reason for the insertion of the little song at this point. Might it, like 6:2, provide a counterpoint to the urban (courtly) world?

Commentary

[6:11a] The speaker is probably the young man, because the garden metaphor is used stereotypically of the woman (six times in 4:12—5:1 alone; but cf. also 1:6 and 2:15). On going down to the "garden," see the commentary on 6:2a. Here it is not merely a garden but, analogous to the "pomegranate park" in 4:13, a "nut orchard." This is the only place in the Hebrew Bible that mentions the walnut tree (*Juglans regia* L.). In contrast to the several Palestinian towns that include רמון, "pomegranate," as part of their name, not one uses אגוז, "walnut (tree)." Apart from Galilee, Israel is too hot for the walnut. Its habitat is farther north. In the post-biblical period of early Judaism, walnuts were still normally imported.[1]

---

1. Löw, *Die Flora der Juden,* 2:31.

The walnut trees may be like the foreign spices and aromatic plants of 4:13-14, giving the garden an exotic note.

6:11b] The purpose of going down is to "look"; the construction has the sense of "checking to see" or of a "joyful contemplation." The word translated "shoots" (אבי) occurs otherwise only in Job 8:12, where it refers to the rapidly growing shoots of a marsh plant. The Akkadian equivalent *inbu* means "fruit, generative power [or 'force']" (cf. Cant. 2:3; Dan. 4:11). Like the nut orchard, the stream evokes a shady, secret area, swelling with life. The Hebrew נחל, "stream," corresponds to the Arabic *wadi*. Both words designate the usually dry streambeds of Palestine/Israel. But it is these areas that first turn green when the early rains fall. In Ugaritic mythology, El, the father of the gods, dreams that the heavens rain oil and the wadis (*nchlm*) flow with honey. These phenomena tell him that Baal, the lord of the earth and of fertility, is again alive and at work.[2] The gardens and wadis, where the return of Baal was first evident, were favorite cultic spots for this god and for deities related to him, like Adonis (cf. Isa. 1:29; 57:3-10; Jer. 2:23). According to an interesting report, the small village of Aphekah near the source of the Adonis River in Lebanon was (still?) surrounded by majestic walnut trees in the nineteenth century.[3] In the context of the Song, however, the interest is not in the return of the fertility-god but in the awakening of sexual powers and the desire for erotic pleasures in the human partner.

[6:11cd] With the mention of the vine, the poet takes up a favorite image of the woman (cf. Ps. 128:3); her breasts are likened to clusters of grapes on the vine (cf. Cant. 7:8 [9]). The metaphor comparing the awakening capacity for love to the budding vine is parallel to the blooming pomegranate trees of 7:12 (13). Like the grapes, the pomegranates also appear as metaphors for the breasts (see the commentary on 4:3cd and 4:16cd). The lack of breasts symbolizes immaturity (cf. 8:8); their appearance, along with the growth of pubic hair, announces that the time for love has arrived (Ezek. 16:7-8). (For blooming pomegranate trees in connection with love apples and lotus flowers, see fig. 102.)

Purpose and Thrust

The patient/impatient checking on whether the time for love has awakened is the theme of a whole series of poems in the Song. It is another example of the sense of partnership and the consideration for the other that characterize the encounter of the sexes in the whole Song. In comparison to the metaphor of the gardener checking on the condition of the garden and doing what is required for it, caring for the blossoms and

2. Baal and Mot 6.iii.4–21; tr. Gibson, 77–78.
3. J. G. Frazer, *The Golden Bough: A Study in Magic and Religion,* part 4, vol. 1, *Adonis, Attis, Osiris: Studies in the History of Oriental Religion,* 3d ed. (London: Macmillan, 1935) 28.

picking the ripe fruit, the more violent metaphor of the soldier storming the fortress recedes into the background (cf. 8:8-10). This caring contact may have its institutional basis in the fact that, before their sexual maturation, young girls were often promised in marriage and engaged to an older cousin (cf. 1:13 on דוד).

Shulammite Is
Too Good for That!

Text

6:12 a   Before I was aware, my [desire] set me
     b   in [the chariots of Amminadib].
13 (7:1) a   Return, return, O Shulammite!
     b   Return, return, that we may look upon you.
     c   Why should you look upon [. . .] Shulammite,
     d   as upon a dance before two armies?

Analysis

Verse 12 seems to many exegetes to be the most difficult in the Song. Krinetzki declines to translate or comment on it at all. Rudolph changes ("corrects") the Hebrew text so it is no longer recognizable. The interpretation presented here follows Gerleman and attempts as fully as possible to understand the Hebrew text as it stands. In the face of the fragmentary character of the text, however, the interpretation is particularly speculative.

Because the first-person narrative of v. 11 occurs again in v. 12, many commentators have seen the two verses as a unit (Gerleman, Krinetzki, Rudolph). But this view overlooks the probability that the speaker in v. 11 is a man, in v. 12 a woman. The motifs suggest that v. 11 is a variation of a favorite theme in the Song, the gardener parody. Verse 12, however, transposes one to the courtly or military world, already encountered in 1:2-4; 1:9-12; 3:6-11; 6:8-10. The most important key words for that interpretation are "armies" and "chariots" (the use of chariots distinguished the most honored soldiers and the several heirs apparent—not so much the king—from the common people; cf. Gen. 41:43; 46:29; 2 Sam. 15:1). In my opinion, the unity of Cant. 6:12 and 13

225

Fig. 126. A high Egyptian official returns from being honored by the king. He stands in his chariot next to the driver; five footmen accompany him. Above the heads of the horses, a man bows submissively to the ground; the women (*left*) enthusiastically welcome the honoree with tambourines, the children with high-spirited dancing. A schoolmaster seems to need a rod to keep his pupils from joining in the festivities (*lower right*). (Painting on the tomb of Neferhotep, West Thebes, no. 49; ca. 1320 B.C.)

(7:1) is just as obvious as the distinction between vv. 11 and 12. Scholars normally see 6:13 (7:1) as the introduction to the descriptive song in 7:1-5 (2-6). But it would be unusual to introduce a descriptive song with this brief disputation. It fits quite well in the world of frivolous courtiers evoked by the term "chariots." Moreover, vv. 12 and 13 (7:1) are connected by the fact that these are the only two verses in the entire Song (apart from those mentioning Solomon—1:1, 5; 3:7, 9, 11; 8:11-12) in which people appear with given names (Amminadib, Shulammite). It is not clear to me why the song was inserted at this point. Perhaps the mention of the "noble daughter" (בת-נדיב) in 7:1 (2) was the occasion for the later addition of this song mentioning Amminadib (which means "my uncle is noble").

Commentary

[6:12] The semiconscious state between sleep and waking was described in 5:2 ("I am already asleep, but my heart is still awake"). A similar intermediate state appears in this verse. The difference is that this time it is the woman's clarity of thought, the understanding of the heart (Deut. 29:4 [3]), that is not (fully) present; instead the speaker is totally controlled by her נפש, by "desire, longing, and passion" (cf. **Analysis** section of Cant. 3:1-5). This desire transports her to the "chariots of Amminadib." The handsome Absalom begins his (unsuccessful) attempt to take the throne by acquiring chariots, horses, and hangers-on (2 Sam. 15:1). A chariot was very expensive, a luxury item (1 Kgs. 10:29). Egyptian tomb paintings only rarely show high officials riding in a chariot. When this scene does occur in figure 126 it produces an infectious enthusiasm among the onlookers. In this poem the plural form "chariots" in v. 12b makes the appearance all the more impressive.

"Amminadib" is a variant of the name Amminadab which occurs about ten times in the OT. It never applies to a particularly important person or one who would be relevant to the themes of the Song. Pope, Rudolph, and others therefore reject the obvious interpretation of the term as a personal name and "correct" the text as they see fit. But such corrections have no binding force. The ancient Greek version and Jerome's Latin translation already saw a personal name here. This reading is supported by the fact that the woman in v. 13 (7:1) is uniquely designated not with a title like "sister," "love," or "beloved" but as "Shulammite."

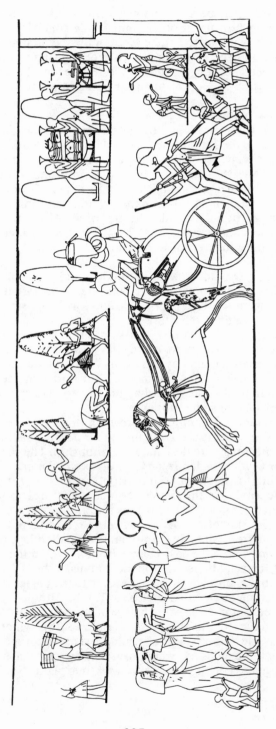

126.

Figures given personal names without having been previously introduced also turn up in other comparable collections of love songs. Gerleman rightly points to Prince Mehi in the Egyptian love songs, who, like Amminadib here, turns up in a chariot, causing confusion.[1] Proper names that mean nothing to modern Western readers but that had meaning for the original hearers also appear in modern Palestinian Arab love songs.

Instead of the usual form of the name, Amminadab, the poet chooses a variation, Amminadib; this change probably means the name itself has been given significance, as in the story of Ruth, where the two men who die early are called Mahlon, "disease," and Chilion, "consumption," while the daughters-in-law, appropriate to their character, are Orpah, "(stiff-)necked," and Ruth, "refreshment." Amminadib means "my uncle is a nobleman." That name could label Amminadib as something of a braggart, a dandy like the ambitious Absalom (2 Sam. 14:25) with his chariots and hangers-on (2 Sam. 15:1), a charmer who inflamed the desire of the daughters of Jerusalem.

[6:13ab (7:1ab)] One must certainly understand these lines as the cries that greet this young woman whose fancy has transported her into these dazzling, arrogant (cf. 1 Kgs. 12:8-11), and forbidden surroundings. The call to "return" cannot refer to a "turn" in a dance, even though many scholars interpret it in this way. It assumes that someone who had been oriented toward those who are calling has now turned away. This turning or alienation is anticipated by the words "Before I was aware, my desire set me in the chariots of Amminadib." But now that she is aware, she turns away. It is also possible that the cry to return comes from her relatives (cousins) or some similar group.

"Shulammite" cannot be a regular proper name, because it is accompanied by the article. Even more than "Amminadib," it is a name used for its meaning or to designate a relationship. The consonants of the Hebrew word evoke the feminine form of שלמה, "Solomon"—שלמית, "the one belonging to Solomon." Understood in this way, the name characterizes the woman as the female counterpart to the legendary Solomon of the Song (cf. 3:7; 8:11). שלמית means the one who is "well," "whole," or "at peace." But the term's vowels are more reminiscent of the Shunammite, "the one from Shunem." Shunem is a small village (now known in Arabic as *sulam*; note the easy change from *n* to *l*) on the eastern edge of the Plain of Jezreel. Shunem was made famous in the OT by the beautiful Abishag, who was brought from that village to the palace to warm David, who had become cold with age (1 Kgs. 1:3-4). Although David had not slept with her, Solomon saw his half brother Adonijah's request for her hand as a claim to the throne (1 Kgs. 2:13-25), which request cost Adonijah his life. "Shunammite" could be a name for a beautiful young woman from the country who unsuspectingly became caught up in courtly intrigues. The third common way to explain "Shulammite" is to

1. Cf. Fox, 64–66.

understand it as a nickname for Ishtar, the goddess of war and love, or for Anat. It is best to regard both "Shulammite" and "Amminadib" as peculiarities of ancient Israelite love poetry whose significance is no longer accessible.

[6:13cd (7:1cd)] These lines indignantly reject the request to make Shulammite the object of voyeurism. It is not clear who voices this indignation. Is it the woman herself, the poet, or the stereotypical daughters of Jerusalem? The unseemly character of the request is expressed by the comparison to dancing between two armies. The soldiers' words brutally reduce the woman to a mere sex object (cf. Judg. 5:30). Decisive battles were preceded by all kinds of crude games, fights, and jokes between the hostile armies (cf. 2 Sam. 2:14-16). If the voices in v. 13ab (7:1ab) are the cousins of Shulammite or a similar group (as suggested there), then they would make up one of the "armies," whereas the other would be made up of Amminadib and his people.

The Prince's Daughter
(Descriptive Song III)

Text

7:1 (2) a How [beautiful] are your feet
     b in sandals, O [prince's daughter]!
     c Your rounded thighs are like jewels,
     d the work of a master hand.
  2 (3) a Your navel [(your vulva)] is a rounded bowl;
     b [may it never lack] mixed wine.
     c Your belly is a heap of wheat,
     d encircled with [lotuses].
  3 (4) a Your two breasts are like two fawns,
     b twins of a gazelle.
  4 (5) a Your neck is like an ivory tower.
     b Your eyes are pools in Heshbon,
     c by the ["Daughter of Many"] Gate.
     d Your nose is like a tower of Lebanon,
     e overlooking Damascus.
  5 (6) a Your head crowns you like Carmel
     b and your flowing locks are like purple;
     c a king is held captive in the tresses.

Analysis

Like other songs of description and admiration (regarding these genres, see pp. 18–22), this one begins in 7:1 (2) with the cry, "How beautiful are . . ." (cf. Ps. 84:1 [2]; 133:1; Cant. 7:6 [7]). The other two extended songs of similar type describe the woman from her head to her breasts (4:1-7) or the man from his head to his feet (5:9-16); this one begins with the feet and works up to the head. Whether from head to foot (2 Sam. 14:25) or from foot to head (Isa. 1:6), the purpose of listing the parts is always to

230

describe the whole; this purpose is made clear in 5:9-16 which describes both head (v. 11) and feet (v. 15) as gold—in other words, the man is completely gold! The song here has similar parameters: the feet of the beloved are those of a prince's daughter (v. 2), and a king is held captive in her hair (v. 6). Thus the whole song has a queenly setting.

The final clause about the captive king departs from pure description. As in other similar songs, the ending depicts the effect on the partner and the transition from observation to praxis (4:6; 5:16ab). Appropriate to the style of descriptive songs, 7:1-5 (2-6) is made up of nominal clauses (cf. the introduction to 4:1-7). As in 4:1-7, similes dominate over metaphors (in the ratio 6:3). The prevalence of similes ("your rounded thighs are like jewels") over the harder metaphors ("your navel is a rounded bowl") gives a tentative, softer character to the two songs about the woman, which character is lacking in the description of the man in 5:9-16, where metaphors dominate (the ratio is 7:5). The song in 7:1-5 (2-6) is the tighter and clearer of the two descriptive songs about the woman because its similes and metaphors are much less frequently supplemented by additions: eleven such additions in 4:1-7 but only five in 7:1-5 (2-6). This impression is strengthened by the content; the animal and plant comparisons of 4:1-7 recede in 7:1-5 (2-6) in favor of comparisons with works of art and architecture and the reference to costly materials (ivory, purple). Even though 7:1-5[2-6], in contrast to 4:1-7, speaks of sex and the womb, the poem has a cooler and more aristocratic effect; it describes not so much a goddess of love and life (4:1-7) as a perfect prince's daughter, proud and reserved.

Commentary

[7:1ab (2ab)] Beginning with the feet focuses the eyes of the observer on the feet of the prince's daughter. Western readers have often been surprised that sandals were thought to make the feet particularly beautiful. But, as figure 116 shows, rural Judean women normally went barefoot. Sandals are seen as decorative items in Ezek. 16:10 and especially in Jdt. 10:4; 16:9. But, along with their aesthetic value, sandals have a juridical value that one dare not overlook. Sandals permit a firm step, in both the literal and figurative sense. In some situations the loosening and removal of sandals expresses a waiver of rights (Ruth 4:7; Deut. 25:5-10). A barefoot person is a weakling (ibid.); to go barefoot indicates mourning (2 Sam. 15:30), poverty (Jer. 2:25), and subjugation (Isa. 20:2-4). This characterization would hardly be fitting for one who is addressed as "prince's daughter."

The word translated "prince" means literally one who is "liberal" or "generous." The clearest sign of nobility in the OT is the opportunity and the ability to be generous (cf. Job 29). Generosity gives social standing and the resultant self-confidence. An ancient Egyptian love poem also sings of the woman's lovely striding feet.[1]

---

1. Papyrus Chester Beatty I, group A, no. 31; cf. Fox, 52.

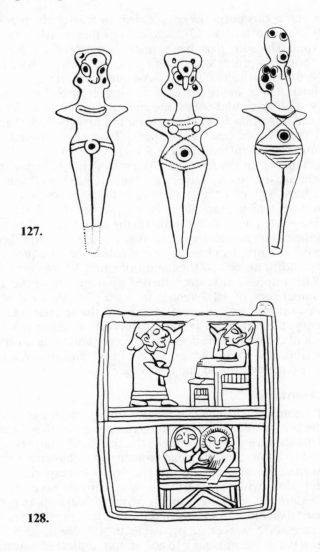

127.

128.

Fig. 127. The bowl-shaped depression in these strongly schematic figures of a Syrian goddess, naked except for her abundant jewelry, sometimes represents the navel (*far right*); but sometimes it is so low that it is better interpreted as the vulva (*far left*). On the interchangeability of navel and vulva, see also figs. 104–7. (Terra-cotta figures; the two to the left are from Hamath; the origin of the one to the right is unknown; thirteenth/ twelfth century B.C.)

Fig. 128. In the upper section a man seated on a throne and a standing woman toast one another from flat bowls (cf. figs. 39–40 and 64); in the lower section a man and woman are seen on a bed (or in a window?); the man presses the woman's breast. (Small soapstone chest, probably from northern Syria; eighth century B.C.)

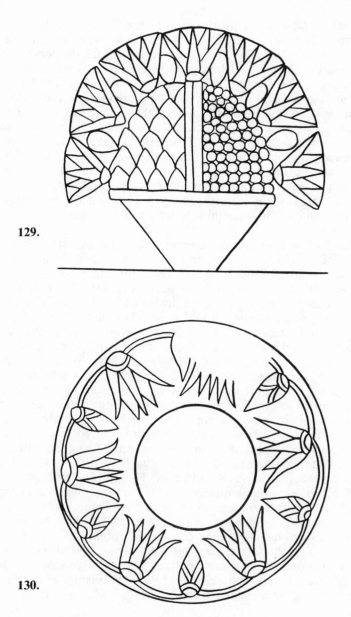

129.

130.

Fig. 129. A bowl filled with love apples(?) and other small fruits is framed with lotus blossoms. (Section of a relief in the tomb of Ramose, West Thebes, no. 55; ca. 1340 B.C.)

Fig. 130. Small stoneware bowl, whose inner cavity is wreathed by lotus garlands. (From an antiquities dealer in Israel; eighth/seventh century B.C.)

233

[7:1cd (2cd)] "Thigh" is frequently used in the OT as a euphemism for "sex organ" (Gen. 46:26; Exod. 1:5—cf. the Hebrew text), as in the expression "under the thigh." In an archaic oath ritual, the person taking the oath touches the one to whom he is swearing "under the thigh" (cf. Gen. 24:2, 9; 47:29). But in this verse the "thighs" do not have this archaic sacral sense. This reference is much more profane; the sculptured quality of the subtle curves of the inner thighs, the buttocks, and the hips are extolled as the work of a master hand. The term used here for "jewels" is elsewhere associated with "ring" (Hos. 2:13 [15]; Prov. 25:12); hence it may designate the other primary form of jewelry, the chain, which is frequently worn around the hips (cf. fig. 127). Artists and artisans belonged to the highest level of society (Jer. 52:15, 24-25; cf. Prov. 8:30). Among the artists, the goldsmiths enjoyed a particularly high rank because of the value of the material with which they worked.

[7:2ab (3ab)] These lines surprise one by speaking of the navel. Pope and Rudolph find this term inappropriate here, especially compared to a round bowl; thus they translate the Hebrew term "vulva" or "pubic area." But the only other place the Hebrew word occurs (Ezek. 16:4), its only possible meaning is "navel" or "umbilical cord." Krinetzki believes "navel" is a *pars pro toto* designation for the whole female genital region. With Gerleman he sees the basis for the bowl comparison in the way the navel is emphasized in ancient Egyptian female figures. The navel is even more prominently featured in the strongly schematic Syrian terra-cottas (fig. 127; cf. fig. 26) than in any of the Egyptian figures. These terra-cottas have also been found in Israel; they were produced in many variations during the entire second millennium, some into the first millennium as well. The figures are naked except for a few pieces of jewelry. On some pieces the small round bowl on the stomach is placed so unmistakably above the pubic triangle that it can represent only the navel. With others it is so low that it could be taken for the vulva. See figures 104 and 106 for the interchangeability of navel and vulva. The unusual wish added in v. 2b (3b) ("may it never lack mixed wine") is an unambiguous metaphor requiring "navel" to be understood here as a euphemism for vulva. The Old Babylonian terra-cottas in figures 111 and 112 show that from the woman's perspective intercourse can be interpreted as drinking. The Sumerian texts for the sacred marriage regularly praise the (wet) vulva as an intoxicating drink for the male partner.[2] Figure 128 associates drinking together from bowls with a clearly erotic relationship, where the man is shown pressing the woman's breast (cf. figs. 39, 40, and 64).

[7:2cd (3cd)] The part of the body praised next is not simply the abdomen in general but the belly (understood as the womb; cf. Judg. 13:5, 7). This part would call to mind above all fertility and nourishment. Wheat was the most important foodstuff in Israel (Deut. 8:8; Ps. 81:16 [17]; 147:14).

2. See Kramer, *Sacred Marriage*, 101.

Wheat and wine could in themselves symbolize a festive diet (Deut. 32:14). Eating naturally follows the drinking of v. 2b (3b). See the commentary on 5:1 on the lovers' eating and drinking. The soft, rounded form of the heap of wheat and its yellowish-brown color—the ideal color of female skin in Egyptian paintings—probably have only secondary significance next to its connotations of eating. This point is confirmed by the phrase "encircled with lotuses." The piles of wheat in the field were guarded (Ruth 3:7) and, as protection against thieves, surrounded with thorn hedges. In Egypt it was a carefully maintained custom to decorate foodstuffs of all kinds with lotus flowers. A bowl filled with fruits and berries pictured in the tomb of Ramose is framed by lotus flowers (fig. 129). Borrowing from Egyptian models, Phoenician artisans produced all kinds of bowls whose inner and outer surfaces were decorated with lotus garlands (fig. 130). The lotus blossoms illustrate the freshness and regenerative powers of the ointments, beverages, and foods served in these bowls (see the commentary on 2:1-2, 16; 4:5). The belly or womb of the beloved produces not only children but also freshness and new life for her lover.

[7:3 (4)] The comparison of the woman's breasts to young gazelles also alludes to her playful, lively, life-giving power. See the detailed comments on 4:5.

[7:4a (5a)] The earlier description of her feet and thighs emphasized the determination and the value of this prince's daughter; now the candid description of her vulva, her belly, and her breasts shows her ability to give new life to the one with whom she shares intimacy. Verse 4a (5a) evokes once more the aloof elegance emphasized at the beginning. When Hebrew uses "neck" metaphorically, the term expresses "pride." Similarly, towers symbolize the self-confident military preparedness of a city or fortress (on all this imagery, see the commentary on 4:4). The more detailed description of the tower as an "ivory tower" (with the article) compels one to think of a particular tower. As in the case of the ivory throne of Solomon (1 Kgs. 10:18), the ivory beds and houses of Samaria (Amos 3:15; 6:4; 1 Kgs. 22:39), and the ivory palaces of Ps. 45:8 (9), the "ivory tower" must have been a structure in which some part—perhaps a tower room—was decorated with carved ivory tiles. Such reliefs have been found in large numbers at several archaeological digs (see the commentary on 3:10d). The off-white color of the precious and artistically fashioned material gave the tower a luxurious luster, producing an almost magical fascination—just like the proudly outstretched neck of the woman.

[7:4bc (5bc)] Here a pool metaphor replaces the customary comparison of the eyes with doves (1:15; 4:1; 5:12). This image matches the general tendency of the poem to prefer comparisons from the cultural realm—indeed, from princely culture. In the ancient Near East, ponds were a favorite royal project (cf. Eccl. 2:6). Pharaoh Amenhotep III (fourteenth century B.C.) celebrated such an undertaking with a commemorative scarab (cf. the Birket es-Sultan, the "pool of the sultan," in Jerusalem).

I have already noted (see the commentary on 1:15) that the metaphorical sense of "eyes" in Hebrew is "gleaming." Hebrew describes a spring as "a gleaming of waters." But in comparison with one small sparkling spring, the gleaming surfaces of two entire pools represents a massive intensification.

Rather than just any pools, the text speaks of the "pools in Heshbon." Ancient poetry prefers to make comparisons with concrete realities, such as the "tents of Kedar" (1:5), the "henna blossoms from the vineyards of En-gedi" (1:14), or the "flock of goats moving down the slopes of Gilead" (4:1); then the whole historical and geographical charm of a particular region lends its meaning to the metaphor. There were probably two pools at the gate of Heshbon. This city, on the eastern fringe of the Transjordan, had an exotic flavor for Jerusalem, especially because it was the capital of a mysterious early kingdom (Num. 21:26ff.). The gate near the pools was called "Daughter of Many," evoking the crowds of people who came from the steppes (cf. Num. 21:16-18, 23, 25) to drink from the pools or to wash and refresh themselves in them. The beloved's eyes have the same effect on the crowds and especially on her lover.

[7:4de (5de)] In rapid tempo, vv. 3-4 (4-5) conjure up pictures that are fascinating and attractive yet maintain respect and distance. The agile fawns of the gazelle are followed by the ivory tower, the gleaming pools by the tower on the highest mountains known to the Hebrews. The comparison of the nose to a tower has nothing to do with a sharply projecting Semitic nose (Krinetzki), because this simile has as little to do with external form as the comparison of the neck with a tower (4:4; 7:4a [5a]). As any lexicon shows, the primary connotation of the Hebrew אף, "nose," is "snorting, animosity, anger." Although the woman's friendly eyes charm and refresh every passerby like royal pools, anyone who arouses her displeasure must reckon with insurmountable resistance. Like the city (6:4), the tower is a symbol of proud military preparedness. Because this tower stands atop the highest mountain (see the commentary on 4:8), it also represents distance and oversight. The text explicitly emphasizes the latter: "overlooking Damascus." Damascus is far from Jerusalem, and only the mightiest of Israel's kings were able to extend their influence as far as that city (2 Sam. 8:5; 2 Kgs. 14:28; 1 Macc. 12:32).

[7:5a (6a)] With its reference to a head "like Carmel," this line further intensifies the notion of dominating height. To be sure, at 1,700 feet (552 meters), Mt. Carmel is of only modest height in comparison with the mountains of Lebanon; but ancient Israel was scarcely able to measure the absolute height of an elevation. The Carmel ridge, which extends 12 miles (20 km.) from the Mediterranean Sea (cf. Amos 9:3) to the Plain of Jezreel, rises abruptly to 1,640 feet (500 meters) above sea level; it has an imposing and dominating effect and can easily appear equivalent to the

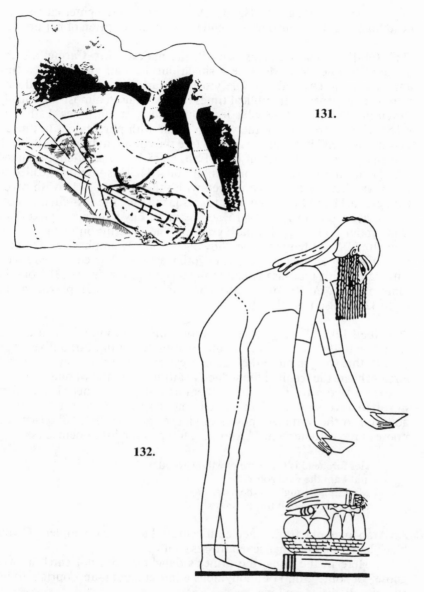

131.

132.

Fig. 131. This girl in a transparent robe is serving drinks at a banquet; the sophisticated artist has arranged the tresses of her hair in such a way as to hide part of her face. (Painting in the tomb of Rekh-mi-Re, West Thebes, no. 100; ca. 1425 B.C.)

Fig. 132. A reclining singer supports her head with her left hand; her right hand rests on a lute. The long tresses of her hair (or wig?) are arranged so they fall far beyond her shoulders on each side. (Sketch on a limestone shard from Deir el-Medina; twelfth century B.C.)

mighty Lebanon range (cf. Isa. 35:2). The prince's daughter carries her head high. But the song does not end with this description of her pride.

[7:5b (6b)] The coastal areas beneath the majestic Mt. Carmel are the home of purple cloth. Because a single purple snail yields only a tiny amount of the coveted dye, the violet or dark-red textiles it produced were very expensive. In biblical times they were used almost exclusively for cultic (Exod. 25:4—39:29; Jer. 10:9) and royal purposes (Esth. 1:6; 8:15). The comparison of the woman's hair with purple does not mean that it was "red" but that it was vital (see the commentary on 5:10), dark and gleaming. In the ancient Near East, black hair was often associated with great vitality (see the commentary on 4:1). This vitality is called to mind whether the hair is compared with (black) goats (4:1), with raven feathers (5:11), with dark-as-night lapis lazuli (see the text cited at note 147 in connection with 5:14-15), or, as in an Egyptian descriptive song from about 700 B.C., with dark grapes.[3] The description of the hair as "dangling," "free-hanging," or "flowing" probably emphasizes its liveliness; it is playful and changeable. Egyptian artists achieved refined effects with hair of this type, as evident in the serving girl in figure 131 from the tomb of Rekh-mi-Re, or the ostracon sketch of a woman playing a lute (fig. 132; cf. also figs. 78–79).

[7:5c (6c)] Like all songs of admiration, this one too ends with a brief reference to the transition from observation to action. But unlike 4:6 or 7:8 (9), this song is more than an expression of the decision to act; one already hears the result of the seductive attraction of the woman's flowing tresses. An admirer is caught in them as though in a net. The ancient Egyptian love song cited in the commentary to 4:9 mentions hair in addition to the seductive power of glances and jewelry: "She casts the noose at me with her hair."[4] Another old Egyptian love poem says:

> Her forehead is the snare of willow wood,
> and I am the wild goose!
> My feet are caught in the hair
> that serves as bait for the snare.[5]

An Arab love song from nineteenth-century Palestine is simpler: "O your black hair hangs down; / seven tresses capture us."[6]

Here in the Song, the prince's daughter does not catch a "wild goose" or some group of anonymous admirers, but—appropriate to her superior qualities—a king.

---

3. Louvre C 100 Love Song; tr. White, 189; cf. Keel, *Deine Blicke,* 20, 105.
4. Papyrus Chester Beatty I, group C, no. 43; tr. White, 183..
5. Papyrus Harris 500, group A, no. 3; cf. Fox, 9; author's translation.
6. Dalman, *Diwan,* 260.

The Tree of Life

Text

7:6 (7) a How [beautiful] and pleasant you are, O loved one,
     b [daughter of all delights].
  7 (8) a You are stately as a palm tree,
     b and your breasts are like [the] clusters [of dates].
  8 (9) a I say I will climb the palm tree
     b and lay hold of its [clusters].
     c [Then] your breasts [will] be like clusters of the vine,
     d [the breath of your nose like the scent of] apples,
  9 (10) a and your [palate] like the best wine,
     b [when it softly submits to "my caresses,"
     c and (still) moistens the] lips [of sleepers].

Analysis

The poem begins quite similarly to the preceding one with the cry "How beautiful. . . ." This similarity may be the reason it was placed here. But the descriptive elements that define the three classic poems of this type (4:1-7; 5:9-16; 7:1-5 [2-6]) quickly fade into the background in favor of a portrayal of anticipated erotic pleasures. What the classic descriptive songs (4:6; 5:16; 7:2b, 5c [3b, 6c]) only suggest becomes the main point here. The song in 7:6-9 (7-10) is related to those in 1:2-4 and 4:9-11, songs that long for and extol love's delights. All three are formally marked by the relation between perfect and imperfect verbs. The statements in the perfect ("How beautiful and pleasant you are . . ."; "You are stately as . . .") provide the basis for the plans, wishes, and hopes in the imperfect ("I will climb . . ."; "your breasts will be . . ."). Equally characteristic are the rapid changes between first and second person; these changes clearly distinguish this poem, which is about the relationship between the two

239

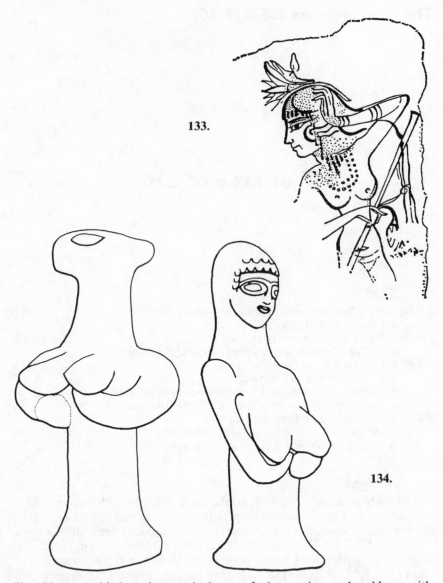

133.

134.

Fig. 133. A very thin lute player, naked except for her earrings and necklaces, with an open lotus flower on her head. Her left hand holds the lute, an open lotus flower, and a lotus bud. (Sketch on a limestone shard from Deir el-Medina; thirteenth/twelfth century B.C.)

Fig. 134. Probably no statues were so widely distributed in Judea from the eighth to the sixth century B.C. as female figures of this type; their bodies are shaped as pillars and their crudely formed hands support full breasts. (The left figure is from Beer-sheba, the right figure from Jerusalem; both found at eighth- century B.C. levels.)

135.

136.

Fig. 135. In the upper section, a goddess is enthroned (*far right*); in front of her is a vase altar, to the left of which stand two worshipers. In the lower section are two date palms on each of which two men are engaged in the harvest. (Cylinder seal from Ur; ca. 2500 B.C.)

Fig. 136. The warlike Ishtar sits on a lion throne. Two worshipers stand in front of her; to their left two women are picking dates. (Cylinder seal of the Akkad Period; ca. 2200 B.C.)

241

lovers, from the song in 7:1-5 (2-6), which concentrates completely on the admiration and description of the "you."

Commentary

[7:6 (7)] This verse addresses "love" itself. But the Hebrew abstract noun "love" surely stands for the concrete "loved one" (cf. Ps. 107:42, where "evil" stands for "the evil ones," and Prov. 12:27, where "indolence" stands for "the indolent"). The result is a one-sided portrait of the "loved one," seeing only those qualities that relate to love—and what kind of love is made clear by the addition "daughter of all delights" (cf. Mic. 1:16 RSV). The words "daughter" or "son" can be used in Hebrew to express the relation between a person and all kinds of things. A "son of rebellion" is a "rebellious man" (Num. 17:10 [25]); a "son of death" is a man who "shall surely die" (1 Sam. 20:31; 2 Sam. 12:5); a "daughter of worthlessness" is a "worthless woman" (1 Sam. 1:16); and a "daughter of delights" a woman who provides all the delights and pleasures of love.

[7:7 (8)] The (tall) stature, which is celebrated primarily in plants like vines (Ezek. 19:11) and cedars (2 Kgs. 19:23; Ps. 92:12 [13]), does not refer to the boylike slenderness so highly valued in women today but serves as an illustration of the expression "daughter of all delights"; it points to the beloved's abundant endowment with "fruits." The huge date clusters look particularly voluptuous on the tall, narrow trunks of date palms. (The Hebrew word here normally means "grapes" or "grape clusters"; but the term can also apply to different kinds of collective fruits; cf. Cant. 1:14.) Egyptian dancers are sometimes pictured with a slender body and relatively large breasts (fig. 133). But a more striking example of full breasts on pillarlike bodies is seen in the so-called pillar goddesses (fig. 134) found frequently at eighth- to sixth-century B.C. levels, especially in Judah.

This ideal of female beauty is still operative in the Near East; but in addition the palm was a manifestation of divinity that may have lent a special intensity to this palm simile. The palm is the archetype for the holy tree pictured countless times throughout the ancient Near East from the third millennium B.C. on (cf. figs. 10, 65, 66, 81). In the OT this tree is known, among other things, as the "tree of life." Images of the tree marked the temple precincts in Jerusalem as a region of life (1 Kgs. 6:29, 32, 35; Ezek. 40:16—41:26). This view of the palm is related, at least in part, to the fact that (also since the third millennium B.C.) the palm was again and again closely connected with important goddesses (in Mesopotamia with Ishtar; cf. figs. 59, 93, 95). A cylinder seal from an early dynasty (ca. 2500 B.C.) shows a goddess enthroned in front of a vase altar, under which is pictured a date harvest (fig. 135). A later cylinder seal (ca. 2200 B.C.) shows the warlike Ishtar on her lion throne with a date harvest next to the throne scene (fig. 136). On the famous wall painting at Mari in Syria (fig. 59), where the goddess is standing on a lion (cf. Cant. 4:8), she is flanked by two large doves (cf. 1:15; 4:1) sitting on date palms (one of which is almost destroyed in the painting); two young men are climbing the palms to harvest the date clusters. The date harvest obviously belongs in the sphere of the goddess. She is the provider of dates.

A fragment of an inscribed vase from an early dynasty shows a goddess, adorned with all kinds of vegetation and a luxuriant coiffure, holding a cluster of dates in her hand (fig. 137); and a well-known Akkadian cylinder seal depicts Ishtar handing a date cluster to the sun-god, who is rising between the mountains (fig. 138). The Sumerian descriptive song cited in the introduction to 5:9-16 says (probably of the goddess Inanna): "My mother is a palm-tree, with a very sweet smell."[1] Various images suggest an identification of the goddess with the palm. On an orthostatic relief from Tell al-Rimah in northwestern Iraq (fig. 139), unfortunately severely damaged, one can recognize a goddess standing between two date palms whose clusters come to rest precisely on her breasts (which she is holding). An orthostatic relief from Karatepe (fig. 140) combines a date palm with a woman nursing a standing child (in the Egyptian manner; cf. fig. 110). An orthostatic relief from Tell Halaf depicts a man who, in contrast to the date pickers in the well-known wall painting at Mari (fig. 59), uses a ladder to reach the ripe dates (fig. 141). In Mari the date harvest was clearly associated with the goddess because it took place in the precincts of her temple. It is probable, though not certain, that the same thing is true in figure 141.

In Egypt, the tree-goddess, who nourishes the dead, occasionally appears in the form of a date palm (fig. 142). In this figure the date palm is given human breasts and arms. The goddess appears twice on an Egyptian sarcophagus (fig. 143), once in purely human form (on the right) and once as a palm. The palm is flanked by the dead, who appear as birds with human heads. Punic steles in Carthage also depict the goddess standing between palms or palms being climbed (figs. 144–46; cf. also fig. 51). Given the nearly three-thousand-year history of these motifs, in an area stretching from Sumer to Carthage, it would be strange indeed if they were unknown in Jerusalem. It is certainly no accident that in several ancient Israelite stories erotically attractive women are named Tamar ("palm"; cf. Gen. 38:6ff.; 2 Sam. 13:1; 14:27). Portraying the woman in the Song as a palm is one of those theomorphisms that say she is the best that could be imagined or experienced in the ancient Near East. Rudolph thinks that because the palm metaphor for a voluptuous woman is also frequently found in modern Arab poetry it has nothing to do with theomorphism. But what is the origin of the metaphors used even in these late, often thoroughly profane poems? The images can often be traced back through centuries. At any rate, the Song itself is fully a product of the ancient Near East; to deny any connections between it and mythic-cultic patterns would be to deprive oneself of an insight into the sources from which many of its metaphors receive the power and intensity that they retain down through the centuries.

1. Civil, "Message," 4–5, line 48.

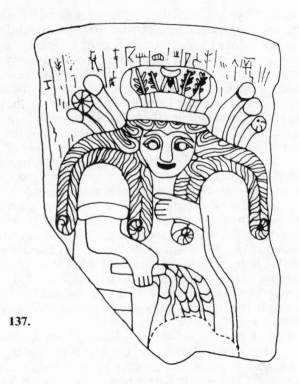

137.

138.

Fig. 137. An enthroned goddess with a luxuriant coiffure has vegetation in her crown and on her shoulders; she holds a cluster of dates in her right hand. (Fragment of a relief on a stone vessel from Telloh, Iraq; ca. 2700 B.C.)
Fig. 138. At the center of this group of gods, the sun-god emerges from the mountains. The winged Ishtar hands him a cluster of dates. To his right are Ea, the lord of fresh water, and his two-faced servant; at the far left is a warrior god. (Cylinder seal from the Akkad Period; ca. 2300 B.C.)

139.

140.

141.

Fig. 139. A goddess, whose upper part is badly damaged, stands between two palms; the date clusters fall on the shoulders of the goddess, who seems to be supporting her breasts. (Old Assyrian relief from ca. 1800 B.C.; reused in a temple at Tell al-Rimah during the Middle Assyrian Period, ca. 1400 B.C.)

Fig. 140. A goddess(?) nurses a standing child beneath a date palm. (Orthostatic relief from Karatepe in southeast Anatolia; ca. 700 B.C.; cf. fig. 110).

Fig. 141. With the aid of a ladder a man climbs a stylized date palm, either to pollinate it or to harvest the fruit. (Orthostatic relief from Tell Halaf; ninth century B.C.)

[7:8ab (9ab)] In view of the tradition just reviewed, the man's plan to climb the palm and lay hold of its date clusters (or breasts) has the aura of a sacral act. This view is quite different from the prophetic perspective, which saw the beginning of all fornication and idolatry in the touching of Israel's breasts by the Egyptians (Ezek. 23:3). Prov. 5:19b-20 adopts a casuistic mediating position. The wisdom teacher recommends that a man find satisfaction only in the breasts of his own wife, avoiding other women. The Song does not deal with issues of this kind; here it is sufficient merely to describe the nourishing, refreshing, and intoxicating effect of climbing the palm.

The prominence of the breasts in this poem and in 4:1-7 is reminiscent of the "pillar goddesses" found throughout Israel during the biblical period (eighth–sixth centuries B.C.; cf. fig. 134). Because of their prominent breasts, goddesses of this type have been called *Dea nutrix,* "nourishing goddess." But such a designation ignores the erotic aspect of the breasts emphasized in texts from that era (cf. Ezek. 23:3; Prov. 5:19; and fig. 128). In the light of those texts, it is noteworthy that naked goddesses of ancient Canaan—as portrayed, for example, on old Syrian cylinder seals (cf. figs. 24–26, 45) or on the so-called Hyksos scarabs from Palestine (fig. 147)—often have no sign of breasts; the whole emphasis is on the reproductive organs (cf. also figs. 104–7). Might this difference indicate a shift from an explicit genital eroticism to one that is less explicit, more interested in sisterly or motherly tenderness? The same difference is noticeable in a comparison of the texts of the Song or the cycles of Egyptian love songs with those of the Sumerian sacred marriage. The sacred marriage existed for the sake of fertility. But fertility was apparently not the purpose in the relationships described in the Egyptian love songs and in the Song—relationships that had no official sanction. The limited possibilities of birth control must have favored a substitution of oral eroticism and petting for genital eroticism—a tendency that would have grown stronger the more strictly the patriarchate punished pregnancy outside marriage and emphasized the value of virginity (cf. Deut. 22:13-22).

[7:8c (9c)] Here the date clusters (breasts) suddenly become "clusters of the vine." Clusters of grapes also sometimes appear as gifts of a goddess. In a work that probably comes from northern Syria, a goddess—naked except for her abundant jewelry—is holding two bunches of grapes (fig. 148). This idea is the theomorphic background of the image here; more tangibly, "vineyard" and "vine" are traditional metaphors for the beloved woman (see the commentary on 1:6d-f; 6:11). In the present context, the vine is probably used to make a transition to the intoxicating wine of v. 9a (10a).

[7:8d (9d)] As stated at 7:4de (5de), when Hebrew uses "nose" in a figurative way, the first thing that comes to mind is not external form but bated breath, snorting, animosity, and anger. Here the reference seems to be to the heavy breathing and the scent produced by passion. It is compared to the scent of apples because apples were considered a fruit that arouses love (see the commentary on 2:5). An ancient Egyptian love song contains a verse with lines similar to this one: "The breath of your nose alone/ is what enlivens my heart."[2] Just like the corresponding Hebrew term, the Egyptian word translated here as "breath" means "scent, aroma, breath." The scents and breath of the aroused woman are what enliven her lover.

[7:9 (10)] Most interpreters radically "correct" the Hebrew text of this verse. The earliest translations into Greek and Latin already offer several variations. My translation and explanation hold to the Hebrew text as it stands, with the exception of only one vowel. The poems in 2:1-3 and 5:9-16 also use the "palate," the "inside of the mouth," to signal the fulfillment of the lovers' deepest longings. Like wine, which sends both gods and mortals into a frenzy of good cheer (Judg. 9:13), thus removing the inhibitions of everyday life, so also the woman's mouth, soft and moist as wine, sends her lover into a state of intoxication when it opens to his pressure. Wine and erotic pleasures are also paralleled in Cant. 2:4; 5:1; 7:2b (3b). In 1:2, 4 and 4:10, the joys of love are placed above those of wine.

The grammar of v. 9 (10)b and c does not make clear whether the palate or the wine is the subject of "submit" and "moisten." The imprecision might be deliberate. The receiver and lender of meaning in the metaphor are all mixed up. Both wine and erotic ecstasy continue to moisten the lips of those who have blissfully fallen asleep, overcome by their frenzy.

2. Papyrus Harris 500, group B, no. 12; tr. White, 173.

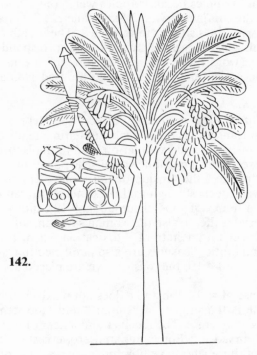

142.

143.

Fig. 142. The Egyptian tree-goddess, who provides the dead with water and food, is sometimes pictured as a date palm, perhaps under Asiatic influence. (Relief from Abusir; thirteenth century B.C.)

Fig. 143. The mistress of palms stands here not within the palm itself but, in human form, next to the palm; she gives water to two Ba-birds (birds representing souls of the dead). (Painting on a wooden sarcophagus from Thebes; ca. 1000 B.C.)

248

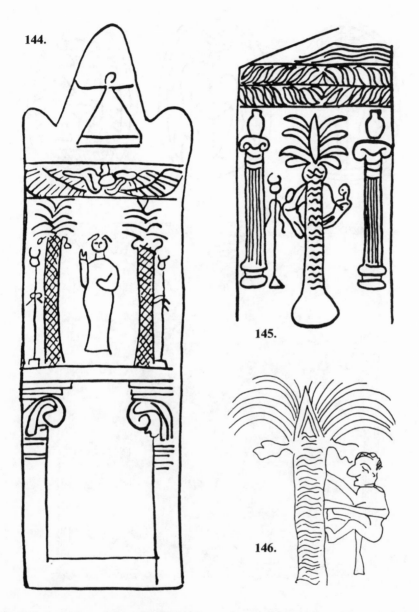

Fig. 144. A goddess giving a blessing appears between two palms. (Grave stele from Carthage; fourth–second centuries B.C.)

Fig. 145. Two men climb a date palm, either to pollinate it or to harvest its fruit. (Relief on a grave stele from Carthage; fourth–second centuries B.C.; cf. fig. 59).

Fig. 146. A man climbs a date palm to harvest the fruit. (Relief from a Punic grave stele; fourth–second centuries B.C.)

147.

148.

Fig. 147. The decorations on three scarabs from Gezer (*left*), Lachish (*middle*), and Tell el-Farah (South) (*right*), from between 1750 and 1550 B.C., show naked goddesses with strongly emphasized sexuality but with no indication of breasts. Fig. 148. A goddess, naked except for her jewelry, presents a cluster of grapes in each hand. She is standing on a mountain; her wings characterize her as a heavenly power. (Electrum tile from northern Syria; ninth/eighth century B.C.)

Lifting the Curse

Text

7:10 [11] a I am my beloved's
      b and his desire is for me.

Analysis

Verse 10a (11a) repeats 6:3 verbatim. But instead of v. 10b (11b), 6:3 has "and my beloved is mine." Verse 2:16a reverses the order: "My beloved is mine and I am his." The numerous occurrences indicate that this formula is common. Many commentators believe that this verse closes the poem in 7:6-9 (7-10), just as 6:3 closes 6:1-3. But the songs of desire in 1:2-4 and 4:9-11, which are related to 7:6-9 (7-10), have no such response. It is more likely that 7:10 (11) functions as the basis for the invitation in 7:11-12 (12-13). The conviction that the two people belong together should find its confirmation in their mutual giving of love. Because of the commonality of the couplet in v. 10 (11) and its loose connection to what follows (or precedes) it, I consider it separately.

Commentary

[7:10a (11a)] At 2:16a I explained at length how this formula expresses an experience of deep solidarity (see also the commentary on the title "sister" in 4:9a). It is futile to speculate whether the man or the woman was the first to discover this solidarity (contrary to Krinetzki), because the formula itself says nothing about this matter. That on all three occasions (2:16; 6:3; and here) it is found in the mouth of the woman shows how important it is to her that their solidarity be mutual.

[7:10b (11b)] This line spells out the reason for this mutual solidarity. The term translated "desire" occurs only three times in the OT: here, Gen.

251

3:16, and 4:7 (the story of Cain). Cant. 7:10 (11) seems to relate directly to Gen. 3:16. There, in connection with the curse of the serpent, the penalties announced to human beings present several of their troubles as consequences of the first sin. One of the woman's troubles is that her longing for love and children produces a desire for the man, but this yearning of the female is used by the male to exercise his rule over her in an oppressive way. Here this line declares the lifting of the inequality that was the basis for such oppression. In the same way that her yearning and passion were directed toward him, his passion and yearning are now directed toward her. Thus the curselike situation is lifted, and the brotherly/sisterly equality given in creation is restored. Love is experienced as a return to paradise.

How Pleasant to Go
to the Fields

Text

11 (12) a Come, my beloved,
   b let us go forth into the fields,
   c [let us rest among the henna shrubs];
12 (13) a let us go out early to the vineyards,
   b and [let us] see
   c whether the vines have budded,
   d whether the grape blossoms have opened,
   e and the pomegranates are in bloom.
   f There I will give you my [caresses].

Analysis

This poem has several things in common with 7:6-9 (7-10). The woman's caresses in 7:12f (13f) correspond to the man's caresses in 7:9b (10b). Some of the plant metaphors of 7:6-9 (7-10) also appear in 7:11-12 (12-13)—for example, the vine in 7:8c (9c) and 7:12c (13c). That the man speaks in 7:6-9 (7-10) but the woman in 7:11-12 (12-13) is probably meant to illustrate the mutuality of love expressed in 7:10 (11) (the verse between the two poems in question).

  The first part of the song consists formally of an imperative (here translated "Come") and three subsequent self-invitations in the first-person plural. A fourth self-invitation ("let us see") corresponds to the introductory imperative in that it leads into another threefold series (this time, of dependent clauses). The song's closing, which is also the motivation for accepting the preceding invitations (in the first-person plural), is the promise (first-person singular) that at the end of the journey ("there") she will allow the lover to share in the pleasures of her love.

253

The content of 7:11-12 (12-13) is reminiscent of 2:10-13, although the similarities have limits. In 2:10-13 the man invites the woman to visit the vineyard (not in his company), because the rainy season is over and the time of new growth has come. The desire to rest together in the open under the trees is expressed in 1:15-17. Going down to the garden ("I [the man?] went down") to check on the buds and blossoms is the theme of 6:11. Yet, despite the connections, each of the four songs clearly has its own character.

Commentary

[7:11ab (12ab)] The woman's invitation to her beloved to go into the fields is reminiscent of an ancient Egyptian love song that closes with the observation: "For one who is loved / how pleasant to go to the fields."[1] The "fields" refers to the open country outside the settlements, whether cultivated land (gardens, vineyards) or wilderness. It is used in the latter sense when the Song talks about the gazelles of the "field" (2:7; 3:5; cf. also Gen. 25:27). One goes into the fields to be alone with someone else, unobserved by others (cf. Gen. 4:8—Cain and Abel; 1 Sam. 20:5, 11— David and Jonathan; Ruth 3—Ruth and Boaz).

[7:11c (12c)] The Hebrew כפרים can be translated either "hamlets, villages" or "henna shrubs" (4:13), but given the connotation of "field" just noted, "villages" does not make much sense in this context. Going there would not achieve the goal of being alone. As shown in 1:14, henna bushes were planted in the vineyards. Whether one translates the accompanying verb "lodge" or, as in 1:13, "lie" makes little difference. The three lines in vv. 11bc (12bc) and 12a (13a) should be understood as strictly parallel statements, not as a sequence of events presented in chronological order—as though they first went into the fields, then rested (or lodged) among the henna shrubs, and finally decided to go early to the vineyards. Such wanderings from place to place are modern. The lovers of 7:11-12 (12-13) wanted to go into the fields to be together undisturbed. Like 1:16-17, this text envisions making love in the open. This outdoor lovemaking has been practiced by lovers of all ages, both because of social necessity and because of the special bond between lovers and the buds and blossoms of new life (see the commentary on 1:16-17). Krinetzki expresses it well in his commentary on 1:16-17: "The lovers are in a hidden place somewhere in a . . . verdant nature, where they can abandon themselves to their loveplay without being disturbed." He points to 7:11 (12) as a parallel. But here his allegorical interpretation, based in depth psychology, has completely taken over. For him, "fields," "villages," and "vineyards" function only as symbols of the "Great Mother" (or of love itself, which is identified with her) and "fertility." Instead of Israel or the church or the believing soul, now it is the *anima* or the Great Mother that is found hiding under every vine. This interpretation

---

1. Papyrus Harris 500, group B, no. 9; tr. Simpson, 302.

obliterates the rich textures of the Song and turns the wonderful variety of ingredients into a monotonous stew.

[7:12 (13)] The reader has already encountered the vineyard as a place for love in 1:6 and 2:13. (See the commentary on those verses.) Verse 12 (13)b-e repeats verbatim 6:11cd, adding the question about the opening of the grape blossoms (cf. 2:13b) to its questions about the budding of the vineyards and the blossoming of the pomegranates. In 2:13 the man points out the new growth to the woman. In 6:11 he is the gardener, checking on the buds and blossoms. Here the woman invites him to go with her to investigate these things. In 2:10-13 the meaning of the awakening of nature is still completely open: Is it merely time for a festival in the vineyards, or is this language a symbol of the woman's awakening to love? The ambiguity is inherent in the image. In 6:11 (see the commentary there) the lover's "disguise" as a gardener suggests that one should probably read the budding and blooming metaphorically. With this poem, the direct closing statement in v. 12f (13f) leaves no doubt: the "blossoms" and "bloom" are to be interpreted figuratively. Regarding the "caresses," see the commentary on 7:8-9 (9-10).

If You Were Only My Brother

Text

7:13 (14) a The [love apples] give forth fragrance,
      b and [at our door] are all choice fruits,
      c new as well as old,
      d which I have laid up for you, O my beloved.
  8:1 a O that you were like a brother to me,
      b who nursed at my mother's breast!
      c If I met you outside,
      d I would kiss you,
      e and no one would despise me.
    2 a I would lead you
      b and bring you into the house of my mother.
      c [You would teach me;]
      d I would give you spiced wine to drink,
      e the juice of my pomegranates.

Analysis

Many commentators (e.g., Rudolph) connect 7:13 (14) with 7:11-12 (12-13). But whereas there the blossoms were just opening on the vines and the pomegranates were in bloom, the images in 7:13 (14)—as in 4:13—are of mature fruit. Furthermore, whereas 7:11-12 (12-13) took place in the open fields, 7:13 (14) talks about a "door," which is more appropriate to the "house" of 8:2 than to the henna bushes of 7:11 (12). Krinetzki thinks 7:13 (14) is an independent song, but it makes more sense to connect it to 8:1-2 (with Gerleman). The perfect verbs of 7:13 (14) provide the basis for the wishes (imperfects) in 8:1-2. Because the love apples are giving off their fragrance and the other fruits lie ready in her house (perfects), the woman wants to bring her lover into the house and refresh him with their juice (imperfects). A similar relation between perfects and

256

imperfects occurs in 7:6-9 (7-10): because she is beautiful and rises like a palm (perfects), he wants to climb her (imperfects). Thus both the motifs (fruits, doors, house, fruit juices) and the grammar (perfects, imperfects) require making a break between 7:12 (13) and 7:13 (14).

Commentary

[7:13a (14a)] The word translated "love apples" (דודאים) means mandrake fruit (*Mandragora officinarum* L. or *Mandragor autumnalis* L.). The Hebrew word sounds the same as the word for "baskets," דודאים (Jer. 24:1). Whether this similarity is accidental or the result of an etymological connection, the small yellowish fruits on their short stems do lie in a rosette of leaves as though in a basket. The plant occurs frequently in Egyptian pictures from the New Kingdom (1540–1075 B.C.). A picture on the lid of a small chest of Tutankhamen shows a man collecting "love apples" while a woman watches (fig. 149). The mandrake was brought to Egypt from Palestine/Syria (cf. fig. 108) at the beginning of the New Kingdom as part of the fashion of importing exotic plants. At the same time Egypt imported Syrian women for the harem, who brought with them the belief that mandrake fruits (or, more precisely, their aroma) were an aphrodisiac (cf. Gen 30:14-15). Although the roots of the mandrake (alraun) played an important role in early Judaism and, above all, in the Middle Ages, in older times only the aroma of the fruit was thought to be significant as Cant. 7:13 (14) demonstrates. In paintings by guest artists in Egypt, women are sometimes seen holding love apples to their nose (fig. 150). The erotic connotation of a small limestone relief from Tell el-Amarna (fig. 151) is even clearer. There a queen holds a love apple for a king, who lazily supports himself on a staff so he can smell the sharp, spicy aroma. What the aroma does not do might be accomplished by the queen's robe, which leaves her lower abdomen almost totally naked. In the unique harem scene from Medinet Habu, the ladies of the harem of Ramses III, who is caressing one of them, bring him bowls of pomegranates and love apples (fig. 152).

An ancient Egyptian love song also describes the effect of the love apple. The man sings:

> If only I were her Nubian maid,
> her attendant in secret!
> [She would let me bring her love apples;
> when it was in her hand, she would smell it,
> and she would show me] the hue of her whole body.[1]

The woman's skin is described in another love song: "Your skin is the

---

1. Cairo Love Songs, group B, no. 21; tr. Fox, 37, modified according to author's German translation. Regarding the translation, cf. P. Derchain, "Le lotus, la mandragore et le perséa," *Chronique d'Egypte* 50 (1975) 77. In one of the love songs of Papyrus Harris 500, the woman's breasts are compared to love apples or mandrakes (group A, no. 3); cf. Fox, 9.

257

149.

150.

Fig. 149. The fruits of a mandrake plant (love apple) are portrayed more or less realistically lying in a wreath of leaves as though in a basket (*center*). A man is picking the fruit while a woman watches. The upper portion of this ivory carving can be seen in fig. 63. (Lid of a small chest from the tomb of Tutankhamen; ca. 1325 B.C.)

Fig. 150. Instead of the usual lotus flower (notice the woman at the right), a woman holds a love apple to the nose of another during a drinking festival (cf. fig. 6). (Painting in the tomb of Nakht; West Thebes, no. 52; ca. 1400 B.C.)

258

Fig. 151. An Egyptian queen holds two love apples and a lotus bud under the nose of her husband. Her robe, which emphasizes her lower abdomen, makes the meaning of her gesture unmistakable. (Painted relief from Tell el-Amarna; ca. 1340 B.C.)

skin of the mandrake, which induces loving."[2] The fragrant love apples incite love. But who is inciting whose love in v. 13 (14)?

[7:13b (14b)] The situation is somewhat clearer with the "choice fruits," already encountered in "The Paradise of Love" (4:12—5:1; cf. vv. 13 and 16). Here, however, the fruits are not hidden in the dark foliage of a locked garden; instead they lie enticingly in the open, at the door of the woman who is speaking (cf. Prov. 9:14). As with the "canals" in Cant. 4:13, one might see the "door" as a metaphor for the woman's womb. But, as far as I know, no philological evidence supports this view. The word used in 8:9c means the "door covering," not the "opening." If the womb were meant in v. 13b (14b), it would not make sense to speak of "our" door instead of "my" door. All in all, it would be wiser not to give a Freudian interpretation to every opening and every space in the Song— seeing these as symbols of the womb. Then nothing would stand in the way of including the mother in the "our" of this verse, especially because, according to 8:2, her house is where the woman is to bring the man (cf. "behind our wall" in 2:9d, and also the commentary on 8:2). This is a still-veiled description of the house of the young woman and her mother as an inviting place to stop off (Gerleman).

[7:13cd (14cd)] Here the fruits that have been described literally are given a subtle metaphorical interpretation. The fruits, "new as well as old," refer to erotic pleasures—both those as yet unknown, coming as a surprise, and those that are old and proved (cf. the householder in Matt. 13:52 "who brings out of his treasure what is new and what is old"—he too begins with the new). As always, where two things are used to describe a whole (merism), the interest is not in the meaning of either of the extremes (new or old) but in the whole—the totality of the experience and the enthusiasm it conveys: *I* have kept *all* treasures for *you.*

The movement is clear: from the rather general aroma of the love apples (whose love apples are fragrant for whom?), through the choice fruits at *our* door, to the sum total of all treasures that *she* has kept for *him.* Krinetzki has correctly noted that the accent lies on this movement. It arises out of the move from a literal to a metaphorical meaning; out of the intensification of what is included, from "love apples" through "all choice fruits" to the lofty merism "new as well as old" (cf. 5:1b-d); but above all out of the increasingly precise identification of the persons involved.

The verb translated "to lay up" can also mean "to hide." But the door opening is not the place to hide something; to the contrary, it is where things are put on display. The fragrant love apples and the choice fruits piled at the door, which in 7:13cd (14cd) become metaphors for the charms of the woman and her readiness for love, are hidden only in the sense that the person to whom she will give them is not yet publicly known.

2. B. van der Walle, review of *Altägyptische Liebeslieder,* by S. Schott, *BO* 9 (1952) 108.

[8:1] The speaker is not ready to give up this hiddenness and intimacy. The contradiction in the previous metaphor between the door open to the public and the things kept hidden for the lover is continued in the relational fantasy of 8:1. The woman wishes her lover were her brother. Nursing at the breast of the same mother would imply intimate familiarity from the very beginning, allowing her to kiss him in public and bring him home. Krinetzki claims such things were not ordinarily done but offers no basis for this conclusion. Indeed, Jacob kisses his cousin in public (Gen. 29:11). The speaker of Cant. 8:1 wants to be able to kiss her lover in public without altering her social status and without being lumped together with prostitutes and adulteresses (cf. Prov. 7:13). The verb in Cant. 8:1e means more than disdaining people or blaming them for something; it means holding them in contempt, ruining them socially (cf., e.g., Prov. 14:21; Ps. 107:40), in the way that prostitutes and adulteresses were socially contemptible. The understandable caution of the speaker in this verse reminds one of the woman in the poem of Cant. 1:7-8, who wanted to find her lover without having to wander around aimlessly looking for him.

The Egyptian love song often cited in reference to this poem has many similarities but makes a different point. There the woman wishes that her mother (or the lover's mother?) would recognize their mutual attraction and arrange an alliance:

> Then I could hurry to (my) brother
> and kiss him before his company,
> and not be ashamed because of anyone,
> I would be happy to have them see
> that you know me.[3]

Whereas the woman in the Egyptian poem wants to have her love publicly known, in this poem the wish that the man were her brother serves merely to make possible the speaker's desire to smuggle him into her house (and the house of her mother) without being caught.

[8:2] The idea of bringing the lover into her mother's house is found already in an earlier poem (3:1-5; cf. v. 4de). There she succeeds by boldly going out to "arrest" him in the middle of the night. Here, though, she wants to have her lover for herself without leaving her familiar surroundings, without accepting the fact that love is an adventure and a risk. Another expression of her timidity and lack of experience is the idea that she needs to be taught by her lover. The context requires that this teaching be understood as instruction about love. The verb "to teach" is used in the same way in Jer. 13:21 where Jerusalem is reproached for teaching the political powers of the Near East to be her "lovers."[4] The consequence of his "teaching" would be that she would give him something to drink.

---

3. Papyrus Chester Beatty I, group A, no. 36; tr. Fox, 55.
4. The text from the Turin Papyrus to which Gerleman refers is too badly damaged to be understood, hence it cannot be used as a parallel.

See the commentary on 5:1cd for a discussion of "drinking" as a meta-phor for erotic pleasures. In Hebrew "I would give you to drink" (אַשְׁקְךָ) sounds very much like the "I would kiss you" (אֶשָּׁקְךָ) in v. 1d. This parallelism is intentional. Wine, which she wants to give him, is related already in 1:2 to kisses and caresses; in 7:9 (10) it is compared to the inside of the woman's mouth; and in 5:1 it is used metaphorically to describe the caresses that intoxicate the partners. Even where the serving and drinking of wine is not a full metaphor for intercourse, its erotic connotations are shown in Egyptian art by having it served by an at-tractive young woman (fig. 153). In comparison with ordinary wine, the offer of "spiced wine" (mentioned only here) intensifies the image. Like fragrances in general, spiced wine was regarded as a means of erotic arousal. The Assyrian incantation cited at 2:5b commends sucking the juice of a pomegranate as an unfailingly effective aphrodisiac. In 4:3 and 6:7 the slit in the pomegranate is a metaphor for the open mouth. Pome-granates were frequently symbols for breasts in Near Eastern poetry (see the commentary on 4:16cd)—an interpretation suggested here by the reference to "my" pomegranates. But in one way or another, the "teach-er's" instruction will surely result in the joys of erotic ecstasy.

Purpose and Thrust

Krinetzki entitles the poem in 8:1-2 "Longing for the End of Secrecy," but that is not what it is about. The poem describes an erotic episode between siblings, forbidden in the real world (Lev. 18:9; 2 Sam. 13:1-9) but invented by imaginative desire. The goal of the woman's fiction is not official recognition of the relationship but merely the opportunity (se-cretly) to entice the lover with the fragrance of love apples and to share with him her wonderful fruits. Here, as in 3:1-5, no settlement is reached between the claims of society and the passions of love, no way is found to "make it legal." These two great powers (social order and passionate love) are so elemental and so strong that often only flights of imagination, filled with cunning and contradictions, can bring them together and prevent the destructive outbreak of open warfare between them.

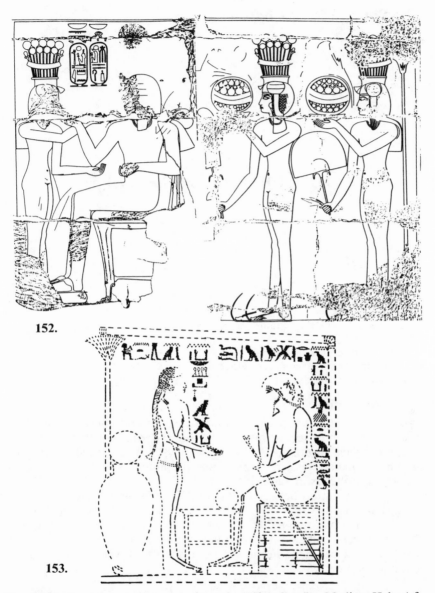

152.

153.

Fig. 152. In the unique harem scene from the "High Gate" at Medinet Habu (cf. fig. 121), the king's "princesses" or "concubines" bring him bowls of pomegranates and love apples. (Relief from the time of Ramses III; 1187–1156 B.C.)

Fig. 153. An attractive young woman presents a vessel of wine (no longer visible) to an elderly man, saying, "Your health! Take this and drink to the health of the herald Antef!" (Painting from the tomb of Antef, West Thebes, no. 155; ca. 1475 B.C.)

Do Not Stir Up Love! II

Text

8:3 a [. . .] His left hand [(lies)] under my head,
   b and [. . .] his right hand [embraces] me.
  4 a I adjure you,
   b O daughters of Jerusalem,
   c do not stir up or awaken love
   d until it is ready!

Analysis

It is no accident that this description of the consummation of love follows the preceding prospect of just such a thing. Because of this connection, many exegetes regard 7:13 (14)—8:4 (or 8:1-4) as a single poem (Rudolph, Gerleman). But here one finds presented as fact what 7:13 (14) clearly describes as imaginative fantasy.

A connection between 8:1-2 and 8:3-4 is also denied by the fact that 8:3-4 repeats verbatim 2:6-7—except that 8:3-4 has no swearing "by the gazelles or wild does." It may be that this oath to "gods" other than Yahweh raised sufficient objections that a version without this line also came into circulation. For more details on this whole poem, see the commentary on 2:6-7.

Who Has Become
So Complaisant?

Text

8:5 a Who is that coming up from the wilderness,
   b leaning upon her beloved?

Analysis

Verse 5a repeats 3:6a verbatim. In both cases, the question follows an exhortation to the daughters of Jerusalem. A prescribed pattern has apparently left its mark here.

Commentary

[8:5ab] But what follows 8:5a is completely different from what follows 3:6a. The commentary there showed that "coming up from the wilderness" implied leaving a wild and inaccessible area. Comparing the beloved woman of the Song to the "lady of the wilderness" and the goddesses of the highest mountain (cf. 4:8) symbolized her majesty, her inaccessibility and distance. Even though she "comes up," her mystery and distance were maintained in 3:6b-8 by the strange litter, the several aromatic substances, and the clattering weapons of the bodyguards.

But the situation is totally different here. In 4:8 the man pleads with the proud "lady of the wilderness" to come down from her peak, to leave her terrifying lions and leopards; but now the woman leans on her lover, supporting herself on him. These two lines come close to mocking her, the wild one who has become so tame and complaisant.[1] The im-

---

1. A familiar theme of Egyptian mythology is the goddess whose wild aspect is symbolized by the mighty Sachmet (lion-goddess) and whose tame aspect by the

pression is strengthened by observing that the interrogative pronoun מִי
("who?") is emphasized by the repetition of its sound in מִן ("from") and
in מִתְרַפֶּקֶת ("leaning"): *Who* is that?

---

complaisant Bastet (cat-goddess); cf. *Lexikon der Ägyptologie*, vol. 5 (Wiesbaden: Harrassowitz, 1984) 325.

From Generation
to Generation

Text

8:5 c Under the apple tree I awakened you,
    d there [where] your mother [became pregnant] with you;
    e there [where] she who bore you [went into] labor.

Analysis

This short poem was probably inserted here because of the catchword
"awaken" (8:4c). Neither form nor content has much to do with what
goes before (8:5ab), and one can make a connection with what follows
(8:6-7) only at a fairly high level of abstraction. The poem's structure is
determined by the adverbs of location ("under," "there," "there") that
open each of the three lines. Giving such emphasis to the place where the
three events occur is meant to provide an inner unity among them and to
present them as one continuous happening; each of the three is expressed
in the perfect tense.

In the present Hebrew text, the woman is the speaker and the man
the addressee. Many exegetes (e.g., Rudolph, Krinetzki) change the masculine suffixes for "you" to feminine forms, because "the claim by a
woman that she has 'awakened' the man's love would, however, be extraordinary, particularly in an ancient Near Eastern poem" (Krinetzki). But
it is primarily in the context of the pervasive patriarchalism of the world
of early Judaism, Christianity, and Islam that the claim would be found
problematic, where one could imagine an initiative by the woman only as
an example of sinful seduction. But this paternalistic view, reserving all
initiative to the man, was less obvious in the ancient Near East, where

goddesses actively courted their admirers. Some of that feminine activism remains in the OT. The Song often depicts the woman as remarkably active (see **Analysis** of 3:1-5). In 4:9 the man admits he has been driven crazy by just one of her glances; in 6:5 he finds her so disturbing that he asks her to stop looking at him. The metaphor of the eyes as doves (1:15; 4:1) signals anything but naïveté and quietness, as the commentary on those passages indicates.

At first glance the reference to the mother seems more appropriate coming from the woman. She is the one in 3:4 who wants to bring her lover into the chamber where her mother conceived her. But 3:11 shows that in matters of the heart the man too was more closely related to his mother than to his father.

Because of paternalistic conditioning, modern readers find the text more palatable if they change the masculine pronouns to feminine, making the man the speaker (as the ancient Syriac translation has already done). But this change clearly smooths out the wrinkles of the received text and offends against one of the basic rules of text criticism: giving precedence to the more difficult reading.

It is the difficult reading that provides another step in the direction of real partnership. The term itself and the conscious movement toward partnership between lovers is admittedly modern. But in the OT, when the man did not carry out his traditional role decisively, the woman could sometimes take over that role in order to advance their common interest; as the story of Ruth shows, such action was often not without its bravado and public recognition.

Commentary

[8:5c] In 7:11 the consuming desire normally reserved to the woman (Gen. 3:16) is ascribed to the man; here the ability to "awaken" or "arouse," normally reserved to the man, is claimed by the woman. In 2:13, where the initiative clearly belongs to the woman, she compares her beloved to an apple tree; she sat in its shadow and its fruit was sweet to her taste. For the erotic connotations of apple trees and apples, see the commentary on 2:3ab and 5.[1]

This verse may be a play on 2:1-3 in the same way that 8:5ab ("Who is that coming up from the wilderness?") parodies 3:6-8. Under the apple tree, as she reaches for apples, she arouses her lover.

[8:5de] It was under this apple tree that his mother conceived him, and here is where she gave him birth. This is one of the few verses in the Song that places the relationship between the lovers in the context of the succession of generations. She arouses his love in the same way that his mother had aroused her lover in order to conceive this very son. Against

1. This text is not a play on the story of paradise and the fall. The tree in the Garden of Eden was only later identified as an apple tree on the basis of a play on words in Latin (*malum*, "apple" = *malum*, "evil"). Genesis 2–3 does not identify the tree.

this background, the awakening of love has something fateful and heroic about it. It brings the woman into the same camp as Lot's daughters (Gen. 19:30-38) or Tamar (Genesis 38), who use the boldest means to ensure the continuity of generations.

This continuity is portrayed by the common location. The apple tree obviously evokes the notion of love under the trees (cf. 1:17), and it is an erotic spot par excellence (cf. 2:3); but beyond that idea it depicts the unbroken growth of a whole race. It represents the family tree (cf. Isa. 11:1; Ezekiel 17) seen from an erotic perspective; this connection gives eroticism a solemnity that it does not possess on its own. By awakening love, conceiving, and giving birth, the woman is a keeper of the family tree—even more, the tree, in whose shadow she nurtures love, grows from her own womb (on the relationship between womb and tree, see the commentary on 4:13a).

Love as the Opponent
of Death

Text

8:6 a [Make me into] a seal upon your heart,
   b [. . .] a seal upon your arm;
   c for [(my)] love is strong as death,
   d [(my)] passion fierce as the [underworld].
   e [Its arrows are flaming arrows,
   f flaming bolts of lightning].
  7 a [Mighty] waters cannot quench love,
   b neither can [rivers] drown it.
   c If one offered for love all the wealth of his house,
   d it would be utterly scorned.

Analysis

In form, 8:6-7b is a petition with rationale. The imperative in v. 6a is followed by three nominal clauses introduced with "for." Their content is further explicated by two parallel verbal clauses in the imperfect tense, describing a regularly recurring event. The conditional sentence in v. 7cd is less closely and less clearly connected. Like a statement of casuistic law, it includes a description of a situation ("If one . . .") and the unfolding of the consequences ("then one . . ."). Complete in itself (in both form and content), it is only loosely related to what precedes it. The connection might come from the idea that a phenomenon related to death cannot be manipulated by wealth any more than the one described in v. 7ab. At a higher level of abstraction, one can also postulate a relation between this poem and the preceding one (8:5c-e): love forges the links between the generations with the same tenacity that death employs in its attempt to destroy them.

270

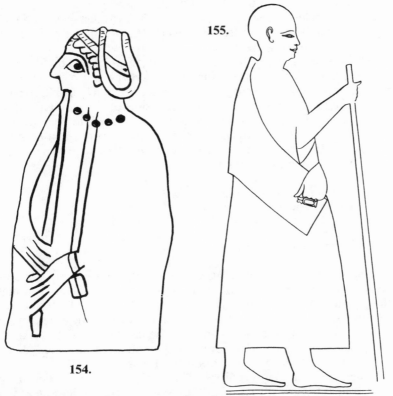

155.

154.

Fig. 154. A woman wears a cylinder seal(?) on her wrist. (Small engraved inlaid tile from Nippur; ca. 2800 B.C.)

Fig. 155. On his finger a vizier wears a seal ring in the form of a cartouche, which contained the name of the king. (Limestone relief from Memphis; ca. 370 B.C.)

Commentary

[8:6ab] A "seal" can be either a cylinder or a stamp. Cylinder seals were normally worn around the neck on a cord (cf. Gen. 38:18). Stamp seals (scarabs, scaraboids, conical seals, etc.) could be worn in the same way, although these were also often attached to a finger ring (Jer. 22:24). Both kinds could be worn on arm bands or on a cord around the wrist, as shown by a mother-of-pearl inlay from Nippur (fig. 154). The Sumerian word for "wrist" *(kishib-la)* means literally "seal bearer," and the Akkadian equivalent *(rittu)* means "stamp seal" when it is preceded by the determinative for "stone."[1] Because about twenty times as many stamp

---

1. W. H. Hallo, "'As the Seal upon Thine Arm': Glyptic Metaphors in the Biblical World," in *Ancient Seals and the Bible,* ed. L. Gorelick and E. Williams-Forte (Malibu: Undena, 1983) 10; *AHW,* 2:990.

seals as cylinder seals (about 8000 to 400) have been found in authorized excavations in Palestine/Israel, and because the cylinder seals come primarily from Late Bronze, pre-Israelite levels (1550–1200 B.C.), this poem probably has a stamp seal in mind.

The woman asks her beloved to make her into a seal on his breast (Exod. 28:29; Prov. 6:21) or on his wrist. (On the use of the Hebrew phrase "set as" with the sense of "make into," cf. Hag. 2:23.) Some scholars have read this request as an expression of the woman's desire always to be at the breast or on the arm of her beloved, to be a precious possession with which he will never part. This interpretation seems to match closely the intention of an ancient Egyptian love song where, significantly, the man makes the wish:

> If only I were her little seal-ring [cf. fig. 155],
> the keeper of her finger!
> I would see her love each and every day,
> . . .
> [while it would be I] who stole her heart.[2]

But to hear the request of 8:6 in this way is to fail to understand its depth; above all, this interpretation does not do justice to the solemn rationale for the petition. Paying sufficient attention to this rationale results in a deeper and more adequate explanation, one already suggested by the seal's location on the breast. As the commentary on 1:13 showed, the breast is the preferred spot for protective symbols of all kinds (cf. the Greek ἐγκολπιον, "that which is upon the breast" = "the amulet"). Israelites were to wear the teachings of their elders as an amulet on the breast to protect them (Prov. 6:20-22). People in the ancient Near East did not wear seals at their breast or on their arm in order to be quickly ready to seal or authenticate something; rather, the seals, with their ornamentation, symbols, and portrayals of the gods, functioned as amulets. The wish to be a seal on the beloved's breast already implies a meaning that is fully substantiated by the following rationale for this wish.

[8:6c] The rationale is well-known: "for love is strong as [not 'stronger than'] death." But what does this saying mean in the context of the OT? The answer needs to begin with the seal amulets. They were meant to protect the wearers from misfortune and disease (the precursors of death), and, positively, to increase their vitality and lust for life. The text in v. 6c speaks only of "love" in general, not of "his" love, "her" love, or "our" love. But when the Song uses the feminine noun אהבה ("love") to designate a particular person *(abstractum pro concreto)*, it is the woman, not the man (see the commentary on 7:6 [7]). The ancient Near Eastern deities that typify love are all female. Based on 7:6 (7), one could also translate v. 6c, "For the loved one [fem.] is strong as death." Although the

---

2. Cairo Love Songs, group B, no. 21C; tr. Fox, 38.

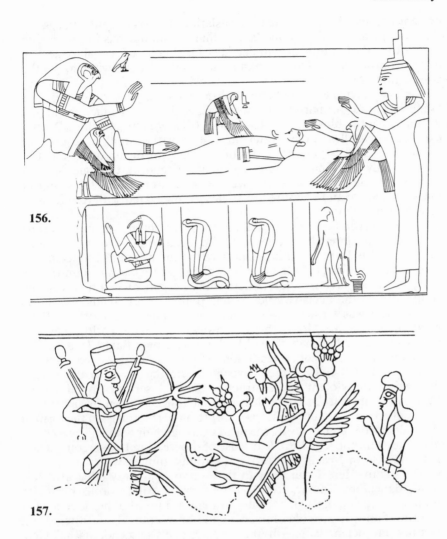

Fig. 156. A dead Osiris lies on his lion-bier. Isis, as a female falcon, mounts his erect phallus (later scratched away) to conceive Horus, his posthumous avenger and heir. In human form (*right*), Isis holds her hands protectively over her dead brother. Horus, with the head of a falcon, witnesses his own conception (*far left*). The two female falcons at the head and foot of the corpse are his sisters, Nephthys and (for the third time) Isis. Beneath the bier (*from right to left*) are a meerkat, two asps, and Thoth, the writing-god, with the head of an ibis. (Painted limestone relief in the mortuary temple of Seti I in Abydos; ca. 1280 B.C.)

Fig. 157. The weather-god holds the chaos dragon at bay with an arrow of lightning; the dragon lurks in the sea, among other places. A worshiper of the weather-god charms the dragon (*right*). (Neo-Assyrian cylinder seal; ninth/eighth century B.C.)

present context disallows such a translation, the same context suggests that it is primarily the woman's love that the author has in mind. The man is to make her into an "amulet," because her love is equal to the task of confronting death. On the man as an amulet for the woman, see the commentary on 1:13-14.

The language of the Song applies metaphors describing "life" or "renewal of life" primarily to the woman. See the commentary on 2:2 (the woman as lotus blossom) or 7:7-8 (8-9) (the woman as palm). Breasts extolled as gazelles among water lilies (4:5) or the womb as a grove of pomegranates (4:13) are not envisioned as organs of reproduction. The Song is only marginally interested in life extending through the generations. Its chief interest is love itself, love as desire and as the source of pleasure. Desire and pleasure are as closely associated with (erotic) love as sorrow is with death.

Yet, given the fundamental nature of the claim that love is strong as death, one dare not overlook the importance of love in the transmission of life. But from this perspective too the woman's connection to love is more evident than the man's. In the Ugaritic myth recounting the struggle of the love-goddess (Anat) with the god of death (Mot), the goddess plays the decisive role. At one point the text reads, "Mot was strong, Baal was strong,"[3] but in the final moment Mot defeats Baal. Nevertheless, before Mot carries him away to the underworld, Anat conceives by him a bull, which will be born as a new Baal.[4] In a similar Egyptian myth, Isis conceives a son (Horus) by Osiris even after his death; Horus will be his father's avenger, restoring power to a beneficial life against the violent and destructive Seth.[5] A series of reliefs in the Egyptian temples to Osiris, dating from the thirteenth century B.C. to the first century A.D., picture Osiris as a corpse on his bier. Isis, in the form of a female falcon, conceives by the dead Osiris an heir who will succeed to his father's throne (fig. 156). Life's use of procreation to overcome death is found also in Israelite narrative traditions, though with a typical Israelite stamp. Here I can refer to the examples already cited at 8:5c-e (Lot's daughters, Tamar, Ruth). Tamar's use of indecorous means to produce offspring through her father-in-law is a proof of her love for her dead husband; it provides him with the only kind of life after death possible in ancient Israel—living through one's descendants (cf. Gen. 25:5-10).

But even in those OT stories that are about the preservation and protection of the life of the loved one, rather than about love as a means of propagating life, it is usually the women who struggle against the ruthless, violent, and insolent assaults of death with an elemental energy equivalent to death's own. Whether it is the cunning Michal (1 Sam. 19:9-17); the determined Abigail, who bets everything on one card (1 Samuel

---

3. Baal and Mot 6.vi.17,18,20; tr. Gibson, 80.
4. Baal and Mot 5.v.18–25; tr. Gibson, 72.
5. Cf., e.g., Lichtheim, *Ancient Egyptian Literature,* 2:83; Assmann, Ägyptische Hymnen *und Gebete,* 446.

25); the wise woman of Maacah, who saves her city (2 Sam. 20:14-22); or the heroic Rizpah, who day and night keeps the vultures and the hyenas away from the bodies of her sons until they can be buried (2 Sam. 21:8-14)—again and again it is women whose love stands between death and their husbands, their sons, their city, and their people (cf. Esther). Of course, similar stories were occasionally told about men. But men normally sought to defeat the weapons of death with the weapons of death, to drive out the devil with Beelzebub; thus in their stories it is usually less clear that it is love that fights against death.

The catchwords "death" and "love" rarely turn up in the kind of stories just cited. But one cannot expect concrete stories to use a hymnic or wisdom vocabulary. Yet, if not in stories like these, where else should one seek the concrete meaning of the heady notion that love is as strong as death?

[8:6d] Here the "underworld" parallels "death," and "passion" parallels "love." The underworld (שְׁאוֹל) is the realm ruled by death (cf. Ps. 49:14 [15]). But in v. 6d, like death, it too is portrayed as a living being. Similarly, Ps. 18:4-5 (5-6) speaks of the snares and Isa. 5:14 of the open mouth of the underworld. Sheol is harsh and unrelenting—it spares no one and never gives up anyone who has come under its power (Hos. 13:14; Ps. 49:7-8, 15 [8-9, 16]; cf. also 2 Sam. 12:23; 14:14). But "passion" (קִנְאָה) is its equal, because like Sheol it too never lets go of anyone who has come under its spell (cf. Cant. 3:4c). The Hebrew term includes not only "passion" but also the phenomena described in English as "zeal" and "jealousy." But in the form of jealousy, passion comes dangerously close to its great opponent, "death" (cf. Prov. 6:34). That relation is the tragedy of the animosity between these two contenders that strangely tends to push them, with all their mutual hatred, ever closer to one another. The narrative tradition of the OT tells many terrible stories about murderous zeal (cf., e.g., Num. 25:7-8, 13; 1 Kgs. 19:10; 2 Kgs. 10:16). It is often hard to see what could justify the means in these accounts, other than the ends; and it hardly needs to be said how questionable that philosophy is. The claim in this verse is not meant to offer a moral judgment but merely to show that the power of love's passion is just as unrelenting and elemental as that of the underworld.

[8:6ef] The notion of love's passion as an elemental force is extended and fortified by comparing its effects with those of flaming arrows (cf. Ps. 76:3 [4]). These arrows are identified in v. 6f as Yahweh-flames, i.e., as lightning. Hebrew frequently combines a noun with Yah(weh) to build a superlative. "Yahweh's noise" is the most impressive sound known to the ancients—thunder (cf. Ps. 29:3-4). "Yahweh's fire" is the most stunning fire—lightning (cf. Job 1:16). The association of lightning with arrows points to the weather god, who is the consort of the fertile land.

[8:7ab] The way the opponents of this fire are portrayed confirms that it was correct to associate lightning with the weather-god. The "mighty waters" parallel the sea and the waters of chaos in Ps. 77:19 (20); 93:4; Isa. 17:13, etc.; and "rivers" does not refer to the Nile or Euphrates but to the dragonlike rivers of the underworld (cf. Ps. 24:2; 93:3; Hab. 3:9) that threaten the realm of life. As many Neo-Assyrian cylinder seals show, the weather-god battles the dragon with his arrows of lightning (fig. 157). Ps. 18:12-15 (13-16) and other texts transfer this picture to Yahweh, the protector of life, who fights against the powers of death that threaten his anointed or his people. Only he can destroy death once for all (Isa. 25:7). Where that destruction has not yet happened, the love between a man and a woman remains as one of the strongest bulwarks against death's dark powers.

The statement about love being as strong as death cannot have a mythical sense in the context of the Song, but to a large degree it owes its strength and the intensity of its images to the several myths about the struggle between the powers of life or love and those of death.

[8:7cd] The conditional sentence—real or unreal (Hebrew has no way to make this distinction)—about the rejection earned by one who tries to buy love has to be understood against the background of the antagonism between life (or love) and death. This sentence is hardly talking primarily about the (unfortunate) custom of the bride price (Krinetzki); rather, given the parallelism between love and death that characterizes this brief poem, it wants to say that purchasing love is just as impossible as buying off death (Ps. 49:7-8). Love can be neither aroused nor abated with money (cf. Prov. 6:30-35). But if love is a force that, like death, defies any kind of manipulation, how can it acknowledge the authority of moral

Futile Pride

Text

8:8 a We have a little sister,
 b and she has no breasts.
 c What shall we do for our sister,
 d on the day when she is spoken for?
 9 a If she is a wall,
 b we will build upon her a battlement of silver;
 c [. . .] if she is a door,
 d we will [strengthen] her with boards of cedar.
 10 a I [am] a wall,
 b and my breasts [are] like towers;
 c [yet in his eyes I am
 d as one who has surrendered].

Analysis

A new poem clearly begins with v. 8. The woman is no longer speaking to her lover; instead the action has a plural subject. This plural subject apparently refers to the older siblings of a girl who has not yet reached puberty. Most interpreters think the speakers in vv. 8-9 are her brothers—though, in this view, they are merely quoted by the woman, who begins to speak for herself in v. 10. These interpreters postulate an introduction for vv. 8-9 that goes something like: "Years ago, my brothers said. . . ." The only problem is that such an introduction does not exist. It is true that brothers were responsible for their sister's honor (cf. 1:6; Gen. 34:11; 2 Sam. 13:22-33); together with their father, or in his place, they were called on to say the decisive word at her wedding (cf., e.g., Gen. 24:50, 55). But the Song does not concern itself with the world of everyday realities. For example, its poems speak seven times of the mother but never of the father, even though in that social reality he had the last word.

Given this fact, the older sisters could certainly be included, along with the brothers, among the speakers of vv. 8-9 (recall the important role played by the "daughters of Jerusalem" in this book). One of these sisters would then be the "I" of v. 10, who is distinguished both from the "we" of vv. 8-9 and from the little sister, who is discussed in the third person. Because as already mentioned, vv. 8-9 are a quotation, I think it is better to put them too in the mouth of the speaker of v. 10. The poem would then be an ironic presentation of the contradiction between the plans of the siblings (imperfects in v. 9) and the rule of love (nominal clauses in v. 10). The theme of the strong, unapproachable woman being brought down by love is already present in 8:5ab. No doubt the recurrence of that theme caused this poem to be inserted here.

Commentary

[8:8] Ezek. 16:7 names the development of the breasts and the growth of pubic hair as signs of puberty (when the girl became eligible for marriage). Young women were often married between ages 12 and 14. It was thought unseemly to wait too long. Thus it is understandable that the parents, especially the father, had the decisive word in the matter (cf. Josh. 15:16; 1 Sam. 18:17; 25:44, etc.). It seems likely that the older siblings also had their say (not only after the parents were dead), and it was not a foregone conclusion that they would agree with the father (cf. Genesis 34). In the freer atmosphere of the Song, the older sisters were also involved in these discussions, which were precipitated by the appearance of an admirer. The "speaking" in v. 8d, as the form of the verb indicates, is an intensive form of communication—wooing and bargaining (cf. 1 Sam. 25:39).

[8:9] All interpreters have noticed the strict structural parallelism between v. 9ab and v. 9cd. They are formally two conditional clauses with exactly the same construction; in terms of content, every word in one clause has its counterpart in the other. The "door" corresponds to the "wall," "strengthen" to "build upon," and the "boards of cedar" to the "battlement."

According to many exegetes (e.g., Rudolph, Gerleman, Krinetzki), the particular interest of these clauses is that, despite all the external similarities, they postulate two quite different situations, and draw opposite conclusions. In my opinion, this thesis would indeed be tempting—if only it did not have to ignore the text.

All commentators agree that the "wall" symbolizes the pride and powers of resistance of the girl who is to be married (regarding tower and city metaphors in general, see the commentary on 4:4; 6:4; and 7:4 [5]; on the "wall" in particular, cf. Jer. 1:18; 15:20; Ezek. 22:30). All agree further that the "battlement of silver"—as an additional wall made of precious material—implies a strengthening and beautification of the wall, similar to the thousand shields on the tower in Cant. 4:4. (The word translated "battlement" means virtually the same thing as "wall" in Ezek. 46:23 ["row" in NRSV].) Thus, the siblings lend their support to their

278

younger sister, who is not ready to go too quickly into a union planned by the parents or assumed by some admirer. It seems totally improbable that these lines refer to shrewd brothers trying to raise the bride price so the sale of their sister will provide them with as much tainted profit as possible (Rudolph, Krinetzki). First, the silver battlement they are building is a thing of real value; second, the harsh tones of social criticism implied in this interpretation are quite foreign to the overall cheerfulness of the Song.

According to the exegetes already mentioned, the next lines make a different point, because the open "door" is the opposite of the wall. The door would then symbolize the sister's open display of her sexuality (Krinetzki). But the text does not talk about an open door. In Hebrew the door opening is the פתח (cf. 7:13b [14b]). But the word here is דלת, which means the board used to close the door opening. To say that a city has "walls, gates [or doors], and bars" is to label it strong and secure (Deut. 3:5; Ezek. 38:11; 2 Chron. 8:5, etc.). Thus this "door" (or door covering) has precisely the same function as the "wall"—to impede or prohibit entry into a city. The planned strengthening of the door with boards of precious cedar (see the commentary on 1:17; 5:15) strictly parallels the heightening and beautification of the wall with a silver "battlement."

Thus v. 9cd not only looks like v. 9ab but is a totally parallel couplet, in form, content, and meaning. The repetition expresses the strength of the siblings' resolution (cf. Gen. 41:32). But how does this proud aloofness, so carefully planned for the little sister, compare with what happens to the older sister?

[8:10] She is a wall. She is not easily approachable. She is no longer flat-chested. She carries her breasts proudly, as a strong city its towers (see the commentary on 4:4; 6:4; 7:4 [5]). But her proud strength is not taken seriously by the one it is meant to impress. To be something "in someone's eyes" refers to the impression one makes on that person. The man who brings the news of Saul's death is, in his own eyes, a messenger of glad tidings, but in David's eyes he is a criminal (2 Sam. 4:10). In her own eyes, the speaker here is a proud and strong city, but in the eyes of her admirer she is like a city under siege, ready to capitulate; according to the Hebrew text, she "sends out peace" (i.e., sues for peace; cf. Deut. 20:10; Josh. 9:15).

The woman's firm intention to maintain her proud distance has no chance against the admirer's optimism and certainty of victory. Reading between the lines, one might say that the woman does not seem terribly unhappy with this state of affairs.

Solomon's Vineyard and Mine

Text

8:11 a Solomon had a vineyard
b at Baal-hamon ["lord of the tumult"];
c he entrusted the vineyard to keepers;
d each one was to bring for its fruit
e a thousand pieces of silver [(annually)].
12 a My vineyard, my very own, is for [me (alone)];
b you, O Solomon, may have the thousand,
c and the keepers of the fruit two hundred!

Analysis

The poem opens with a narrative in v. 11a-c (two third-person perfects). Solomon had a vineyard that was so large he had to entrust it to keepers. Each of the keepers pays (again and again—an imperfect) a thousand pieces of silver for its fruit. This statement closes the first part of the poem. The second part briefly contrasts this situation with the speaker's (first person) personal ownership of his vineyard (nominal clause). There are no keepers here. A second nominal clause sanctions the high profits earned by Solomon and his keepers from their vineyard. The accent of the poem as a whole is on the comparison between Solomon's vineyard and that of the speaker and the contrast between Solomon's twice-mentioned "keepers" (both introduced with the preposition לְ) and the speaker's "for myself" (לְפָנָי).

Commentary

The form and content of 8:11-12 differ so clearly from what goes before that the break hardly requires defending. Nevertheless, it is difficult to explain why the poem is placed in this spot. The word "silver" in 8:9b and 8:11d may have something to do with it. But perhaps even more important is the playfully relaxed and ironic tone common to both units.

280

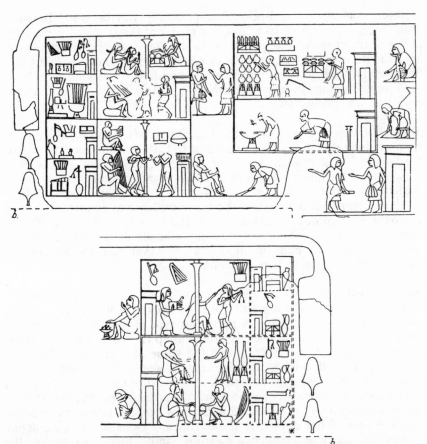

Fig. 158. The women of the royal harem lived in their own dwellings. A watchman sits or stands at each of the four doors to the women's chambers; other male officials are busy in the larder (*upper right*). The women are shown eating, caring for their hair, dancing, and playing music. (Relief in the tomb of Ai at Tell el-Amarna; ca. 1340 B.C.)

[8:11ab] In the metaphorical language of the Song, the "vineyard" usually stands for the woman (1:6; 2:15; 7:8c [9c]; cf. also the related metaphor of the garden in 4:12—5:1; 6:11; 7:11-12 [12-13]). The contrast between Solomon's vineyard and the speaker's vineyard confirms the assumption that the same is true here, because it is reminiscent of the contrast in 6:8-10 between the large harem and the speaker's single loved one; the latter is more beautiful than all the women in the entire harem. The location of Solomon's vineyard also implies that it refers to his harem. The historical or topographical traditions of the OT mention no "Baal-hamon," although many variations of "Baal-*x*" do occur as OT names (e.g., Baal-

281

hermon, Baal-meon, Baal-peor, Baal-perazim). But because "Baal-ha-mon" means something like "lord [or place] of the tumult [or the pag-eantry or the crowd]," one should probably understand it as a name used here for its meaning (cf. the "Daughter of Many" Gate in 7:4c [5c]). Because the tradition remembers seven hundred wives and three hun-dred concubines in Solomon's harem (1 Kgs. 11:3), notions of tumult and crowding are appropriate.

[8:11c] Solomon cannot care for this huge vineyard (or harem) by himself. He must entrust it to keepers. According to Esth. 2:3 the chief "keeper of the women" is a eunuch. In Egypt, however, the harem guards were apparently not eunuchs. The fourteen guards and servants depicted with the harem or at its entrance in a relief from Tell el-Amarna (fig. 158) show no sign of being eunuchs, nor is there any evidence of eunuchs as harem guards in written documents or among the mummies of ancient Egypt. The sources do not reveal whether any officials in Israel (such as the harem guards) were eunuchs. It is clear, however, that there were cas-trated harem officials in Mesopotamia.

[8:11de] Each keeper pays a huge annual sum. A "piece of silver" means a shekel of 0.4 ounces (11.4 grams). For two shekels, one could buy a ram without blemish (Lev. 5:15). A particular type of female concubine (or cupbearer) is worth forty shekels; Amenhotep III ordered forty of them from the king of Gezer.[1] Regarding the value of a vineyard, Isa. 7:23 speaks of one with a thousand vines that is worth a thousand pieces of silver. But this poem does not speak of the cost of the vineyard itself; it values the annual yield at one thousand pieces of silver—an amount that, when multiplied by the unnamed number of keepers, produces an astro-nomical sum. What does this amount mean? Does it stay completely within the metaphor's lender of meaning, simply further expanding the size and value of the vineyard? Or does it correspond to something in the world of the receiver of meaning (the women), and, if so, what? It cer-tainly does not refer to the expenditures for the bride price, which Solo-mon would have paid, not received. Elsewhere in the Song, "fruit" or "yield" can mean erotic pleasures (cf. 2:3; 4:13, 16, etc.). But unless one assumes that the harem functioned as a kind of bordello, for which, as far as I know, no evidence exists, then one must assume that v. 11de belongs only in the realm of the lender of meaning. Solomon's vineyard is im-mense and of great value, which is also the reason he must entrust it to keepers.

[8:12a] Despite 1:6, the speaker here is the man, not the woman. The vineyard that lies before him (לפני) differs totally from Solomon's. The threefold pronoun ("my vineyard, my very own, is for me alone") em-phasizes his certainty that the vineyard is his alone, for his own use. (On the use of "before him" with the sense of "alone," cf. Isa. 53:2; Jer. 49:5;

1. *ANET*, 487.

with the sense of "for his use," cf. Gen. 13:9; 24:51; by contrast, for the Song's sense of mutuality in the relationship, see the commentary on 2:16a.)

[8:12b] The speaker announces that he does not begrudge Solomon the profits from his vineyard or the two hundred pieces of silver earned by the keepers. The question arises again whether this money might not be, after all, a way to ridicule Solomon's harem as a kind of bordello, perhaps involved in sacred prostitution (cf. Astarte of the Sidonians in 1 Kgs. 11:5a). The speaker definitely prefers the direct relationship with his "vineyard" to a more complicated one, carried out through intermediary keepers. In Cant. 6:8-10 the man prefers the one most beautiful woman to the many less beautiful ones; here, in the same way, he prefers a simple, direct relationship to the complicated and expensive operation of a large harem.

A Secret Understanding

Text

8:13 a O you who dwell in the gardens,
    b [. . .] companions are listening. [. . .]
    c Let me hear [your voice!]
  14 a Make haste, my beloved,
    b and be like a gazelle
    c or a young stag
    d upon the mountains of [balsam]!

Analysis

The woman dwelling (participle) in the gardens is notified that comrades (along with the speaker?) are listening (participle). She is called on to let the man hear her voice (imperative). She answers with the words used by the man in 4:6 to announce his plan to enjoy love and by the woman in 2:17 to encourage him to do the same.

The woman dwells "in the gardens"—a passing reference to the garden songs of 4:12—5:1 and 6:11. This agricultural reference may be the reason for the poem's inclusion after 8:11-12 (the vineyard). Verse 8:13c repeats 2:14d (the dove in the clefts of the rock). Verse 8:14 has almost the same wording as 2:17 and 4:6. A speech consisting of quotations and allusions is comprehensible only to those who know the sources. The companions who are listening do not know what all this means—is she calling him or sending him away?

Commentary

[8:13] The address "you who dwell in the gardens" is reminiscent of the "garden fountain" in 4:15a. In both cases, the plural ("gardens") has an intensifying effect. One should not imagine a particular concrete situation here but think of the fountain or the woman in general in the context of the garden. "Companions" are all those who participate in an event—good folks and bad (note the accomplices in Isa. 1:23). They wait attentively for a voice, a signal (Jer. 6:17). Tension is in the air—although the situation is not as threatening as when Susanna went to bathe in the enclosed garden without noticing the elders hiding there (Sus. 15-22).

There is no clear direction here. An indefinite sense of longing governs the scene. The speaker requests instructions from the woman hidden in the gardens, using the same imperative with which the dove hidden in the clefts of the rock was addressed in 2:14d.

[8:14] In contrast to 2:17, where the woman calls on her lover to return, here she urges him to flee. That statement may have made the companions believe she was sending him away. But to those with ears to hear two things betray that what she seems to be saying on the surface is the opposite of what she means: first, her appeal to the man to be like the gazelle and the young stag—animals related to the goddess of love and symbols of the power of life to overcome death (see the commentary on 2:7, 9 and 4:5); second (and most important), the goal of his "flight." His journey, at the speed of a gazelle, will lead him to "the mountains of balsam"—which refer to nothing other than the woman herself; she is described with similar words in 2:17 and 4:6—a wonderful landscape with an infatuating fragrance. Here, though, she replaces the μαλάβαθρον of 2:17 and the myrrh of 4:6 with balsam, the most precious of all fragrances (see the commentary on 4:10c). Thus the cry that the companions hear as a call to separation turns out to be an invitation to utmost bliss. Only a couple with the deepest mutual understanding, who find sufficiency in one another, will be able to shut out the world in this way and coexist with the attentive eavesdropping of the companions, whom the woman had already avoided in 1:7.

Sources of the Illustrations

AOBPs	Keel, O. *Die Welt der altorientalischer Bildsymbolik und das Alte Testament: Am Beispiel der Psalmen.* 4th ed. Zurich, Einsiedeln, Cologne: Benziger; Neukirchen-Vluyn: Neukirchener, 1984. (The German 4th ed. contains some figures not found in the English translation [see *SBW*].)
DBT	Keel, O. *Deine Blicke sind Tauben: Zur Metaphorik des Hohen Liedes.* SBS 114/115. Stuttgart: Katholisches Bibelwerk, 1984.
OLB 1	Keel, O., M. Küchler, and C. Uehlinger. *Orte und Landschaften der Bibel: Ein Handbuch und Studienreiseführer zum Heiligen Land.* Vol. 1, *Geographisch-geschichtliche Landeskunde.* Zurich, Einsiedeln, Cologne: Benziger; Göttingen: Vandenhoeck & Ruprecht, 1984.
OLB 2	Keel, O., and M. Küchler. *Orte und Landschaften der Bible: Ein Handbuch und Studienreiseführer zum Heiligen Land.* Vol. 2, *Der Süden.* Zurich, Einsiedeln, Cologne: Benziger; Göttingen: Vandenhoeck & Ruprecht, 1982.
SBW	Keel, O. *The Symbolism of the Biblical World: Ancient Near Eastern Iconography and the Book of Psalms.* New York: Seabury, 1978.
*	Drawing by Hildi Keel-Leu (usually based on a photograph in the work cited).
1.	O. W. Muscarella, *Ancient Art: The Norbert Schimmel Collection* (Mainz: P. von Zabern, 1974) no. 109bis.*

2. C. Aldred, *Akhenaten and Nefertiti* (New York: Viking Press, 1973) no. 92.*

3. Ibid., no. 123.*

4. A. Vigneau, *Les antiquités égyptiennes du Musée du Louvre*, Encyclopédie photographique de l'art 1 (Paris, 1935) 134–35.*

5. W. Wreszinski, *Atlas zur altägyptischen Kulturgeschichte*, vol. 1 (Leipzig, 1923) 356;* *OLB* 2:420, fig. 302.

6. N. de G. Davies, *The Tomb of Neferhotep*, vol. 2 (New York, 1933) pl. 3.

7. A. Lhote, *Les chefs-d'oeuvre de la peinture égyptienne*, Coll. Arts du monde (Paris, 1954) pl. 113.*

8. E. Strommenger, *5000 Years of Art of Mesopotamia*, photos M. Hirmer, tr. C. Haglund (New York: H. N. Abrams, 1964). pl. 14.*

9. R. S. Lamon and G. M. Shipton, *Megiddo*, vol. 1, *Seasons of 1925–34: Strata I–V*, OIP 42 (Chicago: Univ. of Chicago, 1939) pl. 67, no. 4;* A. Rowe, *The Four Canaanite Temples of Beth-Shan*, vol. 1, *The Temples and Cult Objects*, Publications of the Palestine Section, Museum of the University of Pennsylvania 2/1 (Philadelphia: Univ. of Pennsylvania Press, 1940) pl. 39, no. 14;* E. Sellin, *Tell Ta'anneck*, Denkschrift der Kaiserlicher Akademie der Wissenschaften in Wien, phil.-hist. Klasse 50/4 (Vienna: C. Gerold's Sohn, 1904) 73, fig. 98 and pl. 45, no. 144;* F. Petrie, *Beth-Pelet*, part 1, British School of Archaeology in Egypt 48 (London, 1930) pl. 48, no. 564.

10. Drawing from a museum photograph (Louvre AO 7771).*

11. M. Metzger, "Gottheit, Berg und Vegetation in vorderasiastischer Bildtradition," *ZDPV* 99 (1983) 56, fig. 1; *DBT*, 129, fig. 11.

12. C. R. Lepsius, *Denkmäler aus Ägypten und Äthiopien*, vol. 6 (1849–1858; reprint, Osnabrück, 1969; reduced reprint, Geneva, 1972) pl. 165; *SBW*, 298, fig. 405.

13. N. de G. Davies, *The Rock Tombs of El Amarna*, part 4, *The Tombs of Penthu, Mahu, and Others*, Archaeological Survey of Egypt, 16th Memoir (London: Egypt Exploration Fund, 1906) pl. 22.

14. K. R. Maxwell-Hyslop, *Western Asiatic Jewelry, c. 3000–612 B.C.*, Methuen's Handbooks on Archaeology (London, 1971) pl. 129.

15. R. D. Barnett and L. G. Davies, *A Catalogue of the Nimrud Ivories with Other Ancient Near Eastern Ivories in the British Museum*, 2d ed. (London, 1975) pl. 70, S 172;* *DBT*, 124, fig. 3.

16.   W.M.F. Petrie, *Illahun, Kahun and Gurob* (1891; reprint, Warminster, 1974) pl. 22, no. 5.

17.   A. H. Layard, *The Monuments of Nineveh from Drawings Made on the Spot* (London: J. Murray, 1849) pl. 14.

18.   H. R. Hall, *Catalogue of Egyptian Scarabs, Etc., in the British Museum*, vol. 1, *Royal Scarabs* (London, 1913) 161, no. 1640;* *OLB*, 1:129, fig. 61.

19.   B. Parker, "Excavations at Nimrud, 1949–1953: Seals and Seal Impressions," *Iraq* 17 (1955) pl. 29, no. 1;* *OLB*, 1:129, fig. 62.

20.   F. Lexa, *La magie dans l'Egypte antique: De l'ancien empire jusqu'à l'époque copte*, vol. 3 (Paris: P. Geuthner, 1925) pl. 79, fig. 155; *DBT*, 184, fig. 116.

21.   N. de G. Davies, *The Rock Tombs of Deir el Gebrâwi*, vol. 2, *Tomb of Zau and Tombs of the Northern Group*, Archaeological Survey of Egypt, 12th Memoir (London: Egypt Exploration Fund, 1902) pl. 17; *DBT*, 184, fig. 117.

22.   V. Karageorghis, *View from the Bronze Age: Mycenaean and Phoenician Discoveries at Kition* (New York: Dutton, 1976) 74, pl. 56;* *DBT*, 186, fig. 119.

23.   Drawing from a museum photograph (Metropolitan Museum of Art 74.51.2665);* *DBT*, 144, fig. 39.

24.   Drawing from a photograph of the original (collection of the Biblical Institute of the University of Fribourg, no. 113);* *DBT*, 149, fig. 48.

25.   L. Delaporte, *Musée du Louvre: Catalogue des cylindres, cachets et pierres gravées de style oriental*, vol. 2, *Acquisitions* (Paris, 1923) pl. 195, A 929;* *DBT*, 148, fig. 47.

26.   U. Winter, *Frau und Göttin: Exegetische und ikonographische Studien zum weiblichen Gottesbild im Alten Israel und dessen Umwelt*, OBO 53 (Fribourg: Universitätsverlag; Göttingen: Vandenhoeck & Ruprecht, 1983) fig. 301; *DBT*, 148, fig. 46.

27.   C. McEwan and H. J. Kantor, *Soundings at Tell Fakhariyah*, OIP 79 (Chicago: Univ. of Chicago Press, 1958) pl. 73, no. 44; *DBT*, 150, fig. 51.

28.   O. Tufnell, *Lachish (Tell ed-Duweir)*, vol. 3, *The Iron Age*, Wellcome-Marston Archaeological Research Expedition to the Near East 3 (London, New York, and Toronto: Oxford Univ. Press, 1953) pl. 28, no. 12;* *DBT*, 152, fig. 55.

29.   Tufnell, *Lachish*, vol. 3, pl. 43, no. 58.

30.   Bukowski's Zurich Auctions, "Auction 8 (December 1983): Figurenamulette, klassische Antiken, präkolumbianische Kunst" (Zurich, 1983) no. 131.*

31. D. Arnold et al., *Meisterwerke altägyptischer Keramik: 5000 Jahre Kunst und Kunsthandwerk aus Ton und Fayence* (Montabaur, 1978) 152, no. 226.*

32. P. Amiet et al., *Art in the Ancient World: A Handbook of Styles and Forms*, tr. V. Bynner (New York: Rizzoli, 1981) nos. 3 and 7.

33. Drawing from a museum photograph (British Museum 14594-5).*

34. Drawing from a museum photograph (British Museum 48494).*

35. Drawing from a museum photograph (University Museum, Philadelphia, inv. no. 29-104-55).*

36. Drawing from a museum photograph (University Museum, Philadelphia, inv. no. 61-14-917).*

37. P. Beck, "The Drawings from Horvat Teiman (Kuntillet 'Ajrud)," *Tel Aviv* 9 (1982) 54, fig. 21.

38. J. Leclant, *Ägypten*, vol. 2, *Das Grossreich, 1560–1070 v. Chr.*, Universum der Kunst 27 (Munich, 1980) 185, fig. 166.

39. Winter, *Frau und Göttin*, fig. 248; *DBT*, 149, fig. 49.

40. R. D. Barnett, *Sculptures from the North Palace of Ashurbanipal at Nineveh (668–621 B.C.)* (London, 1976) pl. 65.*

41. Davies, *El Amarna*, part 4, pl. 17.

42. A. and A. Brack, *Das Grab des Tjanuni: Theben Nr. 74*, Archäologische Veröffentlichungen des Deutschen Archäologischen Instituts, Abteilung Kairo 19 (Mainz, 1977) pl. 8.*

43. Winter, *Frau und Göttin*, fig. 519.

44. Ibid., fig. 360; *DBT*, 173, fig. 94.

45. Drawing from a photograph of the original (collection of the Biblical Institute of the University of Fribourg, no. 115);* *OLB*, 1:152, fig. 78; *DBT*, 174, fig. 97.

46. E. Bleibtreu, *Rollsiegel aus dem Vorderen Orient: Zur Steinschneidekunst zwischen etwa 3200 und 400 vor Christus nach Beständen in Wien und Graz* (Vienna, 1981) 68, no. 81;* *DBT*, 175, fig. 98.

47. Winter, *Frau und Göttin*, fig. 42; *DBT*, 133, fig. 20.

48. F. S. Matouk, *Corpus du scarabée égyptien*, vol. 2, *Analyse thématique* (Beirut, 1977) 387, no. 737.*

49. J. Vandier d'Abbadie, *Catalogue des Ostraca figurés de Deir el Médineh*, Documents de Fouilles publiés par les membres de l'Institut Français d'Archéologie orientale du Caire 2/3 (Cairo, 1946) pl. 95, no. 2729.*

50. Drawing from a photograph of the original (collection of the Biblical Institute of the University of Fribourg, loan SK 95).*

51.   Auction Catalogue, "Numismatic Art and Ancient Coins (Thursday, April 17, 1986)" (Zurich 1986) 39, no. 271.*

52.   E. Porada, *Corpus of Ancient Near Eastern Seals in North American Collections*, vol. 1, *The Collection of the Pierpont Morgan Library*, Bollingen Series 14 (New York: Pantheon Books, 1948) pl. 84, no. 601;* *DBT*, 167, fig. 80.

53.   R. Hachmann, *Frühe Phöniker im Libanon: 20 Jahre deutsche Ausgrabungen in Kāmid el-Lōz* (Mainz: P. von Zabern, 1983) 127, no. 25;* *DBT*, 166, fig. 79a.

54.   M. Dothan and D. N. Freedman, "Ashdod I: The First Season of Excavations 1962," *'Atiqot* 7 (1967) pl. 15, no. 9;* *DBT*, 167, fig. 81.

55.   H. Gressmann, *Altorientalische Bilder zum Alten Testament*, 2d ed. (Berlin and Leipzig: W. de Gruyter, 1927) 165, fig. 45.

56.   H. Th. Bossert, *Altsyrien: Kunst und Handwerk in Cypern, Syrien, Palästina, Transjordanien und Arabien von den Anfängen bis zum völligen Aufgehen in der griechisch-römischen Kultur*, Die ältesten Kulturen des Mittelmeerkreises 3 (Tübingen: E. Wasmuth, 1951) pl. 11, no. 26f.;* *OLB*, 2:877, fig. 580; *DBT*, 144, fig. 40.

57.   S. Yeivin, "Jachin and Boaz," *ErIsr* 5 (1958) pl. 11, no. 1;* *DBT*, 145, fig. 41.

58.   A. P. di Cesnola, *Salaminia (Cyprus): The History, Treasures and Antiquities* (London: Trubner and Co., 1884) pl. 14, no. 45;* *DBT*, 145, fig. 42.

59.   A. Parrot, *Sumer (Paris: Gallimard, 1960)* 279–80, fig. 346;* *SBW*, 143, fig. 191; *DBT*, 146, fig. 43.

60.   J. Vandier d'Abbadie, *Catalogue des Ostraca figurés de Deir el Médineh: Nos. 2001 à 2255*, Documents de fouilles publiés par les membres de l'Institut Français d'Archéologie orientale du Caire 2/1 (Cairo, 1936) pl. 29, no. 2218.*

61.   E. Brunner-Traut, *Altägyptische Tiergeschichte und Fabel: Gestalt und Strahlkraft*, 3d ed. (Darmstadt, 1968) fig. 33.

62.   C. Clamer, "A Gold Plaque from Tel Lachish," *Tel Aviv* 7 (1980) 153, fig. 1; *OLB*, 2:917, fig. 614; *DBT*, 157, fig. 63.

63.   K. Lange, M. Hirmer, *Egypt: Architecture, Sculpture, Painting in Three Thousand Years*, tr. R. Boothroyd (London: Phaidon Press, 1956) pl. 36;* *DBT*, 160, fig. 66.

64.   G. Loud, *The Megiddo Ivories*, OIP 52 (Chicago: Univ. of Chicago Press, 1939) pl. 4, no. 2b; *DBT*, 160, fig. 67.

65.   Beck, *Tel Aviv* 9 (1982) frontispiece.

66.   C. Desroches-Noblecourt, "Interprétation et datation d'une scène gravée sur deux fragments de récipient en albâtre provenant des fouilles du palais d'Ugarit," in *Ugaritica*, vol. 3, ed. C. Schaeffer (Paris, 1956) 204, fig. 179;* *DBT*, 170, fig. 89.

67.   W. Orthmann, *Der Alte Orient*, Propyläen Kunstgeschichte 14 (Berlin: Propylaen, 1975) fig. 283b;* *AOBPs*, 342, fig. 493.

68.   J. Vandier d'Abbadie, *Catalogue des Ostraca figurés de Deir el Médineh: Nos. 2256 à 2722*, Documents de fouilles publiés par les membres de l'Institut Français d'Archéologie orientale du Caire 2/2 (Cairo, 1936) pl. 53, no. 2345.*

69.   J. A. Omlin, *Der Papyrus 55001 und seine satirisch-erotischen Zeichnungen und Inschriften*, Catalogo del Museo Egizio di Torina 1/3 (Turin, 1973) pl. 13.

70.   Y. Shiloh, *The Proto-Aeolic Capital and Israelite Ashlar Masonry (Qedem 11)* (Jerusalem, 1979) 23, fig. 13.

71.   E. Strommenger, *Der Garten in Eden: 7 Jahrtausende Kunst und Kultur an Euphrat und Tigris* (Berlin, 1978) 167, no. 134.*

72.   Davies, *Deir el Gebrâwi*, vol. 2, pl. 8.

73.   C. Daremberg and E. Saglio, *Dictionnaire des antiquités grecques et romaines d'après les textes et les monuments*, vol. 3/2 (Paris, 1904) 1005, fig. 4376.

74.   N. Agivad, "The Expedition to the Judean Desert, 1961: Expedition A—Naḥal David," *IEJ* 12 (1962) pl. 22A.

75.   C. F.-A. Schaeffer, "Les fouilles de Ras Shamra-Ugarit: Quinzième, seizième et dix-septième campagne (1951, 1952 et 1953)," *Syria* 31 (1954) pl. 9;* *SBW*, 285, fig. 387.

76.   J. Boardman et al., *Eros en Grèce* (Paris, 1976) 33.*

77.   L. Marangou, *Bone Carvings from Egypt*, vol. 1, GraecoRoman Period (Tübingen, 1976) pl. 43a, no. 126.*

78.   W. Westendorf, *Painting, Sculpture, and Architecture of Ancient Egypt* (New York: H. N. Abrams, 1969);* *DBT*, 182, fig. 113.

79.   Vandier d'Abbadie, *Ostraca figurés*, 2/2, pl. 55, no. 2391;* *DBT*, 183, fig. 114.

80.   F. Muthmann, *Der Granatapfel: Symbol des Lebens in der alten Welt*, Schriften der Abegg-Stiftung Bern 6 (Bern, 1982) 15, fig. 4.*

81.   Ibid., 19, fig. 8.

82.   A. H. Gardiner, A. M. Calverley, and M. F. Broome, *The Temple of King Sethos I at Abydos*, vol. 2, *The*

Chapels of Amen-Rē', Rē'-Harakhti, Ptah, and King Sethos (London and Chicago, 1935) frontispiece.

83. J. Börker-Klähn, *Altvorderasiatische Bildstellen und vergleichbare Felsreliefs*, Baghdader Forschungen 4 (Mainz 1982) no. 227; *DBT*, 127, fig. 7.

84. N. Avigad, "Excavations at Makmish," *IEJ* 10 (1960) pl. 12B.*

85. Petrie, *Beth-Pelet*, vol. 1, pl. 40, no. 477.*

86. Tufnell, *Lachish*, vol. 3, pl. 44, no. 89.*

87. A. Rowe, *A Catalog of Egyptian Scarabs, Scaraboids, Seals and Amulets in the Palestine Archaeological Museum* (Cairo, 1936) pl. 29, S 105;* *DBT*, 167, fig. 82.

88. Drawing from a photograph of the original (collection of R. Brown, Jerusalem).*

89. Drawing from museum photograph (Kunsthistorisches Museum Wien, inv. no. 3896a);* *DBT*, 170, fig. 88.

90. W. Wolff, *Die Kunst Ägyptens: Gestalt und Geschichte* (Stuttgart, 1957) 639, fig. 682;* *DBT*, 171, fig. 90.

91. E. Naville, *The Temple of Deir el Bahari*, part 2, *The Ebony Shrine: Northern Half of the Middle Platform*, Egypt Exploration Fund 14 (London: Egypt Exploration Fund, 1897) pl. 79.

92. H. J. Kantor, "Landscape in Akkadian Art," *JNES* 25 (1966) pl. 15, no. 5; *DBT*, 128, fig. 10.

93. Winter, *Frau und Göttin*, fig. 182; *DBT*, 129, fig. 12.

94. *ANEP*, no. 526;* *DBT*, 131, fig. 16.

95. H. Frankfort, *Cylinder Seals: A Documentary Essay on the Art and Religion of the Ancient Near East* (London, 1939) pl. 35a;* *DBT*, 135, fig. 23.

96. M. Tosi and A. Roccati, *Stele e altre epigrafi di Deir el Medina, n. 50001–n. 50262*, Catalogo del Museo Egizio di Torino 2/1 (Turin, 1972) no. 50066;* *DBT*, 134, fig. 22.

97. V. Haas, *Hethitische Berggötter und hurritische Steindämonen: Riten, Kulte und Mythen: Eine Einführung in die altkleinasiatischen religiösen Vorstellungen*, Kulturgeschichte der antiken Welt 10 (Mainz, 1982) 95, fig. 23; *DBT*, 137, fig. 28.

98. K. Bittel et al., *Das hethitische Felsheiligtum Yazilikaya*, Boğazköy-Ḫattuša: Ergebnisse der Ausgrabungen 9 (Berlin, 1975) pl. 58; *DBT*, 138, fig. 29.

99. C. C. McKown, *Tell en-Naṣbeh*, vol. 1, *Archaeological and Historical Results* (Berkeley and New Haven, 1947) pl. 55, no. 81.*

100. Barnett, *Sculptures*, pl. 23;* *SBW*, 150, fig. 202.

101. Davies, *Neferhotep*, vol. 2, pl. 3.

102. N. de G. Davies, *Two Ramesside Tombs at Thebes* (New York, 1927) pl. 29; *ANEP*, no. 95.

103. C. Desroches-Noblecourt, *Tutankhamen; Life and Death of a Pharaoh* (New York: New York Graphic Society, 1963) frontispiece.*

104. C. F.-A. Schaeffer, "Les fouilles de Ras Shamra-Ugarit: Neuvième campagne (1937)," *Syria* 19 (1938) 322, fig. 49, no. 5.

105. Ibid., fig. 49, no. 7.

106. O. Negbi, *Canaanite Gods in Metal: An Archaeological Study of Ancient Syro-Palestinian Figurines*, Publications of the Institute of Archaeology 5 (Tel Aviv, 1976), 119, fig. 134.

107. Drawing from a museum photograph (Ashmolean Museum, Oxford, no. 1949.305).*

108. Wreszinski, *Atlas*, vol. 2 (Leipzig, 1935) pl. 31.

109. E. Hornung, *The Valley of the Kings: Horizon of Eternity* (New York: Timken, 1990) pl. 62;* *SBW*, 186, fig. 253.

110. A. Mariette, *Abydos: Description des fouilles exécutées sur l'emplacement de cette ville*, vol. 1 (Paris, 1869) pl. 25.

111. Winter, *Frau und Göttin*, fig. 347.

112. Ibid., fig. 348.

113. M. Tadmor, "Female Cult Figurines in Late Canaan and Early Israel: Archaeological Evidence," in *Studies in the Period of David and Solomon and Other Essays*, ed. T. Ishida (Winona Lake, Ind.: Eisenbrauns, 1982) 142, pl. 2.*

114. Ibid., 151, pl. 5a.*

115. Y. Aharoni, "Tel Beer-Sheva," *Qadmoniot* 6 (1973) 82.*

116. Drawing from a museum photograph (British Museum 124907);* *OLB*, 1:75, fig. 22.

117. Mariette, *Abydos*, vol. 2 (Paris, 1880) pl. 14.*

118. Ibid., pl. 3.*

119. O. Masson, "Religious Beliefs and Sanctuaries in Prehistoric Times," *Archaeologia Viva* 2/3 (1969) 52, pl. 7;* *DBT*, 143, fig. 37.

120. E. Pfuhl, *Malerei und Zeichnung der Griechen*, vol. 3 (Munich, 1923) pl. 700;* *DBT*, 143, fig. 38.

121. *Medinet Habu*, vol. 8, *The Eastern High Gate*, OIP 94 (Chicago, 1970) pl. 648.

122. N. Glueck, *Deities and Dolphins: The Story of the Nabataeans* (New York: Farrar, Straus and Giroux, 1965) 114, pl. 52a;* *DBT*, 126, fig. 6.

123. M. H. Crawford, *Roman Republican Coinage*, vol. 2

(Cambridge: Cambridge Univ. Press, 1974), pl. 50.20, no. 409/2.*

124.   A. Moortgat, *Vorderasiatische Rollsiegel: Ein Beitrag zur Geschichte der Steinschneidekunst*, 2d ed. (Berlin: Mann, 1966) pl. 71, no. 599;* *DBT*, 140, fig. 33.

125.   Winter, *Frau und Göttin*, fig. 501; *DBT*, 141, fig. 34.

126.   Davies, *Neferhotep*, vol. 2, pl. 3.

127.   E. Fugmann, *Hama: Fouilles et recherches de la Fondation Carlsberg, 1931–1938*, vol. 2/1, *L'architecture des périodes pré-hellénistiques*, Nationalmuseets Skrifter: Større Beretninger 1 (Copenhagen: Fondation Carlsberg, 1958) pl. 10, no. 5A 846–47;* L. Badre, *Les figurines anthropomorphes en terre cuite à l'âge du bronze en Syrie*, Bibliothèque archéologique et historique 103 (Paris, 1980) pl. 63, no. 19.*

128.   Barnett and Davies, *Nimrud Ivories*, 130, fig. 48.

129.   N. de G. Davies, *The Tomb of the Vizier Ramose*, Mond Excavations at Thebes 1 (London: Egyptian Exploration Society, 1941) pl. 10.*

130.   D. Barag, "Phoenician Stone Vessels from the Eighth–Seventh Centuries B.C.," *ErIsr* 18 (1985) 218, fig. 4.*

131.   N. de G. Davies, *The Tomb of Rekh-mi-Rē' at Thebes*, Publications of the Metropolitan Museum of Art Egyptian Expedition 11, vol. 2 (1943; reprint, New York, 1973) pl. 65.

132.   H. Hickmann, "Miscellanea musicologica," *Annales du Service des Antiquités en Egypte* 49 (1949) 441, fig. 15.

133.   S. Wenig, *Die Frau im alten Ägypten*, Das Bild der Frau (Leipzig, Vienna, and Munich, 1969) 41.

134.   Winter, *Frau und Göttin*, figs. 32–33.

135.   P. Amiet, *La glyptique mésopotamienne archaïque*, 2d ed. (Paris: Centre national de la recherche scientifique, 1980) pl. 101, no. 1346.

136.   R. M. Boehmer, *Die Entwicklung der Glyptik während der Akkad-Zeit*, Untersuchungen zur Assyriologie und vorderasiastischen Archäologie 4 (Berlin: W. de Gruyter, 1965) pl. 32, no. 383.*

137.   Metzger, *Gottheit*, 60, fig. 5; *DBT*, 183, fig. 115.

138.   Winter, *Frau und Göttin*, fig. 183.

139.   T. Howard-Carter, "An Interpretation of the Sculptural Decoration of the Second Millennium Temple at Tell al-Rimah," *Iraq* 45 (1983) pl. 2a.*

140.   Winter, *Frau und Göttin*, fig. 411.

141.   Shiloh, *Proto-Aeolic Capital*, 27, fig. 16.

142.   Winter, *Frau und Göttin*, fig. 464.

143.   Drawing from museum photograph (Heimatmuseum Appenzell).*

144.   A. M. Bisi, *Le stele puniche*, Studi semitici 27 (Rome, 1967) fig. 36.

145.   Ibid., fig. 13.

146.   C. Picard, "Les représentations de sacrifice Molk sur les stèles de Carthage," *Karthago* 18 (1978) pl. 24, no. 9.

147.   R. Giveon, *Egyptian Scarabs from Western Asia from the Collections of the British Museum*, OBO, Series Archaeologica 3 (Fribourg: Universitätsverlag; Göttingen: Vandenhoeck & Ruprecht, 1985) 115, no. 16; O. Tufnell, *Lachish*, vol. 4, *The Bronze Age*, Wellcome-Marston Archaeological Research Expedition to the Near East 4 (London, New York, and Toronto, 1958) pl. 30, no. 47;* Petrie, *Beth-Pelet*, vol. 1, pl. 7, no. 47.*

148.   Haas, *Hethitische Berggötter*, 87, fig. 20.

149.   Desroches-Noblecourt, *Tut-ench-Amun*, pl. 5.*

150.   Leclant, *Ägypten*, vol. 2, 92, fig. 77.

151.   Westendorf, *Ägypten*, 141.*

152.   *Medinet Habu*, vol. 8, pl. 651f.

153.   T. Säve-Söderbergh, *Four Eighteenth Dynasty Tombs*, Private Tombs at Thebes 1 (Oxford, 1957) pl. 15.

154.   W. H. Hallo, "'As the Seal upon Thine Arm': Glyptic Metaphors in the Biblical World," in *Ancient Seals and the Bible*, ed. L. Gorelick and E. Willams-Forte (Malibu: Undena, 1983) pl. 12, no. 1;* *DBT*, 188, fig. 123.

155.a   W.M.F. Petrie and J. H. Walker, *The Palace of Apries*, Memphis 2 (London: School of Archaeology in Egypt, 1909) pl. 25.

156.   E. Otto, *Osiris und Amun: Kult und Heilige Stätten*, Antike Welt (Munich, 1966) 57, fig. 5.

157.   A. Jeremias, *Das Alte Testament im Lichte des Alten Orients: Handbuch zur Biblisch-Orientalischen Altertumskunde*, 3d ed. (Leipzig: J. C. Hinrichs, 1916) 21, fig. 8.

158.   N. de G. Davies, *The Rock Tombs of El Amarna*, part 6, *Tombs of Parennefer, Tutu, and Aÿ*, Archaeological Survey of Egypt, 18th Memoir (London: Egyptian Exploration Fund, 1908) pl. 28.

Abbreviations

AB	Anchor Bible
ACW	Ancient Christian Writers
AfO	*Archiv für Orientforschung*
AHW	W. von Soden, *Akkadisches Handwörterbuch*
AKM	Abhandlungen für die Kunde des Morgenlandes
AKPAW.PH	Abhandlungen der Königl.-preussischen Akademie der Wissenschaften. Phil.-hist. Klasse
ANEP	*Ancient Near East in Pictures*, ed. J. B. Pritchard, 2d ed. 1969
ANET	*Ancient Near Eastern Texts Relating to the Old Testament*, ed. J. B. Pritchard, 3d ed. 1969
AOAT	Alter Orient und Altes Testament
ARE	*Ancient Records of Egypt*, ed. J. H. Breasted
BAW	Bibliothek der Alten Welt
BBET	Beiträge zur biblischen Exegese und Theologie
BEvT	Beiträge zur evangelischen Theologie
BibB	Biblische Beitrag
BKAT	Biblischer Kommentar: Altes Testament
BO	*Bibliotheca orientalis*
BOH	Bibliotheca Orientalis Hungarica
BZAW	Beihefte zur *Zeitschrift für die alttestamentliche Wissenschaft*
ErIsr	*Eretz Israel*
FC	Fathers of the Church
HAT	Handbuch zum Alten Testament
IEJ	*Israel Exploration Journal*
JA	*Journal asiastique*

JBL	*Journal of Biblical Literature*
JEOL:	*Jaarbericht . . . ex oriente lux*
JNES	*Journal of Near Eastern Studies*
JPOS	*Journal of Palestine Oriental Society*
JSOT	*Journal for the Study of the Old Testament*
JTS	*Journal of Theological Studies*
KAT	Kommentar zum Alten Testament
KB	L. Koehler and W. Baumgartner, *Lexicon in Veteris Testamenti Libros*
KHC	Kurzer Hand-Commentar zum Alten Testament
KTU	M. Dietrich, O. Loretz, J. Sanmartin, *Die keilalphabetischen Texte aus Ugarit*
LCL	Loeb Classical Library
LSJ	H. G. Liddell, R. Scott, H. S. Jones, *Greek-English Lexicon*
NRSV	New Revised Standard Version
OBO	Orbis biblicus et orientalis
OIP	Oriental Institute Publications
Or	*Orientalia*
OTP	*Old Testament Pseudepigrapha*, ed. J. H. Charlesworth, 2 vols.
PG	*Patrologia graeca*, ed. J. Migne
PW	A. Pauly and G. Wissowa, *Real-Encyclopädie der classischen Altertumswissenschaft*
RA	*Revue d'Assyriōlogie*
RB	*Revue biblique*
RSO	*Revista degli studi orientali*
RSV	Revised Standard Version
SBLDS	Society of Biblical Literature Dissertation Series
SBS	Stuttgarter Bibelstudien
ST	*Studia theologica*
Str-B	H. Strack and P. Billerbeck, *Kommentar zum Neuen Testament*
TBü	Theologische Bücherei
TZ	*Theologische Zeitschrift*
UT	C. H. Gordon, *Ugaritic Textbook*
ZA	*Zeitschrift für Assyriologie*
ZAW	*Zeitschrift für die alttestamentliche Wissenschaft*
ZDPV	*Zeitschrift des deutschen Palästina-Vereins*
ZTK	*Zeitschrift für Theologie und Kirche*

Bibliography*

Aisleitner, J. *Die mythologischen und kultischen Texte aus Ras Schamra*. BOH 8. Budapest: Akadémiai Kiadó, 1964.

Budde, K. *Das Hohelied*. KHC 17/1. Freiburg im Breisgau, Leipzig, Tübingen: Mohr, 1898.

Buzy, D. *Le Cantique des cantiques traduit et commenté*. La Sainte Bible 6/3. Paris: Letouzey et Ané, 1946.

Caquot, A., M. Sznycer, and A. Herdner. *Textes Ougaritiques*. Vol. 1, *Mythes et légendes: Introduction, traduction, commentaire*. Littératures anciennes du Proche-Orient 7. Paris: Cerf, 1974.

Dalman, G. *Palästinischer Diwan: Als Beitrag zur Volkskunde Palästinas gesammelt und mit Übersetzung und Melodie herausgegeben*. Leipzig: Hinrichs'sche, 1901.

Delitzsch, F. *Commentary on the Song of Songs and Ecclesiastes*. Vol. 6 of C. F. Keil and F. Delitzsch, *Commentary on the Old Testament*. Tr. M. G. Easton et al. Reprint, Grand Rapids: Eerdmans, 1982.

Fox, M. V. *The Song of Songs and the Ancient Egyptian Love Songs*. Madison: The University of Wisconsin Press, 1985.

Gardiner, A. H. *The Library of A. Chester Beatty: Descriptions of a Hieratic Papyrus with a Mythological Story, Love Songs and Other Miscellaneous Texts: The Chester Beatty Papyrus, No. 1*. London: Oxford Univ. Press, 1931.

Gerleman, G. Ruth. *Das Hohelied*. BKAT 18. Neukirchen-Vluyn: Neukirchener, 1965.

Gibson, J. C. L. *Canaanite Myths and Legends*. 2d ed. Edinburgh: T. & T. Clark, 1978.

Ginsburg, C. D. *The Song of Songs*. 1857. Reprint. New York: Ktav, 1970.

Haller. M. *Die fünf Megillot*. HAT 1/18. Tübingen: Mohr, 1940.

Herder, J. G. *Lieder der Liebe: Die ältesten und schönsten aus dem Morgenlande: Nebst vier und vierzig alten Minneliedern*. Leipzig: Weygandsche, 1778.

Hermann, A. *Altägyptische Liebesdichtung*. Wiesbaden: Harrassowitz, 1959.

Keel, O. *Deine Blicke sind Tauben: Zur Metaphorik des Hohen Liedes*. SB 114/115. Stuttgart: Katholisches Bibelwerk, 1984.

Kramer, S. N. *The Sacred Marriage Rite: Aspects of Faith, Myth, and Ritual in Ancient Sumer*. Bloomington: Indiana Univ. Press, 1969.

*For additional bibliography, see Keel, *Deine Blicke*, 193–207.

Krinetzki, G. *Kommentar zum Hohenlied: Bildsprache und theologische Botschaft*. BBET 16. Frankfurt am Main and Bern: Peter D. Lang, 1981.

Maspero, G. "Les chants d'amour du Papyrus de Turin et du Papyrus Harris." *JA* 8/1 (1883) 18–47.

Müller, W. M. *Die Liebespoesie der Ägypter*. Leipzig: Hinrichs'sche, 1899.

Pope, M. H. *Song of Songs*. AB 7c. Garden City, N.Y.: Doubleday, 1977.

Posener, G. *Catalogue des ostraca hiératiques littéraires de Deir el Médinah*. Vol. 2, *Nos. 1109–1266*. Documents de fouilles publiés par les membres de l'Institut Français de'Archéologie orientale du Caire 18. Fasc. 3. Cairo, 1972.

Pritchard, J. B., ed., *Ancient Near Eastern Texts Relating to the Old Testament*. 3d ed. Princeton: Princeton Univ. Press, 1969.

Rudolph, W. *Das Buch Ruth: Das Hohe Lied: Die Klagelieder*. KAT 18/1-3. Gütersloh: Gerd Mohn, 1962.

Schmökel, H. *Heilige Hochzeit und Hohes Lied*. AKM 32/1. Wiesbaden: Kommissionsverlag Franz Steiner, 1956.

Schneider, H. *Das Hohelied*. Herders Bibelkommentar 7/1. Freiburg im Breisgau: Herder, 1962.

Schott, S. *Altägyptische Liebeslieder: Mit Märchen und Liebesgeschichten*. BAW. 2d ed. Zurich: Artemis, 1950.

Simpson, W. K., ed. *The Literature of Ancient Egypt: An Anthology of Stories, Instructions, and Poetry*. Translated by R. O. Faulkner, E. F. Wente, Jr., and W. K. Simpson. New ed. New Haven and London: Yale Univ. Press, 1972.

White, J. B. *A Study of the Language of Love in the Song of Songs and Ancient Egyptian Poetry*. SBLDS 38. Missoula, Mont.: Scholars Press, 1978.

Winter, U. *Frau und Göttin: Exegetische und ikonographische Studien zum weiblichen Gottesbild im Alten Israel und in dessen Umwelt*. OBO 53. Fribourg: Universitätsverlag; Göttingen: Vandenhoeck & Ruprecht, 1983.

Wittekindt, W. *Das Hohe Lied und seine Beziehungen zum Ištar Kult*. Hannover: Orientbuchhandlung Heinz Lafaire, 1926.

Würthwein, E. "Das Hohelied." In *Die fünf Megilloth*, by E. Würthwein, K. Galling, and O. Plöger, 25–71. HAT 1/18. 2d ed. Tübingen: Mohr, 1969.

Index of Biblical References

(The numbers are those of the New Revised Standard Version.)

Index of Biblical References

302

Index of Biblical References